Teaching Technology in Libraries

Teaching Technology in Libraries

Creative Ideas for Training Staff, Patrons and Students

EDITED BY
CAROL SMALLWOOD *and* LURA SANBORN

Foreword by James G. Neal

McFarland & Company, Inc., Publishers
Jefferson, North Carolina

RECENT McFARLAND WORKS FROM CAROL SMALLWOOD (WITH OTHERS)
Library Partnerships with Writers and Poets: Case Studies, edited by Carol Smallwood *and* Vera Gubnitskaia (2017); *Library Volunteers Welcome!: Strategies for Attracting, Retaining and Making the Most of Willing Helpers,* edited by Carol Smallwood *and* Lura Sanborn (2016); *Continuing Education for Librarians: Essays on Career Improvement Through Classes, Workshops, Conferences and More,* edited by Carol Smallwood, Kerol Harrod and Vera Gubnitskaia (2013); *Marketing Your Library: Tips and Tools That Work,* edited by Carol Smallwood, Vera Gubnitskaia and Kerol Harrod (2012); *Mentoring in Librarianship: Essays on Working with Adults and Students to Further the Profession,* edited by Carol Smallwood and Rebecca Tolley-Stokes (2012); *Women on Poetry: Writing, Revising, Publishing and Teaching,* edited by Carol Smallwood, Colleen S. Harris and Cynthia Brackett-Vincent (2012); *Thinking Outside the Book: Essays for Innovative Librarians,* edited by Carol Smallwood (2008); *Internet Sources on Each U.S. State: Selected Sites for Classroom and Library,* compiled by Carol Smallwood, Brian P. Hudson, Ann Marlow Riedling and Jennifer K. Rotole (2005)

ISBN (print) 978-1-4766-6474-3
ISBN (ebook) 978-1-4766-2718-2

LIBRARY OF CONGRESS CATALOGUING-IN-PUBLICATION DATA
BRITISH LIBRARY CATALOGUING DATA ARE AVAILABLE

© 2017 Carol Smallwood and Lura Sanborn. All rights reserved

No part of this book may be reproduced or transmitted in any form or by any means, electronic or mechanical, including photocopying or recording, or by any information storage and retrieval system, without permission in writing from the publisher.

Front cover image of learning concept © 2017 Jacek Kita/iStock

Printed in the United States of America

McFarland & Company, Inc., Publishers
Box 611, Jefferson, North Carolina 28640
www.mcfarlandpub.com

Table of Contents

Foreword by James G. Neal — 1

Preface — 3

Part I: Case Studies and Instruction Methodology

Supporting Student Comprehension through Technology: Scaffolding Techniques in a Virtual Environment
 FRANCISCO J. FAJARDO *and* JORGE E. PEREZ — 6

Guiding Growth: A Modified Constructivist Approach to Instructional Technology and the Framework
 AMY JAMES — 12

Beyond Kicking the Ball and the Physics of Sports: Teaching Process and Product to 9th Grade Science, Technology, Engineering and Math (STEM) Students
 COURTNEY L. LEWIS *and* RACHEL WARRINER BARTRON — 20

Digital Literacy Development at a Public Regional University: The Western Carolina University Experience
 MARK A. STOFFAN — 27

The Benefits of Multiple Instruction Styles in Public Libraries
 AMANDA TOTH — 34

The Accidental Trainer: Instructional Librarianship in the Modern-Day Library
 MONICA M. DOMBROWSKI, MELISSA BERNASEK *and* SHANA LOPEZ — 40

Tech Training 101? Closing the Digital Divide One Device at a Time
 JEZMYNNE DENE — 48

Part II: Teaching Staff to Teach Patrons

Building a Bridge Across the Digital Divide: Teaching Technology in the Public Library
 SAMANTHA DUCKWORTH *and* HAZEL KOZIOL — 56

Show, Don't Tell: Technology Instruction for Front-Line Staff,
Passed On to Patrons
  ELIZABETH TARSKI MCARTHUR   65

Simulating Access Issues: Using Twine to Teach E-Resources Troubleshooting
  KATE LAMBARIA, HEIDI R. JOHNSON and NICOLE HELREGEL   74

On-Demand Tech Training for Students, Faculty and Staff
  ASHLEY J. COLE, HEATHER BEIRNE and BRAD MARCUM   82

Facing Change Together: Overcoming Differing Comfort Levels with
Technology in Librarian and Library Staff Training
  CHRISTINE ELLIOTT, DONGMEI CAO and CHRISTA E. POPARAD   89

Technology Instruction as a Cycle of Instructional Coaching
  SARA FREY   96

Part III: Hardware, Software and Code

Is That Code? Using Google in Undergraduate Math and
Computer Science Research
  AARON J. BLODGETT and JENNIFER L. DEAN   104

Rise or Fall of a Library Intranet: Best Practices, Tips and Hints
  JOSHUA K. JOHNSON   110

Starting a Device Club
  DELORIS J. FOXWORTH   118

How to Design a New Software Class
  JULIA J. DAHM   125

How to Design a Non-Traditional Software Class: PowerPoint for
Conference Posters
  JULIA J. DAHM   132

Ways to Use Digital Badges in the Library: They're Not Just for
Students Anymore
  LAURA BOHUSKI   139

Beyond the One-Shot: Online Video Tutorials for International Students
  MICHELLE EMANUEL   146

Girls Who Code in the Library: Community-Led Programming at Its Best
  JENNIFER BUNTON FORGIT   152

Mobile Computer Lab Services to Tent City Communities: A Case Study
  DANIELLE M. DUVALL and LISA FRASER   159

Part IV: Strategies, Planning and Partnerships

Marketing and Managing Technology Education in the Face of
Library Anxiety
  CARA MARCO   168

Partnering to Teach Technology: Planning a Library-Based Workshop Series
  KATHRYN M. HOUK *and* JORDAN M. NIELSEN   175

Balancing Technology Education with Reference and Instruction
  ELIZABETH NELSON   183

Enhancing Pedagogy with Technology: Librarian-Guided Peer-to-Peer Instruction for Faculty
  EMY NELSON DECKER   190

Information Literacy and Metaliteracy Are the Ties That Bind Librarians and Athletic Coaches
  FORREST C. FOSTER, CARL LEAK *and* TERRENCE JARROD MARTIN, SR.   197

Tech Training and Library Advocacy: Linking the Academic Library with the School Library and Turning Pre-Service Teachers into Lifelong Library Users
  HEATHER BEIRNE *and* CINDY JUDD   205

About the Contributors   213

Index   217

Foreword
by James G. Neal

User instruction is part of the DNA of libraries. In a field characterized by shifting user expectations and needs, creative service strategies, acceleration in collective innovation, radical collaboration, a focus on assessment and demonstration of value, economic challenges, and constant mutability, librarians and other information professionals play a critical role in educating our users and staff to be successful and productive in their use of technology. Librarianship is buffeted by constant revolutions in technology, in the platforms that support our work and our services, in the need to achieve scale and network effects through aggregation, in the devices that enable access, in the explosion of electronic and born digital content, in the tools that support our work, in the networks that connect us with the world, in the maker initiatives in our libraries, in the growing importance of the personal web, 3-D printing, artificial intelligence and geo-everything. Libraries own the responsibility for teaching and developing new skills and knowledge, for improving capability, productivity and performance.

Carol Smallwood and Lura Sanborn have assembled a remarkable group of accomplished and expert authors providing insightful guidance on technology use instruction in a wide variety of library settings and circumstances. This is an essential primer and guide to creative thinking, best practices, and provocative experiences in training and education. The contributors understand and embrace the limitations of resources, time and personnel in our libraries, and focus on very practical and effective techniques of instruction. We learn through case studies and discussions of methodology, through a focus on empowering front-line staff, through software and coding activities, and through valuable thinking about strategy, planning and collaboration. Across 28 essays, we are treated to rich and very helpful grounding on how to advance technology use instruction.

The 21st century information professional must be committed to continuous personal development. Libraries must sustain a strong service ethic which places user instruction as a core value and strategic priority in all settings. These two drivers are part of the larger context of library transformation: a need to change in composition and structure, that is, what we are and what we do; to change our outward form and appearance, that is, how we are viewed and understood; and to change our character and condition, that is, how we do it. We must be virtual, engaged with our users in new and powerful ways. We must be virtuoso, smart but always ready to learn. And we must be virtuous, always embracing and supporting the public interest, and working to improve the experience of those we serve.

2 Foreword

Our users want more and better content, more and better access, convenience, and new capabilities and skills. They want to manage costs and be productive, to control their information environments, and to participate in the use of new technologies. Well-designed and effectively delivered technology use instruction for our patrons, students and staffs is essential to our successful library future. This important compendium of ideas and experiences will help us to even more essential to our communities and to be embraced by both users and decision makers.

James G. Neal is the president-elect of the American Library Association. He will assume the role of president in June 2017. He served as the vice president for information services and university librarian at Columbia University from 2001 to 2014, providing leadership for university academic computing and a system of 22 libraries. Previously, he served as the dean of University Libraries at Indiana University and Johns Hopkins University and held administrative positions in the libraries at Penn State, Notre Dame and the City University of New York.

Preface

Teaching Technology in Libraries is by school, public, and academic librarians in the United States sharing their expertise on teaching the use of technology in their libraries to staff, patrons, and students. In addition to keeping up with technology that advances at a bewildering rate, librarians have the equally challenging task of teaching it to various users when constricted by time, help, and reduced budgets.

The 28 essays written by one to three authors are divided into parts: Part I is Case Studies and Instruction Methodology; Part II is Teaching Staff to Teach Patrons; Part III is Hardware, Software and Code; and Part IV is Strategies, Planning and Partnerships.

Our thanks to James G. Neal, president-elect of the American Library Association for the foreword. Thanks also to Wei Fang, Roland Barksdale-Hall, Vera Gubnitskaia, and Shana Gass for writing back-cover blurbs.

PART I
Case Studies and Instruction Methodology

Supporting Student Comprehension through Technology
Scaffolding Techniques in a Virtual Environment

Francisco J. Fajardo *and* Jorge E. Perez

When one thinks of scaffolding, the image of a building under construction or a support structure comes to mind. These mental pictures are part of foundation of a stand-alone or larger edifice. Similarly, we can apply the concept of scaffolding to education, helping students in learning complex concepts and ideas. Scaffolding supports students in executing difficult tasks and serves both struggling and high-achieving students. By providing scaffolding in a course, instructors are able to fill in the learning gaps while taking on new challenges throughout the academic year (Rollins 2014).

Scaffolding is an excellent pedagogical technique for instructors to emphasize specific content, learning tasks, or material mastery. If executed properly, the approach is flexible and will build upon a student's prior knowledge and support future learning goals. However, this does require the creativity of the instructor and those involved to create meaningful scaffolds to cultivate learning—for example, the use of technology, finding mobile applications or "apps" used as a supplements to a lesson in a course on creating a step-by-step video tutorial on searching for peer-reviewed literature. Teaching faculty and librarians use this method, which draws its influence from renowned Russian psychologist Lev Vygotsky and subsequent learning theorists. Over the years, scaffolding has transcended learning theory and been put into practice with the use of technology, i.e., learning management systems (LMS), and other tools employed by today's information professionals both in and out of the classroom. This essay presents a "how-to" guide to using various tools along with the authors' experience creating streaming video tutorials for a medical course that is easily adaptable to your library's instructional needs. This primer is good for new or seasoned librarians looking for alternative approaches when creating and teaching course content.

With LMS products such as Moodle, Desire 2 Learn, Blackboard, Canvas and LibGuides (a content management system) librarians are able to create active learning environments using videos, screencasts, surveys, polls, images, search widgets, pre- and post-tests, and synchronous/asynchronous collaboration spaces. The goal of scaffolding is not the act of simply putting these items on a web page, but strategically creating interactive elements that build the student's ability to learn and confidence in mastering a subject area. Baker (2014) makes an important distinction between pathfinder-like and

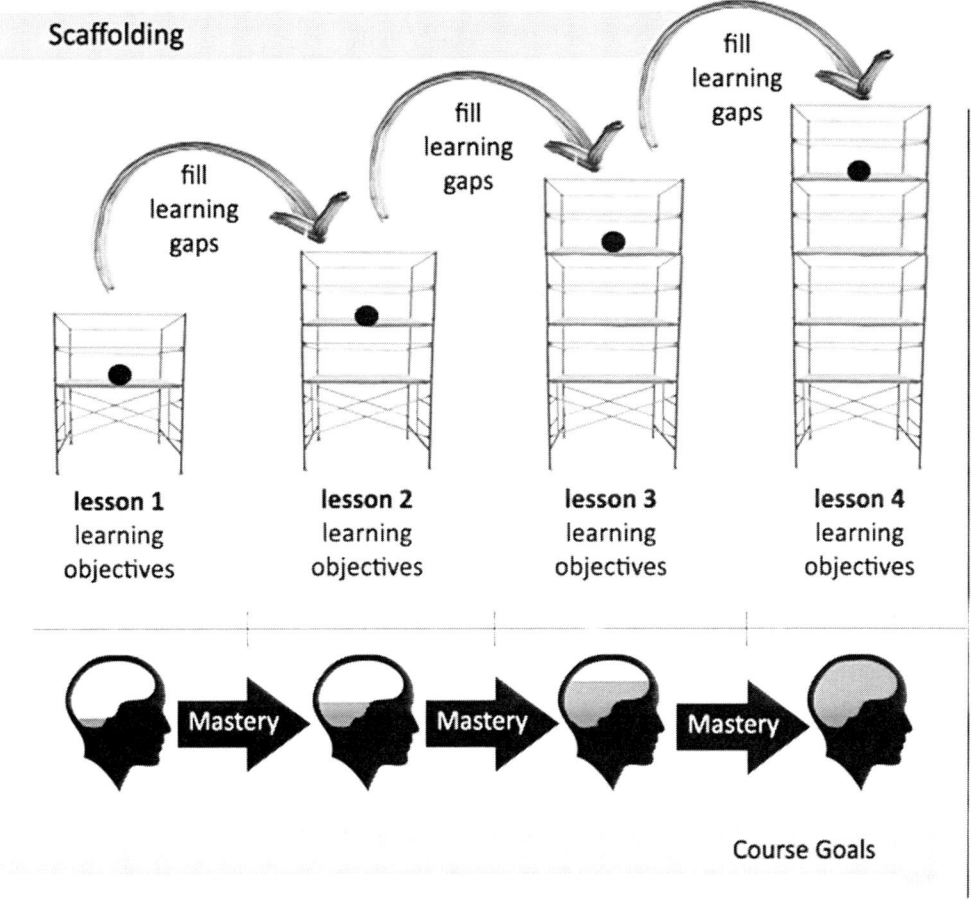

Progression in Learning Lessons

tutorial-type online guides created with LibGuides. The latter becomes a stand-alone resource, with no need for "one-shot" instruction, with resources for students to browse and activities to complete to build their skill level related to a certain assignment. There are many parts to a well-designed tutorial guide, including scaffolding lessons to engage students at their point of need. When creating online guides, the librarian can think of ways to make lessons more interactive and build activities that foster students' skills and comfort-level with the lesson. This may be achieved by creating a short informational video or allowing a space for students to reflect on what they have read by creating a survey or form. One simple approach conducted by the Oakland University Libraries is the addition of a search bar on their LibGuides home page. Librarians track student searches to inform the future creation of online learning objects or use analytics or track use to inform creation decisions (Hess, Greer, Lombardo & Lim 2015). Furthermore, they created decision trees and rubrics to ensure a user-centered tutorial guide. These decision trees and rubrics become scaffolding objects for the instructor or the librarian to ensure standards in the course are met consistently.

Scaffolding in an online environment can take many forms with class meetings completely online, face-to-face, or blended (a combination of online and face-to-face meetings). The LMS environments have helped librarians to embed themselves in courses to reach the students where they meet. LMSs contain online tools to produce interactivity and productive learning environments through scaffolding techniques. Based on findings from the Association of College and Research Libraries (ACRL) Framework for Information Literacy in Higher Education Task Force, scaffolding lessons, termed *threshold concepts*, cutting lessons into bits and pieces, allows librarians to assist Millennials in mastering lessons effectively (as cited in Porter 2014). "While it is unrealistic for librarians to teach students information literacy in one or even a few classroom sessions, helping students to master individual information literacy threshold concepts can lay the foundation for more effective discipline-specific research" (Porter, 2014).

Scaffolding affords an instructor a shift in his or her teaching mindset. The shift occurs when the instructor uses technology to ensure learning or mastery is occurring in the classroom and allowing students to take control of their learning. For example, quizzes or tests are created to assess learning. In the traditional sense, a letter grade corresponds to student performance. Taking the scaffolding approach, the exams can become an opportunity to cement the lesson and ensure mastery. Instructors may use hints to guide a student having issues with a particular question. Similar to games, when a player is stuck, a hint may reveal or show text that can allow the user to remember what to do. Sometimes students guess their answer correctly—never receiving an explanation of why the correct answer is correct. In these instances, it is helpful to have an explanation or a review of the answer in case the student wants to know why the chosen answer is correct or the best of all choices listed. Hints or guiding questions may be activated by prolonged reaction time or by answering the question incorrectly the first time or on-demand not dependent on performance (Hodges, Feng & Pan 2015). In the scaffolding approach, grading can also become a way of building learning levels. If questions were not fully developed or correct, the student may be allowed to review a certain video, receive a hint, or re-do the project. The end goal is for the particular lesson that will further the student's learning to be cemented in his or her mind. Peer grading or participation can assist students in reviewing the lesson.

Synchronous/asynchronous discussion boards or chat spaces can be a way to ensure students are able to communicate their learning effectively through higher-level questioning and allowing peers to participate in constructive discussion. In scaffolding, after the teacher has shown a lesson and worked closely with students, the students are then encouraged to try to complete the lesson and participate in peer groups. Through peer feedback and discussion, students review their learning, which ensures they understand the lesson. It is important to involve peers in constructively commenting on projects created by other students. The critique process allows the person giving and the person receiving the feedback to deepen their learning by revisiting the concepts in the lesson to give constructive criticism. Students are encouraged to transform from passive learners to active learners.

Mobile apps have been important in transforming the way we receive and view information. More students are using mobile devices than ever before, and LMS companies have created mobile apps that update students on classroom activities—bypassing logging in to the LMS for check-ins. Similar to the concept of RSS, Rich Site Summary or Really Simple Syndication, the information is sent to the user in real time. For example, Blackboard has an app titled Blackboard Mobile Learn. From an instructor's point of view, this may open a plethora of engagement possibilities. For one, notifications that pop up may be opportunities for scaffolding lessons. We usually think of notifications as a way to alert a student about an upcoming assignment deadline, a special event, or an upcoming holiday. Scaffolding can be incorporated into student notifications by broadcasting interesting facts or information that support the current lesson. If students download the app on their phone, tablet, or other mobile device, notifications are read like text messages. Interacting with your students is key, and activities such as matching games and flash cards promote further cementing of the lessons and are wonderful tools since they allow students to use what they have learned to complete a task. Besides the literature that supports gaming in education, the interactivity of lessons, individually or in groups, may be helpful to bridge concepts or bring a fuzzy lesson into focus.

Short polls or surveys may be helpful in gaining information from students about where they are having the most issues with an assignment or lesson. The check-in may be during the assignment or after the assignment is completed and can be formal or informal. It is important to note that conducting feedback during the process is imperative to a scaffolding intervention. Surveys created within the LMS, or with tools such as Survey Monkey or Qualtrics, can be helpful by creating a visual representation of data gathered. In addition, with certain apps, such as Poll Everywhere, students can use their phones to interact with the class instructor or fellow students. It is important to change the method as we are bombarded with surveys constantly, and their effectiveness may lessen. One way to avoid surveys is to use statistics or analytics available through an LMS. Instead of surveying your audience, you can simply see what questions were missed on a quiz or test. This information is important in creating a scaffolding mechanism to ensure the lesson behind a particular question can be understood. This data can be found when using your LMS, LibGuides, your database stats, or your YouTube channel.

Home learning, commonly known as homework, is where instructors assign exercises or activities for students to complete at home. Depending on the content, the amount or type of homework is designed to get the most out of what was learned in class. Teachers may assign specific exercises to build on or emphasize a lesson and even provide a bridge to learn other concepts for future courses. Video tutorials have become a wonderful way to flip your classroom in that they allowed students to view certain video lessons before the face-to-face or virtual meeting. Thanks to advances in technology, anyone can create videos and embed them in lesson pages and e-mail through several platforms including social media. Within scaffolding, it is important to divide a lesson into small digestible units. This helps the student to work toward the complete lesson and revisit a particular lesson if a review is needed. Having students create the videos or other learning objects is an activity to consider. Allowing a platform for students to publish their own material is imperative in creating a welcoming learning environment. Turn students into creators of media and masters of their learning.

Experience and Lessons Learned Using Streaming Video as a Scaffolding Technique

The authors of this essay created a number of video tutorials for an evidence-based medical course to allow scaffolding of lesson objectives and reaching students at their point of need. Although it was designed for use with medical students, the process is adaptable for instructors or librarians working with students in any academic setting.

The first step is to identify key concepts and learning objectives for a course. It is imperative that you consult with your faculty or course director to narrow your focus and identify your key concept, for example, teaching students how to search for relevant peer-reviewed literature in a database as well as teaching them what they should do independently for future assignments. Specifically, librarians were tasked with creating a series of online video tutorials demonstrating searches using keywords versus subject headings and identifying the relevant literature. These concepts were applied later when students had to use peer-reviewed published literature to treat a patient.

Next, break down the lessons into digestible units and prepare a narration script. It was decided before the production of the first video tutorial that each title should focus on a lesson and last three to five minutes, though some lessons do require more explanation and time. Another reason for breaking the lessons into manageable units is to make them easy for a student to find if she or he wants to review a particular concept. After identifying lesson areas, begin to write a narration script for the video production. It is recommended you do this before you create your images, animations or PowerPoint presentations. Use simple, clear language and do not assume that your audience will understand all the terms used in your video tutorial. The team also was aware that students learn in different styles—visual, audio and kinesthetic. The audio of each video script was made available for students who prefer audio and do not want to depend only on the visual.

Consider the technology/software for your tutorial. If your library is on a budget, you may use the video editing software that is bundled with your Windows or Mac operating system package or use free open source software such as JING by TechSmith. More advanced editing software, such as Camtasia or Final Cut Pro, provides several ways to emphasize learning concepts. Callouts (items that pop up on the screen), arrows, highlighted text and the like assist students' focus on an area that emphasizes concepts and terms they will use in the future. Some software also allows you to embed quizzes throughout the presentation or at the end to assess learning. Using infographics or data visualizations to support the lesson may be more useful than presenting text-heavy PowerPoint slides. Infographics become a visual mnemonic for concepts or ideas. Collaboration is important, as is seeking feedback throughout the entire process. Share your work with your team. Always edit until you have agreement on your script and visuals; this is crucial as you want a finished product that will serve faculty and students for a long period of time.

Scaffolding in any course involves creativity and is highly dependent on your team. Do not assume that all of your students are familiar with concepts. Simplify your explanations of concepts and words. Use basic language and simple sentences in your descriptions and, when possible, repeat the key terms you want your students to learn the most. Some repetition in your videos is recommended and helps with making the student independent in developing crucial skills you want them to take away. Be creative, use infographics in your videos, and support the words with images. Students respond to visual cues and tend to remember them. Avoid and making lengthy videos with only screencasts or static images. Videos should be short, five to six minutes at most (preferably in series highlighting the most important points for your students)—any longer and you will not engage your audience and they will lose their focus. Make sure you organize the material that you will cover in each video carefully; editing your script is crucial.

Another important consideration when creating your videos is investing in equipment and finding a space suitable for recording. To ensure the best sound quality, look into purchasing a good quality microphone (preferably a condenser microphone similar to those used in a recording studio) with a stand. These types of microphones make all the difference when recording the audio. The voice is usually clearer and more distinct, even when music plays in the background, versus the common USB headsets found at most major retailers. The common headset (with microphone) can get the job done, if budget is a factor. Locating a quiet and well-insulated space in your library to minimize unwanted noise and echoes is paramount.

Go beyond the "one-shot" instruction and embed yourself at any opportunity that presents itself. This means networking with course directors and department chairs, highlighting how the library can provide instruction beyond that "one-shot" and supporting the curriculum in other innovative ways. Whether it is scaffolding or working with other pedagogical approaches, a variety of support mechanisms are available to students and faculty via library resources. Combine efforts and educational approaches, such as scaffolding, as a way to supplement the material and face-to-face lectures. Use web tools to assist in measuring learning outcomes, allowing a space for reflection, and strengthening metacognition. Scaffolding becomes another tool in helping student learning, and if it is used properly, students will use the content what they've learned in one course to support what they learn in later courses.

Does one scaffolding technique work better than another? The answer depends on the materials and content. Use what is appropriate for the type of class and for the environment, i.e., face-to-face, online, or blended formats. Consider all of these factors and learning objectives when you scaffold.

REFERENCES

Baker, Ruth L. 2014. "Designing LibGuides as Instructional Tools for Critical Thinking and Effective Online Learning." *Journal of Library & Information Services in Distance Learning* 8 (3–4): 107–117.
Cayton-Hodges, Gabrielle A., Gary Feng, and Xingyu Pan. 2015. "Tablet-Based Math Assessment: What Can We Learn from Math Apps?" *Educational Technology & Society* 18 (2): 3–20.
Nichols Hess, A., K. Greer, S.V. Lombardo, and A. Lim A. 2015. "Books, Bytes, and Buildings: The Academic Library's Unique Role in Improving Student Success." *Journal of Library Administration* 55 (8): 622–638.
Porter, Brandi. 2015. "Designing a Library Information Literacy Program Using Threshold Concepts, Student Learning Theory, and Millennial Research in the Development of Information Literacy Sessions." *Internet Reference Services Quarterly* 19 (3–4): 233–244.
Rollins, Suzy Pepper. 2014. *Learning in the Fast Lane: 8 Ways to Put ALL Students on the Road to Academic Success*. Alexandria: ASCD. http://public.eblib.com/choice/publicfullrecord.aspx?p=1681152.

Guiding Growth
A Modified Constructivist Approach to Instructional Technology and the Framework

Amy James

There are two main schools of thought when it comes to learning theories: behaviorism and cognitivism. Swiss philosopher and psychologist Piaget wanted to find some middle ground between the two and so he became the father of what we call the constructivist approach to learning (Allen 2008, 30). He believed that gaining understanding and knowledge about the world is a process involving continuous "self-construction" (Allen 2008, 30). Students will ultimately build knowledge and life skills from their past life experiences and pre-existing constructs of the world around them (Allen 2008, 30).

So how does constructivism relate to information literacy instruction? The constructivist approach to learning allows students to work on problem solving in a collaborative way. Students discover how to think critically in order to solve problems. Constructivism is about active learning techniques and allowing the student to learn from the activity rather than learning the information beforehand and applying it during the activity. The activity becomes the vehicle that propels the learning to take place. Oftentimes this approach involves students working together in teams to actively learn while the instructor serves as a facilitator. This approach maintains that the student interacts with the material through an active learning process to create knowledge. Constructivism helps students to think critically, analyze, evaluate, and apply knowledge to real-life situations. Students do this through team tasks and experiences that they have in the classroom in conjunction with their previous knowledge (Allen 2008, 21).

Why is this essay called "modified constructivism" when I just talked up all of the benefits of constructivism? Well, not every student learns in the same way. The constructivist approach might assume that students have some prior knowledge of the subject. The way to combat this is to utilize a mixed methods approach: modified constructivism. You take the active discovery, student-driven teamwork attributes of constructivism but you do not assume prior knowledge on the student's part, unless you know otherwise (pre-session survey, formal or informal) (Allen 2008, 33). When thinking about this approach, Bostock says, "Some students will enjoy the challenges of constructivist learning while others will sometimes find them uncomfortable and need more objectivist [behavioral] instruction. A radically constructivist course would be more difficult to implement within the constraints of large numbers, resources and institutional culture, so it is cheering to think that a partial implementation of constructivist principles may actually be optimal for the majority of students" (Bostock 1998, 236).

With this approach, abstract concepts that are generally more difficult for students to grasp take on meaning because they are attached to the performance of an activity (Allen 2008, 34). When you are developing the curriculum for information literacy instruction, a good approach might be to use a flipped classroom model. The flipped classroom can offer students who don't have as much prior knowledge of a subject a chance to get more familiar with the content before coming to class. Then, when they do come to class, the constructivist methods can come into play. Flipping the classroom is all the rage right now in higher education, but the method actually gained popularity in the mid–1990s (Brooks 2014, 226). This model for learning combines instructional technology (video tutorials, for example) and active learning techniques. It can be a great way to cultivate the modified constructivist method.

Studies in the past have shown connections between the Association of College and Research Libraries (ACRL) information literacy standards, the constructivist learning approach, and Web 2.0 technologies. But not much has been published on how to incorporate the Framework for Information Literacy for Higher Education into a modified constructivist classroom using relevant technologies. In this essay you will learn how to use the framework in your modified constructivist classroom while keeping students engaged through the use of appropriate technology.

The ACRL has long been in support of the constructivist paradigm (Allen 2008, 21). In fact, in looking at the standards that were in existence before the framework, it is made apparent through language like "student-centered learning environments where inquiry is the norm, problem solving becomes the focus, and thinking critically is part of the process" (ACRL 2006). That describes the essence of constructivism. It is active learning, engaging students in the creation of knowledge. ACRL's framework points out that the name "framework" is intentional because it represents a "cluster of interconnected core concepts, with flexible options for implementation" (ACRL 2015). So, since there is this intended flexibility, let's take a more in-depth look at each of the six frames to see how you can focus on the frames by incorporating technology to a modified constructivist classroom.

Authority Is Constructed and Contextual

This first frame focuses on students learning about expertise. Different groups of people have different views on what is authoritative so therefore "authority is constructed." "Authority is contextual" in that the type of information that is needed can help to determine what kind of authority should be expected. This frame is intended to help students think critically about authority with "informed skepticism." It also leaves room for students to reflect on themselves and their own biases so that they can continue to re-evaluate their thinking.

With Web 2.0 technology, students have an even greater opportunity to grasp the concepts of authority and knowledge creation because they can easily create online content themselves. Whether a student is looking at a blog post, website for an organization, or an academic article, this frame points out the necessity for them to be able to look at that piece of information objectively and consider not only the education level of the person(s) who created it, but also any biases that they may have based upon their worldview or culture. Depending on the topic, it's important to remember that some information can be authoritative even if it comes from an unsuspecting place. The purpose is to bring attention to how important it is for students to be able to understand the different facets of authority when they are analyzing a source for its inclusion into a research paper or project (and in real-life application).

One way that you could incorporate this frame into the modified constructivist classroom would be to have your students break into small groups. If your classroom doesn't have computers, you could use iPads (one per group) if they are available to you. Then have the students in each group pick a topic to focus on for the activity. The topic could be a research question, a current event, or another interest. Once students have selected their topics, have them go online and find information on their topic from three social media sites (Facebook, Twitter, blog postings, news websites, etc.). When they are searching Facebook and Twitter they can try using the search bar to search by trending topics or hashtags. Once they find three different posts or articles about their topic they will need to compare and contrast the ways in which the information was presented. This is the time for students to get focused on authority and analyze how the information was presented in each source and think about what biases or worldviews were potentially at play during the creation of the post or article. Greg Bobish's article "Participation and Pedagogy: Connecting the Social Web to ACRL Learning Outcomes" also points out some similar activities to help get students thinking about authority.

This activity allows students to work in teams, use technology that they are likely already familiar with, and learn about the importance of considering all aspects that go into labeling a piece of information as "authoritative." Different cultures, different worldviews, and religions all go into shaping what we conclude to be authoritative.

Information Creation as a Process

Because of the participatory nature of Web 2.0 and the increasing appearance of online only publications, it is important for information seekers to understand the process of how information is created and put out into the world for their viewing. Understanding that process can help students see the potential value in a piece of information. Learning about the review process can help students learn how a piece of information came into being and determine if it is of high quality. This knowledge will give students another opportunity to examine the information that they are reviewing and determine if it fits their needs. The end product should reflect the steps that went into the creation of it.

Students may not have prior knowledge about the publication process or about how different formats are published according to different criteria and standards. It might be a good idea to use a flipped classroom model with this concept and have students watch a short video before the session that covers the information creation process. If you don't have one already created, there are plenty on YouTube that would be worthy of sharing with your students. A video that I would recommend using, created by "Editage Insights," is called "A Manuscript's Journey from Submission to Publication." Then, once students arrive to class, you can answer any questions that they might have. It is also important at this time to mention that information can be published in different formats and that one format isn't necessarily "better" than another. But learning the different steps that a piece of information took before it became published will help clue students in on the quality and usefulness of the information.

Before class, pre-select four sources of information and try to make sure that they are in varied formats (electronic journal, video, academic blog post, etc.). Then have students break into pairs and review each of the sources. Have them make educated guesses about the steps that each source went through before it became published. They can do this by researching the publisher and trying to investigate the publication requirements for that publisher. For example, if they are looking at an academic journal article they could try to figure out which journal it was published in and then look that journal up online and try to find their publishing standards. If they are reviewing a video, they could take a look at the source of the video, find out who created it and see if they can look for more videos from that source or find out the how the video was created and eventually put out on the web for all to see. The more that they can find out about each source, the better. Once they have had time to work with their partner on this, they should try to briefly list the steps that they believe were used to create each piece of information. Then, using polling technology called Poll Everywhere, students can text in their responses and everyone can see them presented on the projector at the front of the class. The librarian would need to create the poll in advance. Then the librarian would facilitate the discussion and students would collaborate with other groups to see which of their ideas differed, which were the same, and why.

This activity combines the principles of a constructivist classroom in a more modified way by incorporating a flipped classroom model. It also allows for students to participate in active learning, work as part of a team, and accomplish tasks that enable them to create their own learning on the process of information creation.

Information Has Value

In the Framework, the idea that "information has value" is about the importance of author ownership and properly giving credit when you use someone else's ideas. This frame is very similar to the previous ACRL Information Literacy Competency Standards standard five, which concentrated on the "economic, legal, and social issues surrounding the use of information and [the ability for the student to] access and use information ethically and legally" (ACRL 2006). This frame encourages helping students to appreciate the work of others and the effort that goes into information creation.

So, rather than go into a lecture about copyright regulations or have students identify parts of a citation, you could try to get them engaged in an activity that will teach them about how copyright applies to the things they see every day. For this activity, librarians would pre-select sources (videos, Tweets, blog posts, academic journal articles, images, Pinterest pins, etc.). Then have students break into small groups and evaluate each source to determine whether or not it can be shared online freely without restriction. If the source is a video, can they upload it to their personal YouTube account? What if you take someone else's Tweet from his or her Twitter account and post it to your Facebook page? Or if you share a journal article PDF that you have downloaded for everyone on your Facebook page to view? Have them try to think about Fair Use and Creative Commons when they are doing their evaluations. In line with the modified constructivist approach, if they don't know much about copyright, Fair Use, or Creative Commons, it might be helpful to pass out a cheat sheet that gives descriptions and examples of each before they start the activity. Have the students work in groups and cover each source that they are given. Then have each group select a spokesperson to aid in facilitating the class discussion. Similar activity suggestions can also be found in Bobish's article previously mentioned.

The American Library Association's (ALA) Office for Information Technology Policy's Copyright Advisory Network also has an excellent list of resources to help you better understand copyright and determine if something is covered under copyright, Fair Use, public domain, etc. (ALA 2015).

Research as Inquiry

This frame, "Research as Inquiry," encourages you to help your students understand that research is a process and that it involves asking a lot of questions. You start off with a research question and then as you learn about your topic you begin to ask more questions. The key is for students to be able to engage with the research process and think about research as an open-ended investigation.

A big part of this concept is for students to be able to take a broad research topic and refine it until it becomes a well-defined, open-ended question that is ready to be explored. One way to incorporate this learning outcome into your classroom is to include an activity that involves mind mapping. Have students break into pairs and create a free account with one of several web-based mind-mapping programs. One program that I would recommend using due to the intuitiveness and easy sign-up option through Google is called Coggle. You can just head to coggle.it and create an account and get started creating mind maps in seconds. Once students have gotten into pairs and at least one person per pair has created a Coggle account, have them brainstorm a topic. They can start by thinking about it in a broad context and then inputting words into Coggle that come to mind when they think of that topic. Together they can take the concepts that they came up with and start expanding on those big picture ideas and then they can begin to refine them. You can encourage them to use this tool throughout the research process. As they start asking more questions about their topic they can use Coggle to keep track of the different facets of their questions. This can also be a great tool to keep track of keywords and synonyms that they come up with as they use databases to conduct their searches.

This activity helps students to see research as an open-ended line of questions that starts off as a broad idea and then needs to be broken down and refined. Using a simple tool like Coggle can help them to keep track of their progress throughout the life of their research.

Scholarship as Conversation

Teaching the principles of scholarship as part of a larger conversation is an important area of discovery for students learning information literacy skills. As students begin doing research and reading journals that are fundamental to their fields, they will start noticing prominent author. They will also start to see authors referring to the other authors that they have already read. One scholar does research and publishes it, another scholar reads their work, and responds to it through his or her own work. Learning this skill takes time to master, and since you can't have your students read entire journals during class it becomes tricky to find a way to incorporate this into your sessions. However, the point is for students to understand that scholarship is about sharing your well-researched ideas and responding to the ideas of others. It's also important for them to understand that at an appropriate level they too can participate in the conversation.

Before class pre-select at least two articles that have a number of references to other well-known researchers' work. Have the students skim through them and highlight sections where the authors mention the work of another scholar and either use that to support or disprove their thesis. When they arrive in class have them write a quick one-minute paper about what they learned from the pre-class exercise. Then share with them that there are ways that they can participate in scholarly conversations in their own fields at an appropriate level. Have them group together with people in the class that have similar research interests or the same major. Then have them begin searching for credible blogs by scholars in that field. Have them use some of the skills that they acquired through frame number one about authority to determine the credibility of the author(s) writing the blog. Most blogs will have a comments section. Once they have found and reviewed the blog, have them select an article from it that interests them. For homework, have each student come up with a well thought-out comment that they can post in response to the article that they selected. Who knows? Maybe the original author or a fellow student will have a response to their comment.

Searching as Strategic Exploration

This final frame is about having the flexibility to alter your search strategy as needed when you make new discoveries throughout the research process. This can be tougher than it seems for students who have spent hours researching a topic in a certain way only to become frustrated when they aren't turning up the right results. But as you go through the research process, you learn new things about your topic and sometimes you find that what you were originally looking for doesn't exist in the same context you expected. So you have to change your mindset and start fresh. This is an important, time-saving skill for students to develop.

For this activity, have students get into small groups and hand them a pre-made note card that contains a vague research question, a Boolean search operator symbol, and a hint at its meaning. They will have a few minutes to brainstorm how to break down their topic into keywords. Then have them go to Google Scholar and start inputting their search terms. Through trial and error and with the help of their peers they will review the results and some will need to revise their search strategy and keywords. To help them revise their searches, have them use the dropdown menu on the main Google Scholar search page that incorporates the natural language version of Boolean search operators. This is where they can use the Boolean search operator symbol and the hint about its meaning to fill in the blanks in the Google Scholar dropdown menu. This will help them work through the search and refine the topic and search strategy with others in the class.

This activity, although not as in-depth as the discoveries that they will make in refining their search strategies in the research that they do on their own, will help students to see the process that goes into creating effective and efficient searches. It will also teach them strategies of narrowing and refining a topic while being open to making changes in their techniques along the way. It incorporates a quick method to learning about Boolean searches through the familiar Google interface. This activity includes hands-on group work in line with the constructivist method (with a cheat sheet card to modify the approach). It also teaches students the technology skills needed to work within an online database through the use of Google Scholar.

Conclusion

The modified constructivist approach to learning is a great way to incorporate those important constructivist principles of active learning and teamwork while also catering to those students who might learn best from a more guided approach. With the constant increase of new technology in the lives of today's students, it is imperative that we teach information literacy skills with relevant, activity-appropriate technology that will engage students and get them actively incorporating these skills inside and outside of the classroom. Incorporating the right type of technology into the classroom can be a difficult task on its own. Adding the concepts of the framework to it and trying to create a fun and effective learning environment is certainly a challenge. Becoming familiar with the framework and using these activities as a launching pad will help as you endeavor to refresh your information literacy curriculum.

REFERENCES

Allen, Maryellen. 2008. "Promoting Critical Thinking Skills in Online Information Literacy Instruction Using a Constructivist Approach." *College & Undergraduate Libraries* 15, no. 1/2: 21–38. Library, Information Science & Technology Abstracts, EBSCOhost (accessed December 7, 2015).
Association of College and Resource Libraries. 2006. "Information Literacy Competency Standards for Higher Education." Last modified September 1, 2006. http://www.ala.org/acrl/standards/informationliteracycompetency (accessed December 7, 2015).
Association of College and Resource Libraries. 2015. "Framework for Information Literacy for Higher Education." Last modified February 9, 2015. http://www.ala.org/acrl/standards/ilframework (accessed December 7, 2015).
American Library Association. 2015. "Copyright Advisory Network." Last modified 2015. http://librarycopyright.net/resources/ (accessed December 7, 2015).
Bobish, Greg. 2011. "Participation and Pedagogy: Connecting the Social Web to ACRL Learning Outcomes." *Journal of Academic Librarianship* 37, no. 1: 54–63. ERIC, EBSCOhost (accessed December 7, 2015).
Bostock, Stephen J. 1998. "Constructivism in Mass Higher Education: A Case Study." *British Journal of Educational Technology* 29, no. 3: 255–240. ERIC, EBSCOhost (accessed December 7, 2015).
Dodge, Lauren, and Jennifer Sams. 2011. "Innovative Copyright." *College & Research Libraries News* 72, no. 10: 596–599. OmniFile Full Text Select (H.W. Wilson), EBSCOhost (accessed December 7, 2015).
Fulkerson, Diane. 2014. "The Flipped Classroom and Media for Library Instruction: Changing Library Instruction." *Against the Grain* 26, no. 4: 17–21. Library, Information Science & Technology Abstracts, EBSCOhost (accessed December 7, 2015).
Halpern, Rebecca, and Chimene Tucker. 2015. "Leveraging Adult Learning Theory with Online Tutorials." *Reference Services Review* 43, no. 1: 112–124. Library, Information Science & Technology Abstracts, EBSCOhost (accessed December 7, 2015).
Magnuson, Marta L. 2013. "Web 2.0 and Information Literacy Instruction: Aligning Technology with ACRL Standards." *Journal of Academic Librarianship* 39, no. 3: 244–251. Library, Information Science & Technology Abstracts, EBSCOhost (accessed December 7, 2015).
Perez-Stable, Maria A. 2012. "Framing a Strategy Exploring Faculty Attitudes toward Library Instruc-

tion and Technology Preferences to Enhance Information Literacy." Reference & User Services Quarterly 52, no. 2: 109–122. Academic Search Elite, EBSCOhost (accessed December 7, 2015).

Ringle, Melissa. 2014. "Redesigning Library Instruction: A Collaborative Process." *Indiana Libraries* 33, no. 2: 68–70. OmniFile Full Text Select (H.W. Wilson), EBSCOhost (accessed December 7, 2015).

Rodriguez, Julia E., Katie Greer, and Barbara Shipman. 2014. "Copyright and You: Copyright Instruction for College Students in the Digital Age." *Journal of Academic Librarianship* 40, no. 5: 486–491. Library, Information Science & Technology Abstracts, EBSCOhost (accessed December 7, 2015).

Roy, Loriene, and Eric Novotny. 2000. "How Do We Learn? Contributions of Learning Theory to Reference Service and Library Instruction." *Reference Librarian* no. 69/70: 129. Library, Information Science & Technology Abstracts, EBSCOhost (accessed December 7, 2015).

Wilcox Brooks, Andrea. 2014. "Information Literacy and the Flipped Classroom." *Communications in Information Literacy* 8, no. 2: 225–235. OmniFile Full Text Select (H.W. Wilson), EBSCOhost (accessed December 7, 2015).

Beyond Kicking the Ball and the Physics of Sports
Teaching Process and Product to 9th Grade Science, Technology, Engineering and Math (STEM) Students

COURTNEY L. LEWIS *and* RACHEL WARRINER BARTRON

The Challenges of High School and STEM Integration

While many schools are focused on the need to attract students into pursuing STEM-related fields, the types of natural interdisciplinary and integrated teaching methods that fit so well in elementary and middle school environments stall when students hit the secondary level. High school science and math curricula are content-focused and schools are subject to both schedules and college admissions pressures, neither of which lend themselves to true interdisciplinary teaching. Layered on top of this challenge are real student fears of the hard sciences and higher mathematics, with many students never having encountered a need for the level of grit and determination required for mastering higher levels of content. Very early in their high school career and often even before arriving in the 9th grade, students decide whether or not they want to pursue a college degree in a STEM-related field (Hutchinson-Anderson, Johnson, and Craig, 2015).

In 2012, Wyoming Seminary, an independent day/boarding school in Northeastern Pennsylvania, received a generous gift from the Maslow Family which funded the foundation of the Maslow STEM School at Wyoming Seminary. This program demonstrates the practical applications and exciting careers related to STEM fields by bringing in speakers and partnering with colleges to demonstrate real-life applications and also by simultaneously designing a framework of courses to expose students to engineering principles and design thinking. This approach is easier at the upper end of a student's career, and the school's robotics, flight, and submersible electives are popular among upperclassmen, but the question still remained of inspiring students at the start of their high school careers to consider STEM-related fields and to pursue higher level science and math classes. From the librarian's standpoint, this foundational class offered a point of collaboration to instill information literacy and technology instruction specific to the sciences that would complement the library's already robust integration with the school's humanities classes.

The 9th grade, formerly a time when the majority of incoming students would take an introductory biology class, was identified as an opportunity to expose students to real-life applications of scientific problems. At the same time, the new 9th grade science class, STEM Foundations, would take a survey approach to the future hard sciences the students would take prior to graduation, covering physics in the fall trimester, a green energy approach to the winter trimester (emphasizing chemistry concepts), and end with bioengineering in the spring.

By covering foundational content and skill elements for physics, biology and chemistry, the goal was to give students a taste of each discipline with an immediate connection between content and real-life application as well as plenty of hands-on lab time, in the hope that the obvious relevancy between science and project would encourage students who otherwise wouldn't consider a STEM-related field to include these topics in future coursework and in college (Hutchinson-Anderson, Johnson, and Craig 2015). Physics was identified by the school's college office as being increasingly important to the college admission process and the inclusion of physics in the STEM course not only fit the overall objectives of the course but also matched the need to demystify the subject to the students who would hopefully take it in increasing numbers (Huang et al. 2015).

The course offers more immediate benefits for freshmen beyond college aspirations. Each year the incoming class is comprised of a mix of students with various backgrounds and differing levels of information literacy and technology instruction. While approximately half of the class are graduates from Wyoming Seminary's Lower School, the remaining students come from a variety of local public and private schools as well as the many international schools whose students attend prior to their arrival. With research on successful STEM programs indicating that not only traditionally considered diversity (ethnic, socio-economic, etc.) is of primary importance to effective STEM project teams, but also that exactly the student personality types that STEM teams most need are the ones least likely to elect to focus in STEM topics, meant the course and its projects needed to appeal to non-science focused students (Chen and Simpson 2015).

Because of the individualized nature of the curriculum at Wyoming Seminary, not all 9th graders take the same schedule of classes. The STEM Foundations class, exclusively for 9th graders, was seen as a great way for librarians to co-teach in the first few months of school and establish a relationship with an audience who may not yet have made the transition to seeing the librarians as information literacy and technological experts, always friendly and ready to help students succeed in any academic discipline.

The Fall Project: The Mechanics of Sports

In 2013, the first year offering the STEM Foundations class, the librarian and course teachers met to discuss a fall term project that would provide a summative assessment for students regarding their mastery of the mechanics concepts taught while also offering a formative assessment of student information literacy and technological mastery. The initial idea of a group video was discarded as having too much of a learning curve since students had not been taught how to write for or edit video in previous assignments. Since the science department had carts of MacBooks and iPads at its disposal and since the majority of 9th graders brought MacBooks to class, the choice was made for groups to produce an interactive iBook.

With approximately 85 percent of the student body electing to do a sport during the school year, the teachers and librarian felt that a focus on having predetermined groups pick a sport and a specific motion within it to analyze had widespread appeal. Students were told that they needed to demonstrate an understanding of the physics principles emphasized throughout the term, particularly regarding the application of kinematic equations. After groups were assigned, students were asked to go over the good group interaction principles taught from the first week of the class prior to lab instruction, assigning roles and emphasizing clear communication as well as total inclusion of all members.

The rubric for the project was shared with students via the class learning management portal along with a timeline and all pertinent details regarding the project (Bartron, Casterline, and Lewis 2013). Groups were given free choice as to the sport and the motion chosen, but were told the following elements had to be present in their final iBook:

- a brief history of the sport;
- an overview of a specific technological innovation within the sport;
- the physics of a specific motion including kinematic equations and a video analysis
- the representation of the sport and motion in art; and
- properly formatted APA References, including all images and video as well as text sources (and the use of parenthetical citations throughout text).

Detailed how-to tutorials and screencasts mirrored the instruction provided in class for future student reference.

Information literacy and technological instruction was offered by the librarian who was present at the start of the project as well as during lab periods throughout the five-week project period. The first session involved an introduction to advanced Google search techniques, exercises surrounding effective keyword searching, and evaluation of websites for authority. Databases taught and used for this project included the Gale Virtual Reference Library, Gale Science in Context and ProQuest's eLibrary Curriculum. A variety of print sources on the physics of various sports were purchased and checked out to the teacher to live in the labs during the project.

Students were encouraged to use a broad foundation of print and eBooks as well as journal and magazine articles in addition to the websites, images and videos necessary for the various elements of the project. Students, already familiar with citing in MLA format, were introduced to the differences in APA citation style, and were led through an understanding of why gender neutrality and source currency were of importance to scientists. Using Noodletools and its shared project feature, group members took turns citing the various sources used for their project. Because questions arose from students regarding the idea of publishing their book via the platform, students also learned about copyright issues and image and video permissions.

While teaching information seeking strategies, source evaluation and ethical use of information met many of the AASL standards, virtually every major component of the ISTE Standards for Students were also addressed (American Association of School Librarians 2007) (International Society for Technology in Education 2007). As they found quality information regarding the above areas on databases and the web, students put information in shared Google documents, storyboarded the organization of their iBooks, and ethically cited sources.

The librarian taught the principles of good design for audience understanding using the iBooks Author software, demonstrating and having students practice using the many widgets available in that program, including labeling interactive images with additional information, embedding and captioning galleries of images (excellent for the art section of the project), importing equations as .jpgs, and finally uploading edited and often original video. Students were taught how to use ClipConverter, either to edit their own video generated from using the Video Physics app on the school iPads or from video illustrating their motion they found online.

Student and Teacher/Librarian Challenges

While all students produced a summative iBook demonstrating understanding of mechanics, there were still challenges. The number one issue was the desire of certain groups to pick too complicated a motion as their focus. Teachers and the librarian counseled students away from this danger, but it took up valuable initial research time for them to realize they didn't have the level of physics knowledge required for this type of analysis. Understandably group dynamics issues arose, but the strong, previously established relationship with teachers as well as the skill set already imparted for lab work during the term allowed students to ask for help and gave teachers a reference point regarding when to step in and when to encourage students to redefine roles or discuss a problem with team members. A few students were English language learners at the intermediate or advanced levels and as such needed more assistance and more time for their reading and writing.

The iBooks Author platform had pros and cons regarding its use. As with many Apple products, the design interface was both attractive to students and intuitive. The various templates provided almost a storyboard of how their information could layout and the interactive widgets, particularly the illustrated images with pop-up information and the gallery feature, had students eager to explain their knowledge about various illustrations or even test reader understanding with embedded multiple choice questions. Students became so comfortable with the interactive features that several groups spontaneously figured out how to do a timeline with image and text popups with no instruction, surprising and delighting the teachers and librarian.

The negatives of the platform are undoubtedly familiar to teachers and librarians offering technology instruction. Obviously the Apple-only platform places a barrier for PC or Chromebook school environments, and the fact that students cannot work collaboratively in iBooks Author meant that one student at a time did the design work or imported previously written text and images from the shared Google folder in which group members were placing content. Teachers and the librarian regularly encouraged the students to cycle the responsibility for elements (one student would work on citations, another work on design elements, another write content), but it's likely that students settled into roles, particularly if one member of the group owned a more recent version of a MacBook and others did not or were using older school computers. Because all students needed access to the latest version of their iBook, the librarian led students through exporting their iBook to the shared Google folder so other students had access to it the next day if someone from the group was absent. Students had varying degrees of success renaming the file to indicate the latest version and this daily chore added a few minutes to the end of each class to make sure this necessary upload was accomplished.

24   Part I. Case Studies and Instruction Methodology

Project Results, Reflections and Long-Term Implications

From a student standpoint, some strengths of the project included the joy students took in the professional and often beautiful finished iBook as well as the degree of creativity they exercised in their choice of sport and motion and the images and text they chose to include. The overall result of their weeks of work made students feel confident and often proud, as they were frequently overheard discussing and demonstrating the features of their iBook to friends. Whether it was archery, diving, the slap shot, the free throw or the eclectic sport of curling, the physics of sports becomes a cross-cultural discussion point in the school during the five weeks of this project.

Like any research project, some students had an easier time finding quality resources than others. The librarian emphasized that a stage of research is insuring a working topic has enough supporting sources to meet the project requirements, but the reality is that there are far more quality print sources on the slap shot in ice hockey versus jai alai. Students continue to struggle with citation details, particularly parsing the original format versus the location the source was found, yet students took the ethical use of information to heart this early on in the 9th grade year.

In another major project occurring two months after the Physics of Sports, the Freshmen Debate Unit, occurring in the other class devoted exclusively to the 9th grade, Literature of Genres, a large percentage of students automatically cited information using Noodletools even though it was not required by the project rubric. Later in the year, the World Civilization required term paper, assigned to a class that many freshmen take, was so free of citation angst despite it being the first time students encountered Chicago/Turabian and footnoting that the history teachers commented on the phenomenon, wanting to know why this year's students were different. No other demographics were significantly different comprising the 9th grade class compared to previous years excepting this change in the school curriculum.

The librarian and teachers got together to debrief the project, looking over the final iBooks, reading student self-reflections and discussing changes for subsequent years. From the librarian's standpoint, the technological instruction was extremely successful and the 9th grade began going more to the library and asking for help earlier in the school year, reinforcing the idea that early, friendly contact (and a significant number of hours) can help a student with the realization that the library program is a wonderful, judgment-free, helpful support. Seeing the many struggles with citation format choice meant that the library program underwent to shift into placing more emphasis on teaching the correct choice of format, with specific games and supporting screencasts debuting on intranet web pages.

The STEM teachers felt that this project has become a pivotal point in the STEM course. Students were excited to learn and to demonstrate mastery of a topic. In addition, students were comfortable enough with iBooks Author to use this format to demonstrate summary knowledge later in the year for the final STEM project. Student behavior was consistent with larger understood trends of student struggle with parsing metadata about information sources, but the exposure to a type of non-traditional digital writing employed by the iBook project is a wonderful addition as more and most selective institutions are asking for strong science writers and greater familiarity with digital writing (Lewis 2015).

In terms of the long-term implications regarding both the course and the project, measurement of alumni STEM majors needs to be taken and compared against other variables to determine if more students are choosing these fields versus before the course's implementation. Similarly, a pre-test of student interests prior to entering the 9th grade and a post-test prior to graduation would also be an interest metric in determining the overall curriculum and its effect on student behavior and interests. The 9th grade STEM course does have an impact on students and the number of AP courses they can take in all disciplines in their junior and senior year, most greatly impacting the highest tier of student who would take more than six AP courses in their final two years of high school. This crunch and other factors limiting student choice has the school hiring a scheduling consultant in 2016 to review how best to accommodate student needs regarding higher level coursework.

From an information literacy and technology instruction standpoint, the project was an enormous success in the areas of

- student familiarity with databases and subject authorities;
- keyword generation and search strategy behavior for databases and search engines;
- advanced Google search techniques;
- familiarity with the Noodletools platform and the APA citation style;
- video creation and basic video editing skills; and
- understanding of copyright laws and the ethical use of information.

While the iBooks Author platform had many benefits, for classroom use, the need for a collaborative, interactive book platform similar to the web-based WeVideo for video editing, is paramount and would allow for not only easy group work but also cross-platform use with non–Apple computer users.

The science teachers and the librarian put the Physics of Sports project in the "win" column for the year, not just due to the student success in meeting learning objectives but as a full-featured collaboration between two departments successfully instructing students in both content and skills. Often teachers and librarians strive for original 21st century projects that can potentially encourage student interest and passions, but fall back on project types that don't inspire the people doing the instruction or the students receiving it. The STEM Foundations course incubated a project that not only met but superseded both content goals for the class as well as the information literacy and technology skills the librarian wished to impart early in the 9th grade experience. Because of its careful construction, hopefully talented students who might not have considered a STEM career now realize that these fields are not out of their grasp.

REFERENCES

American Association of School Librarians. 2007. *Standards for the 21st Century Learner*. Chicago: AASL. Accessed November 27, 2015. http://www.ala.org/aasl/sites/ala.org.aasl/files/content/guidelinesandstandards/learningstandards/AASL_LearningStandards.pdf.
Bartron, Rachel, Renee Casterline, and Courtney Lewis. 2013. "The Physics of Sports: STEM Foundations Fall Term Final Project." Last modified October 29, 2014. Google Document.
Chen, P. Daniel, and Patricia A. Simpson. 2015. "Does Personality Matter? Applying Holland's Typology to Analyze Students' Self-selection into Science Technology, Engineering, and Mathematics Majors." *Journal of Higher Education* 86, no. 5: 725–750. EBSCO Academic Source Complete.
Huang, Shaobo, Kurt Becker, Joel Alejandro Mejia, and Drew Nelson. 2015. "High School Physics: An Interactive Instructional Approach That Meets the Next Generation Science Standards." *Journal of STEM Education: Innovations & Research* 16, no. 1: 31–40. EBSCO Academic Source Complete.

Hutchinson-Anderson, Kelly, Kaileigh Johnson, and Paul A. Craig. 2015. "Students' Perceptions of Factors Influencing Their Desire to Major or Not Major in Science." *Journal of College Science Teaching* 45, no. 2: 78–85. EBSCO Academic Source Complete.

International Society for Technology in Education. 2007. *ISTE Standards: Students*. Arlington: ISTE. Accessed November 27, 2015. https://www.iste.org/docs/pdfs/20-14_ISTE_Standards-S_PDF.pdf.

Lewis, Courtney L. 2015. "Is My High School Senior Ready to Be Your College Freshman?" Paper presented at the Virginia Association of School Librarians Annual Conference, Williamsburg, VA. Accessed November 29, 2015. http://thesassylibrarian.blogspot.com/2015/11/vaasl-2015-is-my-high-school-senior.html.

Digital Literacy Development at a Public Regional University
The Western Carolina University Experience

MARK A. STOFFAN

In early 2015 Hunter Library of Western Carolina University received a Library Services and Technology Act (LSTA) Literacy and Lifelong Learning Grant to develop a digital scholarship lab in partnership with the university's Division of Information Technology (DoIT). The emphasis was on improving digital literacy competencies among WCU students by providing them with the appropriate technology and staff expertise as they make use of library and university resources. The project originated through a similar facility established at another library by a now-retired dean of library services.

The need for this facility was identified through surveys and conversations with faculty across academic departments. In LibQual® surveys conducted by Hunter Library in 2005, 2010, and 2012 faculty, librarians and students consistently indicated that the library does not adequately provide "modern equipment that lets me easily access needed information." In 2011–2012 a campus-wide digital media needs assessment was conducted by DoIT. The survey responses indicated generally low comfort level with technology and a desire for additional development opportunities. A 2014 EDUCAUSE Center for Analysis and Research (ECAR) survey also conducted by DoIT showed that students desired more familiarity with technology, and believed that technology would be better utilized by their classes and in their research if they had improved access to appropriate training and assistance. The 2014 Horizon Report identified the integration of online, hybrid and collaborative learning as a near-term trend affecting higher education, with students shifting from being consumers of information to being creators. (Horizon Report 2014). The rise of the digital humanities also influences how students learn, think, and communicate within the liberal arts, and growing emphasis on STEM (Science, Technology, Engineering, and Math) education at WCU imparted additional attention to the needs within the sciences.

As Hunter Library performed its examination of need for some type of lab facility a number of other trends became evident. As instructors innovate with active teaching methods such as team-based learning and technology-enhanced classrooms, students are shifting from being passive consumers of information to active creators of content. This change is reflected in class assignments; instead of submitting a traditional term paper, a student may participate in multi-disciplinary teams to produce an interactive presentation, video or podcast. The use of new and emerging research methods and tools increases the ability to find, create, share, evaluate, and store information and knowledge, but requires appropriate technology and digital literacy skills that may not be possessed by many students.

Library resources today include traditional print materials, online journals, streaming media resources (both visual and audio), locally-produced digital collections including archival photographs and manuscripts, and institutional repository content. Library patrons need access to the associated tools and software as well as trained staff who can assist them with the technologies used to interact with this wide array of content. "Because digital technologies are assumed in all that we will do in our increasingly visual and connected future, perhaps the most basic definition of digital scholarship is that it is and will be the scholarship of the 21st century" (Sinclair 2014).

Teaching information literacy skills is an area where Hunter Library excels. The library through its instruction program and related services strives to instill a lifelong appreciation for critical thinking. The need for collaborative spaces and technologies is crucial to long-term student success but these were largely unavailable in Hunter Library. The library did not have a digital scholarship lab, digital media lab, or "makerspace" facility. The university had several small departmental computing labs located within various academic buildings, and a technology commons located in Hunter Library and managed by DoIT that offered standard help desk support. Individual departments offering specialized computer resources to their majoring students often did not make their facilities available to students enrolled in other programs. Most of these departmental facilities are basic computing labs with Internet access and Microsoft Office but often lack appropriate tools for working with data in a variety of digital formats. At the same time, librarians were not available in these facilities to help students work with the intellectual content of library resources. In looking at various possibilities, it was apparent that a digital scholarship lab located in the technology commons within Hunter Library would provide students with a modern facility that brought together the strengths of the library and the technology providers. Collaborative programming would help students develop digital literacy skills benefiting their college success and continuing throughout their lives, as they pursue careers where these skills are a routine requirement. Surveys of peer institutions showed us that these newer digital technologies are expanding rapidly due to the "makerspace" movement and changes in pedagogy. Due to post–2008 budget cuts, however, funding was not immediately available nor was adequate staff on hand in the number needed to oversee such a facility. The library's head of digital access and technology services applied for the LSTA grant as a means of getting a facility established as a pilot initiative.

The primary goal of the project is to further develop students' lifelong learning and critical thinking skills in digital literacy. We believed we could best support this effort by (1) providing access to the latest digital technology to undergraduate and graduate students, teaching librarians and information technology specialists; (2) encouraging creativity and collaboration among students, librarians, and IT staff; and (3) fostering lifelong learning and creativity in university graduates. We prepared a LSTA EZ Literacy and Lifelong Learning Grant application with the idea of obtaining startup funds for a basic digital scholarship lab. LSTA grants are administered in North Carolina by the State Library from funds provided by the Institute of Museum and Library Services. In our application, we proposed to create a digital scholarship lab to support development of lifelong learning skills in digital literacy in cooperation with DoIT. The differentiation between scholarship labs, media labs, and makerspaces is often unclear. Goodman has described common features of digital scholarship labs. A true digital scholarship lab

- provides equipment to the community for the creation of video, audio, or other digital content;
- offers members of the community the ability to transform analog media (e.g., cassette tapes, records, etc.) to digital formats;
- offers digital literacy programs on how to create digital content; and
- is a space where content is created in some form rather than just consumed.

Goodman goes on to discuss digital scholarship labs that offer 3-D printing and other means of creating physical output in the context of the makerspace movement. She states that these facilities "may be considered hybrids because they straddle the line between digital and physical [content] creation." A traditional digital scholarship lab focuses purely on creating digital content (Goodman 2014). We wanted to create a space where the campus could use digital technology to work with the intellectual content the library purchases for the entire campus. We decided to partner with DoIT since they had trained personnel available to assist patrons with using the technology and for keeping the equipment maintained. This location was also chosen because it is available to patrons whenever the library is open. A separate facility would have had limited hours due to library staffing limitations. Librarians would offer workshops and would work closely with the technology commons staff to identify target areas for instruction. The technology commons staff would assist students with using the equipment and software and introduce them to online tutorials, software guides, and other self-directed learning tools designed to empower them to explore their creative and technical skills. A partial list of some services to be offered included

- creating virtual exhibits for faculty, students to support coursework and senior capstone projects;
- capacity to enable students to embark on a wider spectrum of projects using a variety of digital media tools (i.e., digital audio, digital video);
- enhanced scanning abilities to support conversion of the library's intellectual content in analog form (books, maps, newspapers) to digital formats (OCR, PDF creation); and
- photo imaging and image editing software for both print publication and the web allows visual editing capacities for academic essays, research and presentation.

Some library faculty and staff had expertise with the associated technology. Hunter Library's head of digital, access, and technology services leads the library's efforts in digitization and scholarly communication initiatives. The digital initiatives librarian has broad familiarity with the digital humanities and engages with faculty on various projects. The library has built extensive online digital collections of archival photographs, manuscripts, and oral histories relating to western North Carolina and the Southern Blue Ridge Mountains, maintains an active institutional repository and online theses and dissertations, and provides data management planning and data curation. The technology commons benefits from this project from closer participation with the library's instructional programs, and access to newer technology. One of the primary strategic goals of the technology commons is to provide support for students in the effective use of instructional technologies. Through collaboration with the library, the commons have a ready-made market of students with a willingness to try new, innovative approaches to class assignments and research.

The grant abstract read as follows:

> We propose to create a digital scholarship lab with the equipment and staff expertise to help students develop lifelong digital literacy skills. The digital scholarship lab will leverage the library's electronic resources, institutional repository, digital collections, and print content by providing students with the appropriate tools and resources to effectively use information in new ways. For example, students might incorporate print material, audio and video files, and their own conclusions into a podcast or a multimedia presentation. 3-D printing is also making rapid inroads into library services and we will offer our students such devices to foster greater creativity. This project will enhance an ongoing collaboration between the Technology Commons and Hunter Library.

In our application, we tied the proposal to the institutional mission and the university strategic plan, "2020 Vision: Focusing our Future." We highlighted one particular goal and initiative:

> GOAL 4.4: Adequately support for scholarship and creative activities in support of Western Carolina University's mission as a regional comprehensive university.
> Initiative 4.4.2: Ensure appropriate institutional infrastructure to support scholarship and research.

We also highlighted three initiatives from the Hunter Library Strategic Plan 2012–2015:

- Provide high quality learning and information services for the discovery and effective use of intellectual content. (Goal: Continue inter-organizational collaboration that enhances information services).
- Provide the information technology infrastructure required to make the identification, acquisition, organization, teaching, access, creation, and delivery of intellectual content convenient, timely, and effective. (Goal: Investigate and implement a user-centered plan for public technology needs within the library.)
- Create physical and virtual spaces and environments that encourage and effectively support all forms of access, learning, discovery, exchange, design, and instruction. (Goal: Make physical spaces conducive to learning and working.)

The goals linked to these strategic directions all support user-centered technology, the exploration of emerging technology, and the enhancement of multiple learning environments.

We identified three intended outcomes as part of the grant application:

- Information access: Improve user's ability to discover information: provide enhanced digital and new media capabilities to empower students to discover and use the library's online resources in a centrally located information-centered location.
- Institutional capacity: Improve the library's physical and technology infrastructure: as a shared informal learning space, the library provides the ideal venue for collaboration among students and faculty to produce digital media to support teaching and learning.
- Lifelong learning: Improve users' formal education: students will develop lasting skills in digital literacy and will use these skills in class assignments. Students will increase their critical thinking skills by focusing on process and outcomes.

We submitted the grant application in February 2015 and were notified of its award in late May. Once the grant was accepted and we had permission to proceed, our focus was on equipping the lab as outlined in the grant. We purchased the following equipment:

- three Dell OptiPlex 920 PC towers with Dell Ultrasharp 34[qm] curved displays;
- two Mac Pro workstations with 32[qm] displays;
- two LulzBot Mini 3-D printers;
- one LulzBot Taz 5 3-D printer; and
- one MDS BookScan 3050 Pro scanning station with LED scanner.

For software, we purchased the Adobe Master Collection for each of the three Dell PCs. We also purchased Solidworks Standard computer-aided design (CAD) software to support 3-D printing. The technology commons staff installed additional software under site license, including Microsoft Office 2010 and software for creating and editing audio and video files. To support 3-D printing, we knew that most users would find advanced CAD applications to be beyond a rapid learning curve. We therefore provided links to Thingiverse.com as a way of providing ready-made, downloadable designs for students. We also debated the merits of mediated versus unmediated printing. In the end, we chose a mediated model where students upload their designs to the online IT Help Desk system, then the staff prints the design for later pickup by the user. To recover costs, we charge for 3-D printing filament at $0.10/oz. As is standard practice when a significant grant is obtained at WCU, the university's Office of Communications and Public Relations produced a press release and covered the event in campus publications and blogs. The current hype surrounding 3-D printing led to a surge in interest that created the potential to shift the project's focus away from digital literacy, but at the same time sparked a wider discussion across campus on potential for creating a true makerspace, possibly by using the library lab as its foundation. The library and the technology commons also did their own marketing. Articles were published in the library and DoIT e-mail and print newsletters, postings made on social media, announcements circulated on the campus digital signage system, and flyers posted across campus. Library liaisons in Hunter's research and instruction services department publicized the availability of the enhanced services to teaching faculty and departments. We also offered an afternoon open house which was widely publicized across campus. Approximately 75 people attended the open house, including members of two classes who were brought in by their instructors.

We also continued working with faculty to determine the focus of workshops to be offered. Interest in 3-D printing was obvious. Other possible topics were identified through the ECAR survey conducted by DoIT. As the digital initiatives librarian was already heavily engaged with faculty on digital humanities topics, she provided more ideas for workshops in textual analysis, GIS, and archiving. Based upon the data collected we decided to offer a series of workshops on editing audio, video, and image files, working with photo of images, 3-D, using Zotero as a bibliographic management tool, and using Geographical Information Systems (GIS) data. We also offered individual consultation on digital technologies, digital preservation/curation planning, digital project management, and intellectual property rights. At the same time, we conducted another survey designed to assess the current digital literacy skills of students using the lab. The survey was linked from a splash screen that appeared when a student logged on to a computer in the digital lab. Students who participated had the opportunity to enter for a chance to win a gift certificate to the campus bookstore.

During the spring, a series of workshops addressed needs identified during the investigations. 3-D printing individual and group sessions attracted over 200 students. Sessions on WordPress, Zotero citation management software, and editing media files were also well received. However, the focus on digital literacy skills was somewhat obscured by the popularity of 3-D printing, which was near the top of the technology "hype cycle" at the time of this project's implementation. So popular was this service that many people referred to the facility as the "3-D lab." While this somewhat detracted attention away from the core mission, it nevertheless benefited students in many ways. Numerous courses used 3-D printing for such purposes as mathematical modeling and interior design projects. The engineering programs also used the facility as a means of reducing demand on their resources.

In conducting the surveys, we underestimated the willingness of students to participate in the process. The lure of a gift card was insufficient to draw participation. To get a valid sample we had to individually recruit people through persuasion. The process was also affected by another survey conducted in the library at the same time as part of a strategic planning initiative under a new dean of libraries. Some people declined to participate in our survey because they mistakenly believed that they had already done so.

While our partnership with DoIT had seemed like a good opportunity for both participating organizations, some issues influenced efficient delivery of services. With the digital scholarship lab being physically separated from the library's reference and circulation desks, it proved more difficult than expected to get staff working between the two areas. Efficient and effective collaboration was affected. In hindsight, instruction would have been improved by locating the facility near the library public services area. While the partnership is successful, we did not see as much emphasis placed on digital literacy as we expected since DoIT's focus was more directed toward the mechanics of accomplishing a task rather than facilitating understanding of the process. The new dean who arrived after the project began would prefer that the lab be relocated to the main floor of the library, where it could serve as the nascent beginnings of a learning commons and makerspace facility.

Future Directions

As the lab has existed for only one semester, we will need to collect and analyze more data before determining what form the facility and its programming may take over a longer period. The library's new dean is firmly committed to the learning commons philosophy, and sees adding enhanced technology as a priority. Conversations on campus arising from this project have identified the library as an ideal location for a makerspace. These discussions are expected to lead to the development of a plan of action during of 2016. One possibility is assimilation of the lab into the library's information literacy program. The Association of American Colleges and Universities identified ten key high impact practices (HIP) for instruction (Kuh 2008) which are currently integrated into Hunter Library's information literacy program, but a missing factor is technology integration. More teamwork between librarians and information technology staff offers potential for improving student success with using library resources and fulfilling the goals of the instructional program. Our research and instruction services librarians who work closely with teaching faculty across academic departments are highly valued for their contributions to student learning. New and emerging opportunities exist for assisting faculty members with data management planning and curation, personal digital preservation assistance, and related areas. There is untapped opportunity to expand the library's services in these areas.

Evaluation of Outcomes

Evaluation is an ongoing process as we collect data in sufficient quantity to perform proper sampling and analysis. In addition to formal surveys of participants to measure the skills, knowledge, and attitudes connected with digital literacy, the number of workshop attendees and the number of individual users are tracked by staff in the technology commons. We also track the number of student projects enabled and the number and type of services provided to faculty. The satisfaction of workshop attendees is being assessed using workshop evaluations that incorporate both qualitative and quantitative measures. We will also convene targeted focus groups during and after the completion of the project to see if comfort level with use of the technology has increased. The project team will survey faculty in courses with large numbers of enrollees who make use of the lab to assess if student success has measurably improved, using standard benchmarks. Survey content is being developed with the help of assessment experts in WCU's teaching and learning center. Over a longer term, we will develop a future directions report from faculty, students and library staff regarding the digital scholarship lab, in the context of growing institutional interest in a makerspace facility that would incorporate elements of the current lab. For the present, the digital scholarship lab provides the university with new technology and related services that address previously unfulfilled demands and gives the library a firm foundation on which to support the changing needs of 21st century scholarship.

REFERENCES

Goodman, Amanda L. 2014. "Digital Media Labs in Libraries." *Library Technology Reports*, No. 6, August-September. http://dx.doi.org/10.5860/ltr.50n6. Retrieved December 17, 2015.

Horizon Report: Higher Education Edition. 2014. Austin: New Media Consortium. http://www.nmc.org/publication/nmc-horizon-report-2014-higher-education-edition. Retrieved January 3, 2016.

Kuh, George D. 2008. *High-Impact Educational Practices: What They Are, Who Has Access to Them, and Why They Matter*. Washington, D.C., Association of American Colleges & Universities. Summary available at https://www.aacu.org/leap/hips. Accessed November 26, 2015.

Sinclair, Bryan. 2014. "The University Library as Incubator for Digital Scholarship." *EDUCAUSE Review Online*, June 30. http://er.educause.edu/articles/2014/6/the-university-library-as-incubator-for-digital-scholarship. Retrieved July 7, 2015.

The Benefits of Multiple Instruction Styles in Public Libraries

Amanda Toth

Technology instruction can be difficult for any librarian or library associate. There will always be hold outs that believe the technology is not needed, or those that are resistant in regards to anything new. So it's up the tech-savvy and those that are comfortable with emerging technology to pass that enthusiasm on to others, or at the very least–the basic knowledge of how it works.

In this essay, we will discuss the benefits to group classes, one-on-one sessions, or "tutor sessions," as well as why offering both options will provide an inclusive environment in your library or information institution. The Lane Public Library in Fairfield, Ohio, offers both options, and I will provide some examples of what is offered in both situations.

It is important to keep in mind that not everyone learns the same, or at the same pace. It is up to any instructor to create a learning environment that makes the class-taker feel comfortable and open to learning. That is why it is best to offer tech instruction in multiple formats. Some patrons, staff members, et cetera, prefer the anonymity of classroom settings. Still others prefer the "learn at your own pace" style that goes along with one-on-one sessions.

At the Lane Public Library, tech instruction for patrons was originally only offered in classroom style, either in a computer lab or with the instructor using a laptop and projector. Several years later, Computer Tutor sessions were established, and they became so popular that the wait list was several weeks long. Initially, staff thought that the creation of the Computer Tutor service meant that they no longer had to offer group classes, but patrons still requested the group setting. It was decided to offer classes in buildings that had the ability, such as those that had computer labs or staff with great knowledge of different technology and programs, and Computer Tutor sessions would be offered at all the branches for those that preferred one-on-one time with a tutor.

At the Lane Public Library, computer tutor sessions are one-on-one 30- to 60-minute sessions with a staff member knowledgeable in the topic of interest. Some staff members know more than others, and are available for a wider range of topics. The Lane Libraries have a dedicated Technology Center, with more advanced programs such as Adobe Photoshop and Adobe Illustrator. Due to this, only the Technology Center has tutor sessions on those programs.

Computer Tutor sessions can be on the following topics:

Computer Basics
Internet Basics
Microsoft Word—Basics, Intermediate
Microsoft Excel—Basics, Intermediate
Microsoft PowerPoint–Basics, Intermediate
Creating and using an e-mail account
Library eBooks and Downloadable services
Library Databases
Adobe Creative Cloud Suite (Photoshop, Illustrator, etc.)

In Computer Tutor sessions, patrons are limited to what the library offers in regards to software, databases, and downloadable items. This excludes topics such as social networking, buying and selling items online, etc. However, occasional classes are taught on these subjects, due to patron interest.

Anyone that has worked at a library understands the importance of statistics and keeping track of program attendance. One-on-one sessions, or "computer tutor" sessions are no different. At the Lane Public Library, the Computer Tutor is listed as one program per month, and each time a staff member tutors a patron, the attendance number goes up. By the end of the month, one "program" that can be worked around staff and patron schedules can have as many as 20, if not more, attendees. The same can be said for staff instruction. While instructional sessions such as this might not count towards official continuing education credits for staff members, any further educational efforts to keep staff well trained and up to date on the latest technology offered by your library looks good on monthly reports.

The benefit of tutor sessions is that they can be done on any subject at any time while classes must be scheduled in advance and are subject to limited availability and a specific subject. Once a patron shows interest in a tutor session, staff members write down their name, contact information, topic of interest, and what time of day they are available. The patron is contacted within the week with a date, time, and the name of a staff member that will be their tutor for the session. Computer Tutor sessions are easy to accommodate as it means only one staff member away from the desk for a short period, and are always scheduled around times when staffing is lean.

When a student is assigned a staff tutor for the session of interest, that does not mean that same staff member must tutor them in every subject. At the Lane Library, we have some staff members that are more comfortable providing training on specific subjects than others. If a patron wishes to be trained in computer basics, any staff member is available to be their tutor, but when they also request Microsoft Excel sessions, a specific staff member is assigned that session. The same situation occurs when training new or advancing staff members. A few employees have the skill level and background in the technology or program, and they are contacted or scheduled to be the instructor for new employees.

Like with many instruction program, handouts are a must. Outlines not only allow staff members to follow a particular lesson plan, but also help the students to follow along and even write in notes, if necessary. Even in a one-on-one, student-guided session, any sort of technology instruction can be a lot to take in at once. Handouts help the student not only process the information at the time, but go back through their notes to practice and better retain the topic later.

In regards to training staff on technology, the process would be very similar. Initially, one or more staff members need to be trained on a topic, and comfortable enough to instruct others. Once a dedicated "training staff" group is created, those staff members will need to sit down with other staff one-on-one and explain the process. Often, libraries can employ the "train the trainer" method. In this method of instruction, one staff member will get the process rolling by training a small group of staff. That small group is now the trainers for the rest of the staff members.

Like with training patrons, handouts are just as helpful for staff to retain information and refer back. With a lot of new technology that is offered at library and learning institutions, there isn't always a lot of demand at the beginning, or until word starts getting around. In that case, it came be some time before staff members use the knowledge that they have gained in the trainings. Handouts help with that retention as well as a reference point for future questions.

The most common thing I have heard as an instructor has been that the patron or staff member is afraid of breaking the computer, tablet, system, etc. For this reason, it is important that the trainees are given time to feel comfortable with the new technology. If it is a computer program, give the student time after the training to sit on the computer and try different options, with the instructor close at hand to answer any questions. If the technology is something physical, for example: a tablet, allow the student to hold it, test out the new features, and get used to the different functionalities.

There are many benefits to one-on-one sessions in regards to tech training; the ability to work around different schedules, the more tech-savvy staff are away from the desk for shorter sessions rather than multiple hour long formal classes, and finally, the student gets a training session that moves at their own pace. The more comfortable a student is made during the training process, the more comfortable they will feel with the subject.

Classroom Style

At the same time, there are benefits to offering classroom style learning as well as one-on-one sessions. While there is a fair amount of people who appreciate a staff member taking time to personalize a lesson for one student, others feel more comfortable in the anonymity of a group setting. There are always people that don't want to be singled out, or who prefer to hide amongst others so they don't feel like they are being judged for how slow they may learn. As much as an instructor may emphasis that everyone learns at their own pace, or there are no silly questions, there will always be those that feel uncomfortable if called upon or if they are made the focus during a class.

Another benefit of teaching in a classroom setting is that the instructor can teach multiple students at once. Compared to the amount of time that goes into doing multiple one-on-one sessions, a class of even as few as six students could mean that a staff member is only away from the desk for less than two hours at once, rather than three to six hours it would take to do the individual sessions.

If a library or information institution only has, for example, one staff member competent enough in Microsoft Excel to be able to instruct others on the subject, this staff member might be run ragged with multiple one-on-one sessions a week, if not multiples in one day. However, one class dedicated to the subject would be able to keep the demand for one-on-one sessions low, and those that are comfortable in a group setting would be able to get the knowledge they need to begin using the program on their own.

A downside to offering a classroom only style learning environment is that there is always the issue of limited seating or computer usage, and scheduling. For example, a class might be offered in the evening, but a patron interested in taking the course might work evenings and would be unable to attend. While one-on-one sessions have the benefit of quick scheduling and working around both the patron and staff member's schedules, classes are often a onetime offering.

Handouts were mentioned previously as an important part of the learning process in one-on-one sessions, and this remains true in the classroom setting, if not more so. Learners that are in the class, but are following along at slower rates than the instructor is going, or those that are looking ahead, can use the handout as a guide of their own. Similarly, topics that might be glanced over in the class due to time constraints or any number of reasons can be gone back over when the student references the handout in their own time.

If your library has a computer room, classes can be a no-brainer, but for libraries that lack a dedicated computer training area, there are still options for training patrons on different programs, library databases, and more. Even if all you have is a screen, laptop, and projector, classes are still a viable option. Students will not necessarily get the hands-on training in the initial class, but they will get the basic knowledge needed to feel confident using the program or technology on their own time.

When it comes to instructing staff in a classroom setting, the same rules apply as instructing patrons. The more staff you can train at once, the faster the knowledge will spread amongst the staff as a whole. At the same time, this means that a multiple staff members are not working the public service desks at one time, which can lead to staffing difficulties and scheduling conflicts.

The Benefits of Using Both Methods

So far we have seen the benefits and drawbacks to both styles of instruction. Together, these two options provide a comfortable learning environment no matter what the learning speed or reservations of the learner. Having both options can save instructors a lot of headaches, and might even save the scheduling issues that come with using only one or the other style.

Having both one-on-one sessions and classes mean that if a class gets full, interested students that find out about the class too late to sign up still have the chance to be instructed on the subject in a one-on-one session. Patrons that wish to attend a class but can't go on the scheduled day can take a tutor session that fits around their work or home schedule.

This also allows an instructor to try out potential class subjects, and judge the interest. For example, if the library is thinking of adding Facebook instruction, staff can first add it to the list of available topics for one-on-one sessions, and if the list for this subject grows, a class can be designed that allows multiple students to learn about the topic at once. Similarly, if a particular subject is only requested by one or two patrons, there is no need for a full, instructor-led class. Instead, a one-on-one session can be offered to the interested student.

The style of instruction also matters in regards to what you are teaching. If the goal of the instruction is to teach staff members or patrons about new features on the library's website, a classroom setting is all that's needed. If a library purchases a new tablet to prompt staff to roam and help patrons away from the desk, one-on-one sessions with an instructor and those using the tablet is more beneficial, as it would allow the students to get hands-on experience with the device. There are always some programs that can be taught either way, one-on-one or classroom style. For example, instruction patrons on social media privacy could be taught in a classroom in a general sense, or an instructor could sit with one student and go through their specific privacy settings one by one.

It is also important to remember that when dealing with tough or intensive subjects, it is better to do it in multiple sessions rather than one long tutor session or class. The more a student has to absorb, the more knowledge will likely be lost by the end of the multiple hour long session, even with handouts and notes. Classes or tutor sessions on subjects such as multiple library databases, the new eBook download service the library is starting to offer, etc., might be best as two sessions, giving the students more time to grasp the new information. This also allows students to ruminate on the subject, and come back with questions about items that were not made clear in the first session. In tutor sessions, if the 30-minute mark has been reached, and the student seems to be getting flustered, it might be in the student's best interest to end the session and schedule another time to continue the next day, or even the next week. This way, the student is not overloaded with information.

Offering both options also allows patrons to feel like they get a well-rounded education on a particular subject. If a student feels that they did not get enough instruction in a particular section of the class, or if the one-on-one session was not enough, a staff member can direct the student to the other options offered by the library or information institution.

Conclusion

No matter what type of instruction your library or institution prefers, handouts should be a given. Handouts are handy for staff members to use as a go-to outline for the course, as well as a great way for students to follow along and take notes. The more writing space, the better, but don't scrimp on the subject just to allow more note-taking space.

Everyone learns differently, and everyone feels comfortable in different types of environments. In the effort to be more inclusive to all learners, offering multiple options gives interested students a variety of choices to fit their learning style. Traditional classes mean more people learning at once, but slower learners and those uncomfortable with technology in general will get more out of a one-on-one session with an instructor than if they hide themselves away in a classroom setting.

For libraries that lack a dedicated computer room or instruction space, tutor sessions can be done on a laptop or mobile device anywhere in the library. Even classes are still an option without a typical classroom, as long as the instructor has access to a laptop, projector, and screen or white wall.

Formal classes require prior scheduling and sign ups, which is a great option for those with open schedules, but the open spots can fill up fast. Tutor sessions are a great alternative to offer interested students that can't make the class due to scheduling conflicts, or having to settle for the wait list if the class is at capacity.

No matter what type of instruction the student receives, it is important to allow the learner time to get comfortable with the new program, device, or technology. Dedicated time sitting at the computer or with the device, with an instructor close by to answer questions, is helpful to reinforce the training received, as well as allows the student to explore other features on their own.

Not every topic will have enough interest to warrant a full class, or the use of an entire computer room for a class of only a handful of students. Topics that have a small interest group might be better served as tutoring sessions, saving larger space and staff time for more popular and asked for subjects.

While many of the above techniques speak about instructing patrons, the same goes for instructing staff members. An extra benefit involved in training staff members one-on-one or in small groups is that those staff members can then become trainers themselves for other staff, if they feel confident and comfortable enough with the material.

Giving students the option to choose between classes and one-on-ones sessions puts the power in the hands of the student. No matter the comfort level, learning style, or interest, having multiple formats is the way to go for libraries and information institutions. Librarians and technology instructors are there to provide the information necessary for students to keep up in today's technology heavy world, and multiple teaching formats is just another tool in the librarian's belt.

The Accidental Trainer
Instructional Librarianship in the Modern-Day Library

MONICA M. DOMBROWSKI,
MELISSA BERNASEK *and* SHANA LOPEZ

"I think all I did this evening was tech support." The moment Melissa Bernasek, Director of Information Services at Gail Borden Public Library, heard this from her staff, she knew the tide had turned. The situation at Gail Borden Public Library was no doubt being repeated at libraries across the country. Providing an answer from a book or webpage was no longer enough. Increasing numbers of patrons were seeking greater response and support from library staff when using computers and devices.

In a matter of a few short years, transactions about finding a website were replaced by questions about obscure tablets, Excel functions, and cloud storage. "We were out of our league," recalled one Gail Borden Library staff member. Every desk shift felt like a potential sojourn into fear, embarrassment, and inadequacy.

Reaction vs. Response

The ability to handle technology questions loomed large. Even though all staff had completed device training, some were unable to integrate the information into patron interactions. Others were well trained, but a single customer question out of left field was enough to shake their confidence. For a few staff members, the amount of information was just too much. They demonstrated symptoms of being overwhelmed and ultimately resisted training. The result was an Information Services team who could handle most technology questions, but relied heavily on the two most technologically-skilled staff members in the building when a problem arose. The underlying fear had not been adequately addressed.

Meanwhile, library staff continued to teach Internet and e-mail classes sporadically with reservations. Since librarians led the way with effectively searching the Internet decades ago, teaching others to do so was an obvious outgrowth. The increasing number of technology questions at the Information Desk indicated the need for more classes, but staff were adamant: "I'm a librarian, not a teacher!" Though bibliographic instruction was a standard part of library school curriculum, the nuts and bolts of how to teach digital immigrants to attach a file to an e-mail was not. The truth was on the table and the department's response would dictate its path into the coming years.

Teachers Without Training

Patrons clearly needed formalized instruction so Information Services librarians ventured into unknown territory: developing and teaching classes on topics like buying an eReader or using Pinterest. At the same time Gail Borden Library's Community Service & Program Development Department hired contract trainers to teach classes like Microsoft Excel and File Management. While both solutions addressed patron demand, they only provided short-term fixes because budgets fluctuated and the librarians remained overwhelmed and uncomfortable. The Administrative team knew it was time for a more permanent solution.

Identifying a Staffing Need

It was clear from attendance numbers that library district residents wanted more technology classes, so in 2014, the administration team created a position whose sole focus would be on technology training at the library: Technology Education Manager. This position would allow the library to become a place for community members to explore new technologies and learn to use them (McGettigan 2015). They could achieve this faster if they applied a more methodical approach to technology training with a leader at the helm. Was the best candidate a librarian or trainer? Administration crafted a job description that included a wide array of skill sets and experience to entice both type of candidates and began their search.

Finding the Right Person

Human Resources received 33 applications for the position and invited 11 to do a first interview via Skype. The hiring team chose this platform because, according to Division Chief Miriam Lytle, "it provided evidence of the candidates' technology competencies and allowed us to get a feel for their professionalism in non-traditional platforms."

After the Skype interviews, one candidate stood out: a degreed librarian with a corporate training background who was working at a small career college. The hiring team appreciated her diverse background; open, easy approach; and enthusiasm for tackling their challenges. The team invited her in for a two-part interview during which she taught a class on Tumblr and spent time answering questions about her experience and vision.

After seeing her in action and hearing her ideas for expanding training efforts at the library, the hiring team offered Monica Dombrowski the job and she joined Gail Borden Public Library in the role of Technology Education Manager.

Analyzing the Situation

Monica knew she would be wearing two hats in her new role, so she immediately began assessing the situation concerning both staff and patron training. After some preliminary investigation, she saw a more urgent need on the patron side as staff had some interim training solutions in place. She started talking to contract trainers, staff, and patrons to learn how public classes were designed, taught, and reviewed at the library. These conversations uncovered that nearly all the library's class offerings were taught by contract trainers who created classes and materials with no input from the library. The others were designed and delivered by librarians with no consistency from one to the other. Furthermore, because it took too long to create classes, the library was unable to respond to patron requests. It became clear that a formalized design process was needed.

Next, Monica analyzed the previous year's class surveys and noticed that while overall feedback was positive, comments indicated problems such as covering too much content, unclear progression of concepts, and little or no hands-on practice. Based on her analysis, Monica drew two conclusions that informed her actions: (1) The classes offered by the library needed to be redesigned and (2) library staff would need to teach classes to expand offerings within the existing budget.

Formulating a Plan

Monica realized that redesigning the 30 classes offered at two library locations would be easier if she had a series of templates to use for the materials, so that is where she began. She used Microsoft Word to create her documents because she knew it was commonly-used software that most people were able to use. Next, she reviewed the existing class materials and found that all classes lacked Design Documents (lesson plans) and most lacked activity sheets which meant those classes were lecture-based instead of interactive. From her knowledge of information literacy and instructional design, Monica knew hands-on practice was critical to helping learners process what they'd learned and apply the knowledge to other situations (Kaplowitz 2014, 88). In addition, handouts ranged from one-page charts 35-page PowerPoint presentations and class surveys—though administered—needed to ask more valuable questions. Monica's once medium-sized project instantly ballooned beyond what she could manage; it was clear she would need help to bring forth change.

Monica set up meetings with existing contract trainers to discuss her ideas and establish a more collaborative design process. The trainers were excited because they knew the system would improve the patron experience and make it faster and easier for them to develop classes. While continuing to teach with existing materials, the trainers began moving their content into the templates and submitting their drafts to Monica, who reviewed them and made suggestions for improvement. This back-and-forth dialog during her first eight months with the library dramatically improved material quality and allowed Monica to step in, with confidence, if a trainer suddenly had to miss a class. With the success of this new model, Monica set her mind on tackling the next project: using library staff to expand class offerings.

Expanding a Role

The 2016 Edge Impact Survey reports that 60 percent of public access technology users received one-on-one help at the library in the last year with 12 percent of those users taking a computer class (Crandall 2016, 5–6). When Monica approached Melissa to discuss the possibility of using librarians to train, Melissa was already on board. She saw the librarian role expanding to include instructor and knew her staff needed to help. Melissa identified two obstacles to overcome before the librarians would be able to train: (1) They did not have time or skills to develop classes and (2) they did not know how to teach. Monica asked if the idea would be feasible if she provided the content and trained the librarians. Melissa agreed, and set about promoting the idea to her staff.

Sandra Nelson, Library Consultant, accurately summarized the situation Melissa faced: "People, often library managers, who initiate a change have invested time and energy in analyzing a situation and identifying a new or different way to manage that situation. These change agents are enthusiastic about their new ideas and they hope that others will also see the benefits of their ideas" (Nelson 2016). Although Melissa was indeed enthusiastic, initial reactions among her librarians were split: some were excited about teaching and some were skeptical. She knew that what appeared to be resistance from staff might really be insecurity, a lack of understanding of the change, or unanswered questions.

Melissa held one-on-one conversations with her team to uncover their concerns and found that they ranged from personal humiliation to providing inferior service to patrons. She worked hard to help reassure staff that Monica's model would help them look like professionals and dramatically improve service instead of making them look foolish. In the end, her staff agreed to be open minded and attend Monica's session on how to teach a class. During the training, Monica walked through topics ranging from how to prepare for class to how to redirect disruptive participants. Staff was engaged and asked questions throughout that allowed Monica and Melissa to assuage their fears and make the idea less frightening. In the end, all the librarians agreed to try training a class, and the two moved ahead to piloting the model.

First Steps

The pilot consisted of four librarians each teaching a class in the four-part Computer Basics series. Monica and Melissa chose this series because it was for seniors, who tend to be a little more patient when things go wrong, and it required the lowest levels of user proficiency. Monica provided the class materials ahead of time and made sure she was there at the start of each class to provide moral support. She listened from the office next door so she could jump in if needed. To the librarians' credit, Monica heard only solid instruction, great questions, and lots of thanks from participants. After successful initial efforts, Monica and Melissa replicated the model for the next six months, allowing the librarians to gain confidence with the basic classes before adding in more advanced topics.

As the pilot continued it became clear that there were varying degrees of skill level in teaching technology. Melissa used this knowledge to begin aligning staff to the areas of service that best fit with their skills. Some took on greater teaching responsibilities while others took on greater public desk duties. Monica began teaching those in the first group how to design classes, which allowed them to take their skills and interests to a higher level. Also at this time, Monica took on her first full-time staff member, Shana Lopez, who assumed some of the administrative duties so Monica could focus on working with the librarians. These efforts allowed Monica and Shana to expand the library's stable of classes and by the end of 2015, they had more than 80 to offer patrons with more in development.

Replicating the Process with Librarians and Other Staff

Integrating librarians into the training schedule was only one piece of the puzzle. Monica and Shana lacked the luxury of designing all the classes the library needed to offer while still accomplishing their jobs. They wondered how other libraries did it and reached out to peers for ideas.

Monica and Shana uncovered a number of interesting approaches to technology education at other libraries. For example, at Skokie Public Library in Skokie, Illinois, they had successfully implemented a model where most staff members developed a class or two based on their interests and then taught it each time it was offered. Learning Experiences Manager, Mick Jacobsen, said this model worked because staff got to develop something they had a passion for and had a chance to cultivate deep knowledge on the topic (Jacobsen 2016).

Ephrata Public Library Executive Director Penny Talbert worked with her leadership team to develop staff competencies which allowed all staff to provide technology support on public desks. By setting clear expectations, providing training resources, and holding people accountable for meeting the competencies, she had a fluid staff that could meet the needs of their community. Inspired by these, and other, innovative training models, Monica continued her plans to involve librarians in training and designing classes at Gail Borden Library.

She knew that the core of her model was a formal design process for creating class materials. Once librarians became familiar with using the templates and following the style guidelines, it would be easier for them to share their knowledge. This model also would allow others to teach classes they did not design because everyone could follow a clear content outline. To make this happen, Monica and Shana created four standardized document types for class materials that incorporated specific style guidelines. These templates provided a starting point for creating classes while leaving room for the librarians to infuse their creativity into the content.

Creating the Skeleton

The first of the four document types was the Design Document, which provided a road map for teaching the class. Similar to a lesson plan, it contained information about the audience, class materials, and required technology. It provided smart objectives to ensure learning occurs and specific, sequential, talking points for instructors to follow. Most importantly, it included information about when to guide participants through learning activities to reinforce concepts.

The second type was the Activity Sheet. This was critical because adult learners needed opportunities to practice new concepts in a safe and comfortable setting. Each topic in a design document was followed by a corresponding activity that promoted hands-on practice. Frequently, these entailed following step-by-step directions to complete a task, such as calculating a formula in Microsoft Excel.

When participants left class, it was common for them to want to practice new concepts so the third type—a handout—summarized key concepts and gave them a jumping off point for independent exploration. Handouts used screenshots, terminology, labels, and other visually-rich methods to reinforce learning and aid in independent exploration (Crane 2014, 69–70).

The fourth type—a PowerPoint presentation—was useful for complex topics or when live demonstrations are not feasible, such as in libraries with slow Internet connections. They included specifically staged screenshots to illustrate key concepts in the same manner that a live demonstration would.

In addition to creating these documents, Monica redesigned the class survey because she realized it needed to ask a more specific set of questions to capture useful inputs. For example, there were no questions about the instructor—which left a gap for providing feedback—and no questions asking whether participants had learned something that would be useful outside of the class.

Help! I'm New to the Design Process

As the librarians began developing materials, Monica saw a problem arising that was common to new instructional designers: too much information. Without experience in breaking down concepts into digestible pieces it was easy to overload patrons with too much information. It was even more difficult to determine how much information would comfortably fit into a 90-minute instruction session without previous design experience. Monica realized she could help the trainers by employing one of two coaching methods: short-term fixes or staff development.

Initially, it was quicker and easier for Monica and Shana to adjust content during the copyediting process and then print the revised materials, but that model could not be sustained over time. If they simply continued to fix the errors without coaching the librarians, they would not have a chance to improve their design skills. Working directly with staff to increase their instructional knowledge would provide a better return on investment over time so it seemed a logical next step.

As more classes were developed, Monica and Shana worked with the librarians through a collaborative feedback process filled with examples and constructive suggestions. They engaged the librarians to uncover their thought processes and worked with them to adjust the content accordingly. The two-way review process worked because it incorporated both theory and functionality on a topic. In the case of one tech-savvy recruit, he came to understand that less, more focused content was better for learning than covering multiple topics superficially (Kaplowitz 2014, 82).

In time, four librarians successfully followed the new model and created classes on topics ranging from library resources to electronic devices. This led Monica and Melissa to wonder if their efforts to create and use this type of training approach could help other libraries who didn't have their resources and wanted to offer classes. Further, they wondered if they could secure a grant to create some sort of online tool for sharing content with other librarians. Gail's Toolkit was about to be born.

Gail's Toolkit

Monica and Melissa knew they would need administrative and financial support to create the portal they envisioned. Following a nod from library administrators, the search for a grant began. One that seemed to fit was ALA Publishing's Carnegie-Whitney Grant, which would allow them to create a content portal and resource bibliography for those training in libraries. Three months after submitting their application, they received an acceptance letter and the first round of funds to proceed with the project.

The team—which expanded to include librarians, staff, and a grant-funded intern—worked for six months to prepare materials and the portal. In September 2015, they launched Gail's Toolkit and began promoting it within the library community. The Reaching Across Illinois Library System lent their support to the project by financing the website and providing opportunities for the team to speak at their events. By March 2016, Gail's Toolkit had 6,942 page views from 1,613 users. It was clear that the portal addressed the needs of other librarians who found themselves in the same situation as the librarians at Gail Borden. Halfway through the grant, the team continues to add content and is seeking a long-term partner to take over management of the Toolkit when the grant ends in 2017.

Lessons Learned

Two years after implementing their model, Monica and Melissa realized some important lessons, despite the model's success.

> Lesson One: Don't put a square peg in a round hole. It's okay to urge staff to try new things but not to expect them to continue long-term if it's a mismatch for their skills. Sometimes people are scared to try new things and they need someone to give them a gentle push. However, if it becomes clear that someone is beyond their capacity, stop pushing and figure out another plan.
> Lesson Two: Address the elephant in the room. Why are staff resistant to training? Initiate an honest discussion that will help you uncover what's really holding them back. Take time to reassure them, and draw comparisons to times when they've tried new things and found success.
> Lesson Three: Don't be afraid to re-align staff to meet changing patron demands. Do your best to place staff in roles where they can best use their skills. Skills usually are directly related to interests and people better engage in what fully interests them. Re-aligning staff may require some uncomfortable conversations at first, but will make for a more productive and happier staff in the end.
> Lesson Four: Talk to the key decision-makers to secure their support early in the process. Have a plan in mind and a potential road map along with a list of benefits. Tie it in directly to your library's strategic plan and initiatives so you can show the link to improved service for your community.
> Lesson Five: Hire based on where you need to go versus where you are now. What roles will staff need to play in the future and what types of skills will they need to possess? Evaluate your job descriptions every time someone leaves the organization to see if it should evolve. Be sure to advertise that teaching others technology will be one of the requirements, even if it's on an individual basis (one-on-ones).
> Lesson Six: It is worth the effort. As information moves online, it's inevitable that public-serving library staff will have to teach patrons about some type of technology as part of their jobs. It's critical to set staff up for success by providing them with skills to give patrons a great experience. Just because the education offered in libraries is free doesn't mean it can't be world-class. By investing in training and getting staff

comfortable with this expanded area of library service, we ensure that the library continues its relevancy in the community.

References

Crandall, Michael, and Samantha Becker, comps. 2016. Cumulative Report of Impact Survey Results. Report. January 22. Accessed March 8, 2016. https://impactsurvey.org/sites/impactsurvey.org/files/cumulative_report.pdf.
Crane, Beverley E. 2014. *How to Teach: A Practical Guide for Librarians*. Lanham, MD: Rowman & Littlefield.
Jacobsen, Mick. 2016. E-mail message to author, March 11.
Kaplowitz, Joan R. 2014. *Designing Information Literacy Instruction: The Teaching Tripod Approach*. Lanham, MD: Rowman & Littlefield.
Lytle, Miriam. 2016. E-mail message to author, March 11.
McGettigan, Liz. 2015. "6 Tips for Public Libraries in the Technology Tsunami." LinkedIn. December 9. Accessed March 8, 2016. https://www.linkedin.com/pulse/6-tips-public-libraries-technology-tsunami-liz-mcgettigan.
Nelson, Sandra. 2016. E-mail message to author, March 16.
Talbert, Penny. 2016. "Competency Handouts." Guerilla Librarian. Accessed March 8. http://www.pennytalbert.com/competency-handouts—information.html.

Tech Training 101?
Closing the Digital Divide One Device at a Time

JEZMYNNE DENE

The Portneuf Library is a small library located in Southeastern Idaho. The library faces a wide digital divide issue, as many users do not have access to personal computing or the Internet at home. Before beginning this project, the majority of the staff had minimal experience with computers and smartphones or tablets. Staff who did have cell phones had older models and did not use any mobile technology. The library began to cultivate digital collections, such as eBooks and audiobooks, but found that only a few staff used the tools and were able to help users adopting use of the electronic materials. As the popularity of the eBooks and audiobooks began to rise, library staff faced frustrating challenges when approached with questions they could not answer. The few staff that understood how the digital collections worked found themselves overwhelmed with answering all reference questions relating to the use of the digital eBooks and audiobooks. All staff found the situation frustrating; many could not answer questions, and few were overwhelmed dealing with a backlog of unanswered questions. Facing this challenge, the library decided it needed to do some creative brainstorming to create a program training staff in order to help train the users.

The library was lucky enough to participate in the Gizmo Garage program sponsored by the Idaho Commission for Libraries (ICfL). Funded by Library Services and Technology Act (LSTA) grant money, ICfL purchased a variety of mobile devices representing popular operating systems. These "Gizmo Garages" were distributed out to the Special Projects Library Action Team (SPLAT) members in the four areas of Idaho. The Portneuf Library was lucky enough to have a SPLAT member on staff, and therefore acquired the Southeast Idaho Gizmo Garage containing e-readers, Android tablets, a Microsoft Surface, and an iPad. It is with this Gizmo Garage the library began to approach training library staff on the different mobile operating systems and popular devices.

Initially, the library held all staff training meetings where the gadgets were placed on tables for staff perusal and exploration. These meeting lasted approximately an hour or so, and the staff were expected to interact with the devices and examples of the library's digital subscription purchases. However, these meetings did not work well for training the staff, as staff interacted with a few devices for a very limited amount of time. Staff milled about the meeting room, often clustered around one device at a time with one person doing something with a device while the remainder of the staff observed. The training meetings were unfocused and did not provide enough goals and objectives to encourage exploration and discovery. Most staff did not have personal smartphones or e-readers, and did not have enough familiarity to truly experience each device. Furthermore, staff were timid, stating things like "I'm afraid I'll break it" or "What if I touch the wrong thing?" The training meetings did not inspire the staff nor facilitate familiarity to ensure that the majority of the library's employees could answer patron questions. The library needed to implement a more innovative training method.

The library director created a new training plan that also met professional development requirements, which are required for staff for promotion. Staff members received a loaned gadget from the Gizmo Garage along with a list of core competencies. The Core Competencies were device agnostic concepts the director felt staff members should fully understand in developing a familiarity with the inner workings of any device. Staff had a month to take the device home and use it as if it were their personal item. Staff were assisted in either creating an account to use the device (Google for Android, iTunes for the iPad, or Amazon for the Kindle) or use an account created by the library specifically for training purposes. In addition to working with the list of Core Competencies, the library director requested the staff connect the device to the library's digital content, containing of audiobooks and e-books. To sweeten the likelihood staff would use the device, staff were authorized to count use of the device as work time while at home, up to a certain amount set by the library director. After the allotted loan period with the device was up, the staff member returned the device along with a summary of likes/dislikes or pros/cons, which showed their interaction through reflection and assessment. Staff did not have to write an essay; bullet points and lists were accepted. These assessments demonstrated staff interactions with the device as well as critical thinking skills. These assessments were shared back to ICfL, as well. Staff created the documentation on work time and felt their input was valuable as it was used by ICfL to assess the value of the Gizmo Garage Project. After returning the device and the assessment report, the staff member received a new device while the returned one cycled to another staff member. Each device rotated through the staff until every staff member had experience with an e-reader, the Microsoft Surface, a Kindle, an Android device, and the iPad.

The Core Competencies grew from the need to help the staff explore devices in a meaningful way. The director took her own experience to create a list of common or important skills a mobile user ought to have. The Core Competencies are concepts that span across device and operating system, such as finding the settings, making settings changes, connecting or disconnecting from Wi-Fi, power cycling the device, closing applications, and the like.

This training strategy was a far more successful training program than the tedious meetings with staff poking at devices on a table for a short period of time. At the conclusion of the program, a large majority of the library's staff had a familiarity with the most popular mobile platforms and was prepared to answer basic user questions. In addition, the library experienced an unexpected development of "Subject Specialists" to certain operating systems or devices.

One staff member took a Samsung tablet with Android home, returning the next day frustrated and in tears, saying she was "too old" for the technology. She expressed frustration with trying to use the keyboards and interacting with apps. The director encouraged her to try again with the iPad, and after a few days, the staff member returned

Table 1. Core Competencies

Basics	Know how to install apps on the device
• Power cycle device	Know how to force close apps
• Adjust light and volume	Know how to organize apps
• Change display timeout	Browser vs. apps—know the difference
• Turn the Wi-Fi on/off	E-Ink vs. Tablet—know the difference
• Turn Bluetooth on/off	Understand your library's materials
Settings	• eBooks
• Navigate settings to adjust for personal preference	• Audiobooks
• Add accounts	• Streaming/downloading
• Email/iTunes/Google Play/Amazon	• Magazines
• Add an email	• Articles
Pictures	
• Take pictures	
• Email/send pictures	
• Take a screen shot	
Keyboarding	
• Use the shift key	
• Use numbers	
• Turn caps lock on/off	
• Use special characters	
• Emojis	

the iPad as she had bought her own, and later bought an iPhone. She is now the resident iOS expert for the library and regularly answers detailed and complicated questions for users and staff.

Another staff member fell in love with the Microsoft Surface in the Gizmo Garage, and asked the library to purchase her one for library use when her outdated system came up for replacement. She became the library's resident Microsoft expert, and is the go-to person to answer any mobile Windows question or to help library staff and library users with MS 8 or 10 questions. She takes her Surface tablet out into the community and uses it for presentations in classrooms and for community organizations.

Similarly, another staff member who did not have Internet at home or a personal computer, clicked with the Android operating system, eventually purchasing his own Samsung phone and tablet for personal use. He's learned so much about the Android system that he handles all the complex questions asked by library staff and users alike.

After the program, each of the library's staff operated as an ambassador for the library's digital content, and many continued to use the audiobooks, eBooks, and other streaming services the library provides. With a large amount of internal users, the library became a stopping point for the community struggling to connect with digital resources. Library users often take their devices to the service points asking technical questions regarding the library's eBook and audiobook services, and staff are in a position to help because of their understanding of the resources in question.

Furthermore, with the staff each using different devices and operating systems, the staff felt confident to tell users to fearlessly explore devices at retail establishments until they found the device that fit them best. Nearly all the staff experienced disliking a device or platform, and knew that just as every book its reader, every device its user. When users came in asking, "What's the best device to buy?" staff answered instructing the user to explore various options and provided them with copies of the core competencies. The core competencies sheet gave the user activities to perform on each device to gain a better understanding of how the device would work for them, just as it did for the staff.

Once all the staff experienced the variety of mobile devices and felt comfortable enough to answer basic questions, programming became the next goal. The programming team created a "Gizmo Garage" event for the public, planning to place the state owned devices on a table in a room and inviting the public to come, explore, and ask questions. The event was advertised in the paper and on the library's Facebook to coincide with the beginning of the holiday season, when library users may be thinking of choosing mobile devices as gifts. Two staff members ran the event.

This program, while a noble attempt, was chaotic and challenging. Without thinking, the library staff created the exact same structure as the initial failed all-staff meetings; the devices were put out on display, and users were expected to explore the devices and ask questions. In reality, only one of the attendees came in to see the offered devices, the remaining users brought their own devices and their own questions, from the very basic to time intensive and complicated. The two staff quickly became overwhelmed with the large number of attendees requiring long periods of staff time per interaction. The library staff were not prepared for this scenario; an extra staff member was pulled off a service point to assist, and staff raced from person to person trying to answer questions. Library users clustered in the room and overflowed into the area outside, waiting for a turn to ask a question. The hour long program quickly became two, and at that point users had to be turned away.

Reflection on this event encouraged changes to the library's open sessions. The programming team initiated a 3:1 user to staff ratio, capping attendance with signup sheets for group sessions. The director dusted off the Core Competencies previously used for staff training for the events. During the remainder of the holiday season, the open sessions continued. The state owned devices remained available, but the majority of library users brought their own devices in. At the beginning of the sessions, the core competencies sheet was distributed to each attendee. Staff would answer a question, and instead of allowing users to monopolize staff time, library staff would break from the interaction with the statement "Work on that and I'll be back to check on you in a few minutes" while moving on to the next individual. If the library user's question was answered and they had a natural break in thought after the one-on-one staff time, the library staff member would encourage the user to go through the competencies sheet. It is important to note that library staff did not handle personal devices or accounts for potential liability reasons, rather patiently guided users through necessary steps on their device. This new class structure distributed staff time across the attendees better, answered more questions, and provided more direction for the library users. This model continued well into the new year after the holiday season.

The library staff realized that nearly all attendees were older adults in the Baby Boomer generation. The staff learned that the vast majority of these users never had Internet at home, nor a personal computer. Some claimed to have used computers at work before, but felt intimidated by the mobile devices gifted to them by their children and grandchildren. These users were entering into Internet access for the first time via cell service or free Wi-Fi available in town. The vast majority of the user's questions rotated around basic Internet usage, such as using e-mail and understanding account usernames and passwords. Frequently, library staff had to assist users with connecting to the library's Wi-Fi, as few library users had Internet at home. As a result, the library staff made sure to clarify data and data use to help the users understand device behavior that might negatively impact their bill. Furthermore, the staff created bookmarks listing all the locations of free Wi-Fi in town and distributed these bookmarks to users.

Previously, the sessions were open to all ages, but after hearing experiences from the majority, the programming team felt modifications were in order. As attendance died down from the open sessions, a discussion group called "Silver Surfers" grew. The library sponsored a discussion group once a week at the same time, encouraging Boomers to come in during that time to network with peers and ask questions. Many times, users came with a specific question or problem, but regular attendees enjoyed networking with new found friends affectionately calling the time "Appy Hour," where library users shared their favorite apps with each other. Library staff kept a small, portable projector on hand with device dongle attachments, so tablets and smartphones could project their screens onto the walls for better sharing. Library users loved this and happily interacted with their peers while showing off their devices.

The unintended outcome of the development of the subject specialists in the different devices broadened the library's ability to help users who came in with questions beyond simply connecting to library resources. The library began to use the subject specialists it developed from its training to offer one-on-one, in-depth appointments. Anyone could book an appointment with the Android expert, the iOS expert, the Microsoft expert, and the Kindle expert. The appointments lasted no longer than an hour, and mimicked the already established reference appointments and homework help programs. There are rules for these appointments; users are required to bring in their power cords (it was too often the case a user would arrive for an appointment with a dead device and no way to charge it), and users are required to bring in any usernames/passwords for accounts. The last rule resulted from tremendous problems encountered in the open sessions and discussion groups. Often, users arrived with a device gifted to them by a child or grandchild. The child or grandchild, meaning well, would set up the device for the user, but would fail to provide usernames and passwords for Google, iTunes, and Amazon. Staff ended up walking users through complicated password resets, or turning users away altogether who did not know their e-mail address to even begin a password reset process. Once the rule was enforced, Boomers arrived for appointments with papers and notebooks. Documenting e-mail addresses and passwords became a crucial part of the appointment process for the user in order to ensure that the user always knew what their e-mail address was, and passwords for various accounts. Often, library staff would encourage the user to discard old scribbled out passwords and begin the documentation process anew with a fresh page. It was too easy for users to become confused with so many usernames and passwords written down. Occasionally, the library staff would teach a user who did not have good writing ability, and to save user time and frustration, help sheets were created and printed for the user. It was a simple matter to assist with a laptop on hand to quickly type up workflows and URLs. URL snipping services, like Bitly or TinyURL were used to shorten complicated URLs in documentation. It turned out that the very basic needs of knowing an e-mail address, a username, a password, and the name of different services were the most common needs addressed in the one-on-one tech appointments.

Born from the one-on-one appointments, the library director approached local continuing education groups to offer free introductory classes as library outreach. Already the local academic institution offered hour-long sessions, and it was an easy step to teach

Android 101 and iPhone 101 classes. Again, the Core Competencies sheet came into play, and special emphasis on mastering the settings of individual devices were covered. Each session also included the suggestion to explore the device with a paper and pencil, noting any changes or clicks so users could follow a trail to undo a change they did not like. Finally, the instructor reminded attendees that this was nothing more than something new, and they could master the device, and that they had the crucial critical thinking skills from a life of learning to lean on. Many attendees claimed feeling poorly because they were not adept, but at no fault to their cognitive abilities, and this gentle reminder instilled confidence in class attendees. Users simply needed to know it was new, and required attention to master, just as once learning to ride a bike did. Of course, the director encouraged the class attendees to take advantage of the Silver Surfers discussion group and the library's one-on-one appointments. Attendees were not alone, and the library was there to help.

The library furthered its outreach programming by offering drop in, open sessions of an hour at local senior centers. Once a month, one to two library staff members would visit participating senior centers with copies of the Core Competencies. Attendance varied from a few users to several. The first step upon beginning the program was to sort users by operating system, and sub-categorize by question (for example, at the Android table the Facebook questions sat together). Each person was given a copy of the Core Competencies with the instruction to work with their operating system team as the library staff member rotated from group to group or among individuals asking questions. Library staff members honed the skill of ending an interaction after sufficient time to allow for movement throughout the groups. While the groups waited for a turn, they were asked to work together or individually on their group question or the Core Competencies, or to share favorite apps, or discovered tricks. Users chatted and sessions were lively with discussion. The attendees learned from each other through sharing discoveries, making friends, and helping to mentor new mobile device users. Mentors told library staff they felt confident and secure answering mentee's questions, and felt a sense of accomplishment and a higher level of comfort through feedback forms. The sessions were hugely successful and valued by the community.

The Portneuf Library was lucky to participate in the state's Gizmo Garage program, and use the program's devices to enable the staff to master proficiencies with mobile devices in order to answer library user's questions. However, the Idaho Commission for Libraries' program is unique and may not be readily available for libraries. Libraries can create their own Gizmo Garages for staff training. The latest tablet or smartphone is not necessary for training staff proficiencies with operating systems. Libraries can buy used tablets at a lower cost specifically for training programs. Libraries with thin budgets can create a group where each library purchases a used device, pooling them together allowing each library to have the Gizmo Garage for a set period of time. Additionally, libraries can solicit donations, which are tax deductible, from board members, Friends groups, and library users for training purposes. It's not necessary to have the latest and greatest to teach staff how the different operating systems work. Older, outdated hardware suffice in a pinch for illustrating how each operating system works on different devices.

In conclusion, the Portneuf Library continues to experience successful library user service due to its unique training program. Currently, the vast majority of the staff now own personal devices and regularly use the digital content owned or licensed by the library, and as such can provide basic assistance helping library users establish accounts and access on their own personal devices at service points. The library's Subject Specialists continue to offer one-on-one appointments with users to assist users with detailed and complicated questions, much to the delight of the library's community. Outreach classes are still taught and open sessions are held for community members, which may or may not be a library user. Additionally, the library creates goodwill with users by offering the classes, and it's often the case non-library users express interest in the library after attending tech help sessions and classes. The program is hugely successful and has marked the library as a tech savvy, helpful place for the community to go for connecting to digital materials or to help users learn to use their personal devices.

Part II

Teaching Staff to Teach Patrons

Building a Bridge Across the Digital Divide
Teaching Technology in the Public Library

SAMANTHA DUCKWORTH *and* HAZEL KOZIOL

Portland Public Library (PPL) is located in the largest city in Maine, serving a diverse community that includes immigrants and refugees, entrepreneurs, professionals, college students, retirees, islanders, and families. PPL has a staff of 53 full-time equivalents who work across the Library's four branches and bookmobile. The system has more than 65 computer stations, over 300,000 materials, and numerous daily programs, serving the city of over 66,000 residents and, as an area resource center for Southern Maine, over 784,000.

PPL is managed through a team-based structure. Subject teams were developed in accordance with community interest and organizational needs, and are both internally focused, such as Technology Infrastructure and Health & Safety, and external, Arts & Culture, Business & Government, Health, City of Readers (fiction), and Science & Technology. Each staff member is assigned to a team, and allotted five hours of paid time per month in addition to his or her regular schedule to devote to team activities, which allows the Library to support and facilitate professional development while advancing the broader organizational mission, vision, and values.

Professional development guidelines advise libraries to provide a flexible plan for staff digital literacy development that includes all levels and ranks of employees (Koerber 2015). We can look to management scholarship that uses addiction treatment behaviors to understand how technology savvy staff can share and impart their skills with their less digitally comfortable colleagues. Peer support, acknowledging small successes, replacing old habits with new ones, and aiming for progress not perfection, are edicts that Friends of Bill W. advocate (Ferrazzi 2014). Successful professional development takes many forms, and technology skill building is very much aligned with these 12-step tenets.

- **Peer support: Peer-to-peer training**—This includes programs through library consultants at the Maine State Library, like the Technology Petting Zoo and districtwide Information Technology and eCommunications group meetings, as well as internal meetings that allow library staff to share knowledge, skills, problems, solutions, and experiences. Peer-to-peer training is a fundamental component of

professional development, as it provides a casual setting where staff are not afraid to ask questions, and have an opportunity to broaden skills in other areas of library service.
- **Acknowledging small successes: Opportunities for staff to try new technologies**—Making new technology available for staff to experiment prior to public release is crucial to building staff confidence. Whether patrons ask questions about technology in a formal setting like a class or workshop, or on the floor more casually, staff need to have confidence in their own ability to use technology, which is best gained from practice and experimentation. Understanding the nuances and common pitfalls when using technology helps staff experience success before modeling it to others.
- **Replacing old habits with new ones: Institutionalized support of professional development**—Staff are encouraged to attend conferences, workshops, and meetings. Institutionalizing the importance of professional development—at any dollar amount—is a good way to promote skill building among staff. Discrete training opportunities allow librarians to focus on learning new skills, transition to new ways of using technology, and provide occasions to acclimate to modified digital habits. Even when professional development budgets are unavailable, libraries can support learning by providing off-desk time for staff to follow webinars, read literature, experiment with emerging technologies, and attend local trainings.
- **Aiming for progress not perfection: Staff should utilize patron resources**—With technology, there will always be exceptions and anomalies, so it is important for staff to learn that change is not a single event that occurs once with each new database or equipment acquisition, but that change is a constant state. Staff should regularly use the resources accessible to patrons, and those who put themselves in patrons' shoes are better equipped to offer their knowledge at service desks, and can better work though higher level difficulties.

Each staff member has the potential to exponentially increase the library's educational effect within the community, when the time and resources are made available to do so. Within the library, it is often made to seem as if the task of equipping patrons with skills for digital success is a unique departmental specialization, but the ability to teach digital proficiency must be a fully institutionalized responsibility. This is only possible when all staff are well-equipped with the same skills that patrons need to access information. The Library's administration must value professional development and training for staff to be able to impart these skills to the community.

While there are many ways to prioritize staff development, PPL achieves this through a team structure that governs library operations. As staff are encouraged to explore new ideas and topics that will help build confidence in their daily work, they are simultaneously pursuing the Library's mission and values. This grows the organization's resources and commitment to each topical area, expanding with each hour a staff member devotes to his or her team. Team-based management encourages an environment of intentional cross-training, in which the sharing of experiences is a priority, not an afterthought. Staff who attend conferences commit to presenting on what they learn to a larger staff audience, and these presentations often take place before start of business to maximize attendance. With these opportunities for interpersonal and interdepartmental learning, even a small staff becomes capable of meeting community needs.

Going Public

Library staff who are motivated to be digitally literate are the mortar for a bridge across the digital divide. By training staff to understand that change and learning are constants while making institutional support available in pursuit of the advancement of information at all levels, a library is practicing what it is teaching. Not everyone will be taught typing skills in school, and not everyone has access to a computer at home—indeed, not everyone even has a home. In 2014, Portland homeless shelters housed over 2,200 adults, many of whom were public library users (City of Portland 2015). Twenty-one percent of the city's population is estimated to live below the poverty level, and focusing only on the population who live in the same downtown zip code where PPL's Main Branch is located, the population living in poverty rises to 31 percent (U.S. Census Bureau 2014). In order to help these patrons gain occupational skills, employment, and regular housing, technology skills are crucial. To ensure that library staff are able to succeed in providing public computer access, technology assistance and education must also be included in a comprehensive vision of library provided literacy. In 2015, PPL staff met with 196 patrons for individual tutoring sessions, 307 patrons came to classes and workshops, and assistance was requested at 8 percent of all computer sessions. While the demand will never completely disappear, the ability to meet appeals for assistance becomes easier when there is a structure for how patron needs are met.

Given the extent of this need, digital literacy programs—especially those that favor one-on-one interaction—can pose staffing constraints; however, these are critical services and libraries with all types of staffing constructs can provide a structure to help adjust patron experiences of computer and Internet utility. Every day we greet new patrons who require assistance with digital tasks, and as those who have never had cause to use a computer are deciding that it is finally time, librarians will only be called upon more by our communities. We need to be ready.

Step 1: Identify the Challenges and Boundaries

Teaching introductory computer skills to novice users as a digital native presents a unique set of challenges. In an instructional library environment, *language barrier* can mean one of three things.

- **Language**: The most common use of *language barrier* describes the mis/communication between people who do not speak the same language. English is not a common language for many patrons seeking computer help at PPL. The city of Portland is home to native speakers of, most commonly, Somali, Arabic, Spanish, French, Vietnamese, Khmer, and Portuguese (Portland Public Schools 2015). Many of these patrons seek opportunities for computer education from the Library.
- **Language literacy**: *Language barriers* can also exist between the patron who is unable to read and understand the content from or about which she is learning.
- **Jargon**: This is most unique language barrier to digital learning. Using unfamiliar technical jargon can create both patron-teacher and patron-content barriers, potentially leaving even the patron who is able to read and speak the same language as her teacher stuck on the wrong side of the bridge across the digital divide.

While the teacher has the responsibility in any of these situations to meet the patron where he or she currently is, but it is also in the best interest of both if the teacher is able to encourage the patron out of his or her comfort zone. A one-on-one, hands-on approach is best in that it favors demonstration when verbal communication is either unproductive or unfeasible due to *language barriers*. When possible, an assistant teacher in a class setting is ideal, as skill and language barriers can quickly derail the class's agenda, lowering the threshold so that the only productive learner is the patron with the lowest skills. Still, it is not always easy to adequately provide this ideal kind of support to patrons on the floor with one designated staff member responsible for attending to the needs of many users.

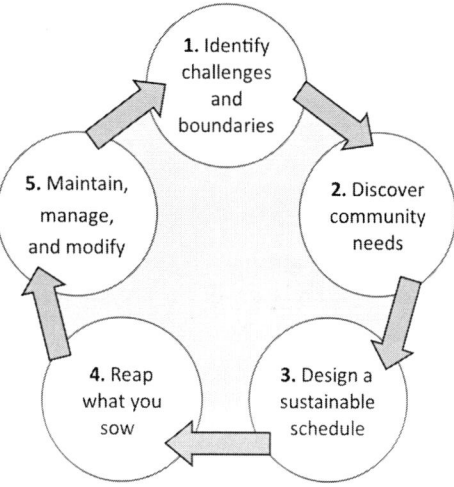

The Key Steps to Constructing a Library Bridge Across the Digital Divide

1. Identify challenges and boundaries
2. Discover community needs
3. Design a sustainable schedule
4. Reap what you sow
5. Maintain, manage, and modify

There are distinct boundaries that libraries need to recognize, from a daily time limit on computer use, to the necessary access restrictions when fines are due. These are boundaries that libraries should recognize as surmountable by coaching staff on appropriate reasons to extend time computer sessions, and allowing patrons to pay fines in installments. While maintaining fairness in a greater context, it is also important to recognize these policies as potential barriers to patron access and learning, and to demonstrate policy flexibility when it is appropriate.

An additional boundary that should be addressed by libraries is how staff interact with non-library owned equipment and devices. PPL has an expectation that staff should verbally walk a patron through using equipment that is not owned by the library, which has mitigated the burden staff feel around messing up and being liable for future problems on others' devices. This also fosters a culture in which the patron must use his or her own device, and even with staff guidance, the user will ultimately be the one to reach the solution. In the Public Computing area, PPL staff model this behavior whenever possible so patrons can better understand that technology skills *can* be learned, and that the problem *can* be solved—moreover, that *they* can be the ones to solve it—with the right information on how to proceed. In class and tutoring settings, laptops are provided so patrons can work through an activity to reinforce what they are learning. Phrases like "I'm going to let you drive" or "You won't break the machine, give it a try!" are encouraging words that help users begin to understand that they can stop expecting staff to "just do it for me."

Step 2: Discover Community Needs

Personal instruction in computer use is an enormous task for library professionals. At PPL, Public Computing staff are trained in the best practices of providing technology assistance on demand, but it is almost impossible for anyone who regularly uses computers to remember their first few hours using it, and each new user brings unique learning styles, abilities, and intentions. As is true of education more generally, there is no one-size-fits-all approach, and the vast possibilities and applications of modern technologies prove that this is truer now more than ever before.

Just as learning to read takes hours of practice sitting with a patient teacher, learning to operate a computer requires patience and understanding on both sides of the teaching experience. An important facet of helping to impart digital literacy is being quick to respond to needs, and making excuses to avoid change is applying an analog mindset to a digital need (Stephens 2014). Technology training for public patrons requires that change is acknowledged as constant, not a task to temporarily mobilize around. This should be institutionally internalized and modeled by staff development, as described in the first section. Libraries should include regular revisions and updates to their digital literacy trainings. There is a multitude of foundational digital skills and curriculum guides freely available on the web (see appendix). Having well-maintained collection materials with foundational computer literacies offers an access point for reluctant learners who may be more comfortable with books, and tenacious weeding of outdated materials is crucial to avoid information fatigue as patrons browse relevant materials.

Another key element of a successful digital literacy plan is maintaining an internal list of frequently asked questions and topics. These recurring patron questions should inform class development, as will targeted surveys in print formats to allow non-computer users to provide input, too. This will help tailor the content of group classes to specific community needs. Libraries can work with available staff times, and look for patterns of staffing levels and patron traffic that lend themselves to a sustainable program. For example, if statistics show that Tuesday mornings are slow, that would be a good time to offer tutoring, especially if the desk staff will still be managing the desk while adding one-on-one assistance to their services. In addition, offering a basic computing class once per month is better than never, and patrons will eagerly look to the next available class when they are struggling with a topic or task.

Step 3: Design a Sustainable Schedule of Classes and Tutoring

Over the course of an 18-month development period, PPL has found a pattern that meets the needs of its community, and works with available staff time. PPL offers

- ten individual half-hour tutoring appointments each week, including morning, afternoon, and evening appointments to maximize accessibility. Patrons attend these sessions primarily for instruction in (1) introduction to computing, (2) using eReader software to access library materials, and (3) creation and basic use of e-mail and social media accounts.
- one 90-minute drop-in computer assistance session per week. Some weeks have six patrons throughout that time, other weeks have just one or two. Since scheduled tutoring sessions can get booked out for a few weeks, it is beneficial for staff and patrons to structure a time when patrons can seek more in-depth assistance on a topic.
- regular, topical classes, rotating seasonally. Usually, these are held once per week for two months, a month break, and then resuming for another session. They are

presented as a sequential series, but can be taken à la carte, which offers options for the varying patron needs and skill levels.
- "on call" desk hours, designed to allow the solo desk staff to call for help so that more time can be spent with a patron on a specific, time-sensitive task. When a public desk is staffed by a single person, having periods of back-up support is a valuable way to accommodate patrons who need in-depth, unscheduled assistance.

Ideally, a mix of on-demand tutoring and drop-in computer assistance should form the backbone of a library's digital literacy program, scaled to community size and staffing availability. Digital literacy volunteers can provide the content of these services, but library staff are essential to train the trainer, and to develop a model of service, curriculum goals, and facilitation. Smaller libraries can look to their communities for aid in providing computer training to the public.

Step 4: Reap What You Sow

As a digital literacy program takes shape and matures, staff should look to create connections to build a self-sustaining class cycle. Focused engagement with patrons who move through the program will contribute to its longevity. Former students possessing newly acquired technology skills develop a digital expertise they can offer back to others, which in turn fortifies their own knowledge. As the classes move along, regular students will emerge, and librarians who share the goals and needs of their digital training programs will successfully recruit recent students of the programs as volunteers. People who have adapted well to technology are so grateful for their digital freedom, they are often happy to give back—either financially, or in-kind as volunteers. Looking to the students and cultivating relationships will have a lasting impact on the success of a digital literacy program. There are other types of potential community support for digital literacy:

- **Young people**: Pre- and early members of the workforce seek opportunities to volunteer as a means of augmenting college applications and early résumés or fulfilling community service requirements. The millennial generation is the first to grow up surrounded by our fast-moving technological world, some since birth, and PPL has had success framing volunteerism as an opportunity to build a career path.
- **Immigrants and refugees**: These patrons are valuable and unique members of the Portland community (and many other communities worldwide). As new residents, some seeking asylum, there are many steps required before one is able to obtain a work permit. While government processes can take months, or even years, these people are often excited to have meaningful opportunities to share their rich knowledge and add high quality work to their resume. Immigrants and refugees can also provide digital literacy instruction in non–English languages, which subverts the *language barrier* to learning for those who do not speak English natively. At a time when the desire to work is strong but the legal requirements prevent it, volunteering technology skills can help provide a stopgap measure while paperwork is processed.
- **Digital Literacy Tutors**: A third type of distinct volunteers require special brand-

ing, which cultivates talent and desire to help others acquire technology skills. PPL provides community tutor tables for other organizations to use, and heavy use of these areas shows both a steady need for literacy training and mobilized supply of volunteers. People are always willing to help others succeed. Soliciting volunteers who can help support people in pursuit of technology literacy goals is another way the library serves as an information connector. Librarians do not always know the answer to questions, but do help provide access, and facilitating a human connection to digital learning is an important facet of our services in this century.

Step 5: Maintain, Manage and Modify

Digital literacy programs in a public library are a moving wheel, powered by change and the persistent call from digital novices seeking help. The tools patrons use, as well as the program content, need to be maintained, managed, and modified to account for physical degradation, obsolescence, and new developments in the technology landscape. Planned review of all aspects of a digital literacy program is important to empower staff and patrons to teach and learn. It begins with public desk staff voicing patron needs, moves through higher levels of library administration supporting these needs, and results in regular updates and new equipment as possible. Staff who are not system administrators need to advocate for the maintenance of the area, and openly communicate issues. Systems and machines cannot be fixed if administrators do not know they are broken.

- **Maintain**: Public access computers must be running as cleanly as possible. Libraries can facilitate this by implementing reboot-to-restore solutions (free and low-cost options available), many of which include software updating. Regular software refresh is a crucial step to easily avoid errors new technology users might experience with a less than optimally running computer.
- **Manage**: Public library budgets rarely allow for frequent equipment upgrades to state-of-the-art machines, but paying attention to the age of equipment and software is imperative if libraries are to maintain their bridge across the digital divide. Staff should be champions for replacement and upgrades every three to five years, with special attention to the shorter time frame for software. For example, basic usage and document accessibility was a concern as Office 2003 stopped interacting easily with other services (printer software, interoperability with patron owned-equipment). Upgrading equipment on a consistent schedule will ensure patrons who have learned basic digital skills stay relevant in their access at the library. Equipment leasing programs, thin clients, cloud-based computing, and refurbished machines are all options that libraries can explore.
- **Modify**: As teaching digital literacy becomes part of daily business in a library, offering modifications and alterations to the regular offerings will help strengthen the library's bridge. People who have acquired basic skills may seek further development, so providing lessons on special topics—social media, basic (or advanced) web design, digital privacy, ethical hacking, alternative operating systems, for example—will position the library as a community resources for sought-after topics. Volunteers are well-suited to teach these topics, and local experts are often

happy to share their knowledge, especially when it boosts visibility for a small business or other community resource. Being open to modifications to a technology literacy program when requested by the community is a final component of a healthy and strong library bridge across the digital divide.

Conclusion: Overcoming the Barriers to Bridge Building

It is our job as teaching library professionals to understand what a patron hopes to achieve and then to help them identify the steps they can take to get there. In addition to the question of *how* (e.g., a job searcher asking, "How do I get an e-mail address?"), users who lack digital literacy skills often struggle with the *what* as well (e.g. that same patron who knows she needs to apply for a job online may not even know that she needs an e-mail address to do so, or perhaps even what an e-mail address is or does).

The hardest aspect of teaching anything is to remember what it was like before *you* knew, and to put yourself there with the patron. We must remind ourselves that just as a new reader would not begin with *Ulysses*, a digital novice will not dive into advanced web design, or even Excel, right away. Especially for new learners, it is important to encourage computer use of any kind, as there are useful skills to be acquired in all areas of computer use. Casual social media use has the potential to familiarize patrons with ubiquitous Internet elements and tools while computer gaming fosters mouse and keyboard dexterity. This practice of encouraging learning in judgment-free environment is one with which librarians are already familiar.

There will never be a shortage of new computer users. As technology continues to advance, more people are being left behind in the wake of ever-expanding options. It is no longer possible to be not willing to learn technology, and libraries need to be prepared to help everyone understand how to access essential services that are only online.

The good news is that most patrons, in our experience, only require enough instruction to get the ball rolling. Libraries that provide basic skills can inspire beyond the scope of library technology instruction. PPL staff witness newly educated patrons willing to share their recently acquired skills with others, an interaction that is invaluable for all stakeholders. Investing time and energy to empower self-sufficient users creates an environment in which staff can apply those resources to improving and maintaining equipment infrastructure and designing programs that delve deeper and reach further.

Appendix

http://www.digitalliteracy.gov/resources-by-term/81 Curated database of digital literacy lesson plans, sorted by topic

http://digitalliteracy.us Extensive teaching resources (including digital toolkits) for librarians teaching digital literacy skills

https://www.digitalliteracyassessment.org/ Eight assessment modules covering basic computing, Microsoft Office, Internet and e-mail

https://www.digitalpromise.org/ Blog addressing techniques, trends, and other topics in digital literacy education

http://www.gcflearnfree.org/ In-depth tutorials for basic computing, social media and e-mail, Windows and OS X, Microsoft Office, and more

References

Anglada, Lluis. 2014. "Are Libraries Sustainable in a World of Free, Networked, Digital Information?" *El Profesional de la Información* 23, no. 6: 603–611.

City of Portland, Maine. Health and Human Services Department. 2014. "Oxford Street Shelter & Community Overflow Shelters Year End Report FY 2014." Accessed Feb. 11, 2016. http://www.portlandmaine.gov/DocumentCenter/Home/View/6569.

Ferrazzi, Keith. 2014. "Managing Change, One Day at a Time." *Harvard Business Review* 92, no. 7/8: 23.

Gonzales, Amy. 2015. "The Contemporary US Digital Divide: From Initial Access to Technology Maintenance." *Information, Communication & Society* 19, no. 2: 234–248.

Koerber, Jennifer. 2015. "Manage the Device Deluge: Create an Effective Program to Train Staff to Teach Tech to the Public in a Time of Rapid Change and Gadget Proliferation." *Library Journal* 140, no. 9: 28–31.

Portland Public Schools, Portland, Maine. 2015. "Fast Facts Fall 2015." Accessed Feb. 11, 2016. https://www.portlandschools.org/UserFiles/Servers/Server_1094153/File/District%20Information/Fast%20Facts%20Fall%202015.1.compressed.pdf.

Stephens, Michael. 2014. "Always Doesn't Live Here Anymore." *Library Journal* 139, no. 17: 51.

U.S. Census Bureau. 2010–2014 American Community Survey 5-Year Estimates. Accessed Feb. 11, 2016. http://factfinder.census.gov/bkmk/cf/1.0/en/place/Portland city, Maine/POVERTY/BLW_LVL_PCT.

Show, Don't Tell
Technology Instruction for Front-Line Staff, Passed On to Patrons

Elizabeth Tarski McArthur

Show. Don't tell. This tried and true method of training was adopted as our instruction motto when we overhauled our library's student staff technology training program. This simple motto helps us focus on three overarching goals:

- Increase customer satisfaction.
- Answer every question (even if the answer is "Let's look at that together").
- Help staff feel more knowledge, comfortable, and empowered.

Training frontline staff at a small academic library requires a variety of techniques, but the one I have found most important is hands-on technology training. The student workers who constitute the bulk of our frontline staff are part of the digital generation, but they still need instruction on both the library webpage and online catalog. Additionally, there are many Internet search techniques they have never learned and it is extremely important that they feel comfortable troubleshooting much of the technology in the library. When training, we model the behavior we would like our frontline staff to pass on to our patrons; namely: showing not telling. Then, our staff does the same when helping patrons. This impacts the tech skills of everyone our staff-members interact with throughout their tenure at the library.

While these techniques have been used to train student staff at our library, they are applicable for any frontline library staff, and for many who work in the back of the building. We consider technology training to be the basis of building patron trust. The most frequent questions asked at our desk address basic technology problems: the printer won't print or a file won't open, etc. If we turn away patrons looking for basic help, how can we expect them to come to the desk when they have an in-depth reference question? Making technology training a priority truly helps establish a relationship of trust with our patrons.

Because of this need for trust, technology instruction is important for every member of a library staff—whether they are of the digital generation or not. In addition to training frontline staff, this requires "programs that both address digital fluency training in librarians, along with the faculty and students they support on campus" (Johnson et al. 2015, 24). Frontline staff, however, are the first piece of this puzzle. In order to avoid a slide into the obsolete, we train our frontline staff with a series of hands-on techniques. After being trained, they know to use these same "showing" rather than "telling" techniques to help our patrons better learn how to use the library website, as well as computers, printers and more. There is a popular belief in the idea of "see one, do one, teach one" as a way of truly mastering a new skill. This idea is backed up by the library literature, which maintains "the most effective way to teach someone a new technology is to encourage them to keep playing with it" (Koerber 2015, 31). As we go through the training process below, it will become apparent that our training plan correlates to this three-step process.

Background

Training was formerly based on a series of documents created at various times. Student staff read these documents during their first shifts. While they contained useful information, and their key points are certainly still incorporated in our current instruction processes, simply reading documents about key policies and procedures did not adequately prepare students—our frontline staff—for the technology questions they are required to answer. Through a series of gradual changes, we adapted our current technology training program, which is interactive and focused on showing staff members how to do things rather than talking at them and hoping they retain the information.

We were committed to using resources to which our library already had access. In our case, this meant finding tools that would integrate with LibGuides, but it would be possible to train staff through a WordPress account or even the staff intranet. Once we committed to both computer and hands-on tech training, we tried a variety of tools and techniques before settling on what worked best for us. It was quickly determined that a formal orientation session was needed at the start of each semester, but that training sessions should also be continuous. A typical agenda for our orientation session would look like this:

- Documents to Hand Out
    - Contact sheet
    - Full Schedule
    - Contracts
    - Meeting dates list
    - Bingo Cards
    - Payroll items
- Things to Go Over
    - Icebreaker and introductions
    - Read contracts out loud and add meeting dates to planners
    - Scheduled individual training
    - Building tours—seven at a time. Other seven—Library bingo.

While students expect some of their learning to be done online, they also consistently still want face-to-face teaching, so we try to accommodate those differing needs (Newland, Byles 2014). This first meeting with the whole team, as well as twice-monthly staff meetings, are important because they bring everyone together. This builds a team mentality, helping staff support each other and strive for success together. The pace and tone of this orientation meeting informs staff that this job is both important and complicated. It is expected most new staff members will leave orientation feeling overwhelmed, but this is acceptable because their individual training begins as soon as they arrive for their first shift.

Initial Training

During the first few weeks of each semester, training is our first priority. The student workers each have a training checklist, which is longer or shorter based on their tenure as a library staff member. To complete the checklist staff must

- familiarize themselves with the everyday tasks of the circulation desk;
- familiarize themselves with all the technology in the library;
- shadow a more experienced worker;
- meet each full-time librarian individually and introduce themselves;
- interact with each item in our equipment cabinet; and
- go through several role-playing scenarios.

(To see a checklist for a new staff member in its entirety, please see Appendix A.)

Training checklists are typically one sheet long and go over the bulk of a frontline staff member's responsibilities. Each item on the checklist is very important for the development of a good team member. It is important to note that while we make sure each piece of technology our students will need to use is on the checklist, we do not follow the checklist in order. We do all of our training at the desk, so answering patron questions is part of our staff members' job from day one. If a patron asks a question about a piece of technology on our list, we answer the question and use that real-life example to train. For instance, if a patron comes up and says that they can't print from the computer they are using, the trainee and the instructor would, together, walk over to the computer. The instructor would introduce the trainee and explain they were training. Then the instructor would verbally go through the different ways to check that a printer is installed and/or how to install a printer. The trainee would physically carry out the tasks on the computer. The instructor would ask the patron if he or she had any questions and address them. Once back at the desk, the instructor would ask the trainee the same question. Once all questions were resolved, we would check "printer troubleshooting" off of the training checklist.

This same scenario will happen throughout the training period. Whether a patron needs help with scanners or computer programs, the trainee and instructor work on the problem together. The instructor will go through the steps while the trainee carries out the tasks. If a patron doesn't happen to ask about a certain item on the checklist, we will still train in the same manner—the trainee is always the one physically completing the training task. Some of the more complicated technology tasks are completed by the trainee in this manner, and are later reinforced with role playing. The instructor acts like a patron and the trainee completes the task without verbal prompting, unless they ask for assistance. These role-playing scenarios are invaluable. Telling someone how to check in items with multiple barcodes or look up varying due dates will not teach them how to do these tasks. Allowing them to complete each task, make mistakes, and fix them is a much more effective technique.

A new staff member is more likely to learn from a returning staff member, hence the shadowing, but this also helps returning staff members "because when you teach someone a skill or show them a neat feature, you set it more firmly in your own mind and you might learn something from them in return" (Koerber 2015, 31). This also frees the instructors for other work tasks.

We believe staff members can more successfully checkout equipment when they know how to use it and what it can do, so we set aside time in one of their first shifts of the semester for a "technology sandbox" activity. To complete this, they check out a digital camera, a laptop, a projector, a tablet, and a webcam and play with each item. We allow them the autonomy of playing however they would like (watching YouTube videos or checking their Facebook page) which makes it seem like a fun activity, rather than work. It also means they actually interact with the technology and learn how to use it. While not strictly technology instruction, the self-guided librarian introductions are also a useful training tool. Staff are instructed to talk to each librarian in their office, which allows them to get to know the different office locations. Originally, they had introduced themselves and asked a pre-selected question, but we have changed this policy and now allow the students to pick their own questions. This has led to more natural conversations and some great questions. In the past semester alone, students have asked about favorite books, strange food, and what subject the librarian would study now if they went back in time to college.

The most important part of the checklist is to maintain a standard of hands-on learning. By having the students do everything themselves, starting with verbal cues, and moving on to just overseeing as they help patrons and adding a helpful idea when necessary, you set a precedent. Then, when they go to help patrons, they tend to be naturally enthusiastic about the different items and to model the same behavior—showing not telling. It's also important to note that our training checklists change each semester. These changes are based on what new technology we have gotten in the library, as well as feedback from the previous semester. With technology training, in particular, it is important not to get attached. As tech changes, so must your plan.

Ongoing Training

The importance of ongoing training cannot be exaggerated. As in any library, there are many moving pieces to working at our circulation desk. Staff members, particularly part-time staff members, cannot be expected to remember how to complete tasks that only come up once every few weeks or months without continuous training. In our library, after the orientation session and initial checklist, continuous training consists of

- a computer-based problem of the week;
- a computer-based game of the week; and
- twice-monthly meetings.

Training staff with a "show, don't tell" motto enables patrons to better use the library because our staff members, in turn, train patrons who then help each other. Once they understand our resources, patrons are also able to successfully use the services we provide remotely, such as online books, journals and articles, as well as music scores, videos and sound recordings (Garner 2016).

For most of our online training, including both the Problem of the Week and the Game of the Week, staff members complete quizzes and games. For most of these, we use two free platforms: Typeform and Purpose Games. There are a few others that we use for specific training, for instance LCEasy teaches the Library of Congress classification system, but we create the vast majority of our online training on these two websites. Both of them allow for complete customization. With a little bit of innovation, we are able to train frontline staff members on exactly what is expected at our library, or from our specific collection. Typeform, in particular, embeds very well in LibGuides. This is key because our staff website is located on LibGuides.

The Problem of the Week is usually an online quiz. Sometimes they are about recent changes in policy, such as a new way to log non-college community members into the computers. Typically, we introduce changes in our staff meeting and then use this quiz to make sure the new policies were correctly understood and absorbed by staff members. Occasionally we use this platform to get feedback about different displays. Before completing the online portion of these particular quizzes, staff members are required to go interact with the display extensively.

Typeform is extremely versatile, which allows us to use this space for a variety of tasks. Some of our most successful problems have been mock reference questions. While we have librarians staffing the desk to answer reference questions 30–40 hours per week, the library is open over 70 hours per week. This means students need to feel comfortable and empowered to use the library website and assist people with basic reference questions. In order to familiarize staff members with the intricacies and quirks of the library website, it is vital that they have a reason to explore it. Online scavenger hunts and interactive problems motivate staff to understand this resource. Their understanding is vital, as usability tests have shown that university students, as well as faculty and staff, utilize basic search functions far more than advanced search functions (Hanrath and Kottman 2015). Instruction cannot stop, however, at the library website or catalog. As we are all aware, users have more access to more information today than ever before, but have very little instruction on how to assess this information or even process it. As reported in the *NMC Horizon Report: 2015 Library Edition*, this is changing the expectations of what library staff should know. Without technology training, libraries risk becoming obsolete (Johnson et al. 2015). To combat this, in addition to reference quizzes based on the library website and catalog, our problems of the week also require staff members to complete in-depth Google Scholar searches and advanced Google searches.

The Game of the Week usually takes a little less time than the Problem of the Week and is generally a way to reinforce earlier training. One game, for instance, required staff members to match up the names of everyone who works in the library with their job title. Another was a blank map of the library they had to label correctly, and a third was a picture of the desk, which asked them to identify where different supplies are located.

Once each staff member has completed the problem and game, the supervisor goes over the answers with them. If there are just a few wrong answers to discuss, that's all we do. If, however, the staff member obviously doesn't understand the concept, and has many missed answers, we would go back to our modeling standard and use verbal cues to get them to re-do the problem successfully.

At our twice-monthly staff meetings, we get everyone together for teambuilding and announcements. These meetings are admittedly when our training veers into "telling" territory. It's impossible not to tell someone how to do their job at certain junctures. But even during these meetings, we include hands-on activities. We meet in the library instruction lab, which features computers. This allows everyone to log on and learn search techniques together. We also end each meeting with a round of "Less Good Thing / Very Good Thing." During this game, every member of the student staff names a less-good thing and a very good thing that has happened to them at work since the last meeting. In addition to improving staff communication, this game frequently brings up new technology problems that we add to our regular, ongoing training.

Communication

The importance of communication cannot be overstated. The literature shows that supervisors' communication affects employees, especially in regards to satisfaction and turnover. The way supervisors respond to communication can predict employee reactions and behavior in the future (Garner 2016). This is reinforced by the fact that our library has experienced very low staff losses since implementing the new training program. Of 25 students trained under this new technology program, only 2 have stopped working for us before graduating.

If the lines of communication are not open, you'll never have any idea how effective your training is, or whether anyone on staff understands how to use the different types of technology they help patrons with each day. In addition to our staff meetings, we have frontline staff members fill out an End-of-Shift Survey during the last few minutes of each shift. We use our staff LibGuide to host this survey as well, and it is also made on the Typeform platform. The survey is divided into basic reminder questions and more in-depth communication questions.

Basic questions include the following:

- How was your shift today?
- Do you wish you had more work or less work today?
- Was the library busy, empty or in between?
- Did you fill out your timesheet?
- Is the desk area neat?

In-depth questions include the following:

- Did you have any reference interactions today?
- Did anything out of the ordinary happen today?

These surveys are crucial for communication purposes. The basic questions, in addition to providing good reminders for everyday tasks, also give the supervisor an idea of how things are going. The "How was your shift today?" question offers staff emoji options for answering which range from "Super happy" to "Angry." This is an easy way for our frontline staff to communicate their feelings. Then, the more in-depth question about out-of-the-ordinary happenings allows staff to expand on something that may have gone wrong (or right) during their shift. Dissent (communicating negative things) improves business and employee satisfaction (Garner 2016). Therefore, giving staff members a way to show dissent, or to share a job well-done, is vital.

Also vital is the reference question in the survey. Because students do have to cover the desk without the assistance of a reference librarian for several hours each week, this question helps us to follow up with patrons who have had reference questions answered by students. It also helps us keep tabs on when the library and desk are busy, so that we can adjust reference hours accordingly.

Adaptability, Possible Issues and Conclusion

These methods are highly adaptable to any library. While we measure everything in semesters, which is obviously not done in public or special libraries, many libraries also don't have our high turnover rate—we strive not to keep anyone for longer than four years. Perhaps having an orientation meeting each time you get a new staff member isn't possible, but incorporating some of the orientation session goals into individual training or whole-staff meetings would certainly work. And training staff members one at a time would actually make the checklist process much easier. Typeform and Purpose Games work very well for our library, but there are many different platforms to consider. While not specifically aimed at libraries, the website Free Technology for Teachers has reviews of many different game and survey websites. Other websites such as Lifehacker, Wired and the ProfHacker blog at *The Chronicle of Higher Education* also review a variety of very useful technology.

There are, of course, possible issues associated with this training method. First of all, those who would naturally be in the "trainer" or "instructor" role are not always comfortable with tech themselves and need their own training (Newland, Byles 2014). I would argue, however, that not knowing what you're doing with technology is the first step to training someone on technology. Many, many problems with computers, printers and the like involve walking to the device and trying some things. Restart it. See what the settings look like. In other words: you don't have to know everything to teach others. One of the reasons our training program is constantly growing and changing is that our instructors learn more and want to pass on this new knowledge.

A related problem is that technology is constantly morphing and changing, which means your training program has to be flexible and your instructors have to continuously learn new things that they can then pass on to staff. This is why it is so useful to move away from paper training. With the use of LibGuides, Typeform and other online platforms, we can get our frontline staff members off on the right foot and help them train throughout their tenure with us.

Lastly, the literature suggests it's also possible to put the responsibility solely on the staff to do independent training and use their search skills to find new and exciting things, and then learn how to do them in their downtime at the desk (Koerber 2015). While we are exploring this as an option, we feel it doesn't necessarily work with our current setup.

Promoting digital literacy in a library has to start with training all staff to be not just digitally literate, but also able to show others the skills they have (Johnson et al 2015). Our modeling techniques help our frontline staff members feel confident and empowered to answer questions—even if their answer is "Let's go look at it together." Because our technology instruction for them is hands-on and led by the trainee, they pass their skills on to our patrons by modeling the same behavior. We feel that our training methods have positively impacted our frontline staff and our library patrons and believe they are both useful and adaptable for all frontline library staff.

Appendix

Training Checklist

General Training
- Customer Service
- Greeting people/coworkers
- Homework, tasks, attention, voice volume
- Timesheets & Schedule Change sheets
- Different types of call numbers/Collections
- Circulation & Reference Desk
- Phone/Intercom
- Receipt Drawer
- Security Gate & Security
- Working the Circ Desk Website (End-of-Shift Survey)
- Location of Office Supplies
- Typeform Basics
- Computer Troubleshooting
- Printer Troubleshooting (including printers 1&2, color printer, poster printers)
- Scanner Troubleshooting

Library of Congress
- Voyager
- Catalog/Website
- LC Easy
- Cart (regular, children's, mixed cart)
- Shelve (Reference & Circulation)

Tasks
- Equipment Sandbox Hour
- Explore the Library

Scenarios/Role Playing
- Checking in & out plus equipment
- Tours/Guests
- Poster Printers & Scanning
- Journals & ILL
- Phone

Individual Training
- Library Policies
- Individual Responsibility
- Week One Problem of the Week & Game of the Week

Reference

Dent, Nelson. 2015. "Digitarians @ Your Library." *Oklahoma Librarian* 65, no. 2 (March/April): 40–41.

Garner, Johny Thomas. 2016. "Open Doors and Iron Cages: Supervisors Responses to Employee Dissent." *International Journal of Business Communication* 53, no. 1 (January): 27–54.

Hanrath, Scott, and Miloche Kottman. 2015. "Use and Usability of a Discovery Tool in an Academic Library." *Journal of Web Librarianship* 9, no. 1: 1–21.

Johnson, L., S. Adams Becker, V. Estrada, and A. Freeman. 2015. *NMC Horizon Report: 2015 Library*

Edition. Austin: New Media Consortium. http://cdn.nmc.org/media/2015-nmc-horizon-report-library-EN.pdf.
Koerber, Jennifer. 2015. "Manage the Device Deluge." *Library Journal* 140, no. 9 (May 15): 28–31.
Newland, Barbara, and Linda Byles. 2014. "Changing Academic Teaching with Web 2.0 Technologies." *Innovations in Education and Teaching International* 51, no. 3 (May): 314–325.

Simulating Access Issues
Using Twine to Teach E-Resources Troubleshooting

Kate Lambaria, Heidi R. Johnson *and* Nicole Helregel

Patrons of academic libraries often experience difficulties when trying to access online library resources from off campus, and sometimes even from on campus. Teaching library staff how to successfully troubleshoot these difficulties can be challenging. Even though documentation of recommended steps may exist, truly learning and digesting the process can be difficult if only looking at words on a page.

At the University of Illinois at Urbana-Champaign library staff at the virtual reference desk and various in-person service points are constantly asked to troubleshoot access to the library's e-resources, especially online journal articles in databases. The only helpful documentation to refer to is an internal web page with text instructions and additional hyperlinks. In order to provide successful training on how to troubleshoot e-resources, two graduate assistants, with the help of librarians and staff, used interactive fiction and gamification to develop a tool that simulates these issues with the intent of emphasizing the preferred order in which troubleshooting steps should be taken. Twine, "an open-source tool for telling interactive, nonlinear stories," was selected to create the simulation, which is titled *Adventures in Access!* (Twine n.d.).

This essay will describe the processes of creating the various storylines, utilizing Twine's available features, and testing the game with graduate assistants and other library staff at Illinois. The development and implementation of *Adventures in Access!* serves as a model for using Twine for training and instructional purposes in a variety of library settings.

Literature Review

Interactive fiction (IF), which we define as text-based games that require readers to make choices that influence the plot, has a long and varied history that pre-dates the Internet. The *Choose Your Own Adventure* book series from the 1970s is an example of older IF in print. Computer-based IFs roots date back to 1975, with Infocom's *Adventure* (Farber 2015). Now, with online software programs and applications like Twine, Inform, and inklewriter, IF is easier than ever to create, and the possibilities for its use as an instructional tool are promising.

IF teaches essential skills in critical thinking which has a positive effect on learning (Farber 2015). IF can be more effective than just providing a list of instructions and it even has benefits over traditional stories for teaching purposes, since players often feel a sense of responsibility for the outcomes in the game (Green and Jenkins 2014, 488).

IF can also incorporate game elements, which is known as gamification. Several researchers have explored the development of gamification and its various definitions (Kim 2015; Seaborn and Fels 2015). Although there is no agreed-upon definition, we have accepted a common understanding of gamification as "the use of game elements outside of a game," where "a pre-existing process is augmented ... with characteristics borrowed from games" (Landers 2014, 756). In the case of *Adventures in Access!*, pre-existing information was used to create a simulation that employed meaningful combinations of selected game elements, such as variables and value-laden outcomes, without creating a fully developed game. In contrast, serious games have a primary goal of education and incorporate a mixture of all game elements (Landers 2014). A discussion on serious games is outside the scope of this essay. However, it is important to distinguish between serious games, which are fully-fledged games, and gamification, since *Adventures in Access!* is not a serious game, but instead uses IF to create a gamified tool for instructional purposes. (Although it does not meet the criteria to be considered a serious game, *Adventures in Access!* will be referred to as a "game" throughout this essay.)

Different learning theories, such as behaviorism and humanism, suggest different means of education. One learning theory in particular supports the argument for using IF specifically: constructivism. Szurmak and Thuna discuss how narrative mirrors the cognitive processes that comprise learning from a constructivist viewpoint (Szurmak and Thuna 2013). Narratives provide the structure by which the brain can grasp both the big picture and the details, mirroring what the brain does when it learns (Szurmak and Thuna 2013, 546).

Szurmak and Thuna conclude that there are three elements of narrative that make it an effective instructional tool: (1) narrative makes abstract ideas more understandable, (2) narrative provides the framework into which new knowledge can be incorporated, and (3) narrative provides affective experiences that students easily remember (Szurmak and Thuna 2013, 550–551). Thus, constructivism as a learning theory supports the argument that interactive stories facilitate learning, leading to behavioral changes.

Design Process

The creators of the *Adventures in Access!* believed that library employees at the University of Illinois would learn more effectively from an interactive game than they would from simply reading or hearing about a list of instructions. Another reason to use this method was that the order of steps taken during the troubleshooting process is key, and this could be best taught through a game in which order makes a difference for the final outcome, mirroring the actual real-life troubleshooting process.

The design team first selected XMind, a free online mind-mapping software, for authoring the different storylines. XMind allowed the design team to keep track of all of the different choices written into the game, and it provided a nice visualization of the

76 Part II. Teaching Staff to Teach Patrons

different paths. They then determined the best or "correct" path for troubleshooting access to electronic resources. For this they considered the steps that must be taken primarily from virtual chat interactions, but with other types of reference interactions in mind as well.

To write the text of the game, the design team first consulted an internal library web page on Electronic Resources troubleshooting. The page contains instructions for troubleshooting various issues involving access to articles contained in the University's subscription databases. The web page is used by librarians, staff, and graduate assistants who work at the reference and virtual chat desks. The web page contains information on

- finding out if a user is on or off campus;
- determining who is considered an authorized user;
- Googling the problem, in case vendors or other users have posted information about it online;
- checking the user's IP address to verify if the user is on or off campus;
- solving VPN (Virtual Private Network) issues (a particular Group setting must be selected when the user signs on to the VPN);
- clearing the browser cache;
- dealing with specific error messages, such as hostname error, certificate warning, or too many simultaneous users;
- checking subscription information in SFX to make sure the University has access to the resource (SFX is a link resolver that directs users from the library website out to subscription-based journals and databases);
- filling out ERTech tickets (the type of ticket specifically for access issues that gets sent to the Electronic Resources Librarian); and
- resolving Library Catalog login issues.

Next, the authors of the game studied and condensed these instructions and put them in a logical order that made the most sense—troubleshooting from the most general, most common, easier-to-troubleshoot issues to the narrower, least common, or most challenging issues. First, the library employee would need to make sure the patron is an authorized user of e-resources, which is done through a commonly used initial canned chat message that asks if and how the patron is affiliated with the University. Because most library employees working at virtual reference use this canned chat, the message was built into the game script

Then the authors included the step of confirming that Illinois affiliates have access to that particular article. This is important because sometimes users request articles that are not a part of Illinois' subscriptions, and without this step any other troubleshooting efforts would be futile.

Next, the authors included the step of finding out if the patron is on or off campus. This information is important for determining whether the patron must use either the VPN or proxy server or can go directly to the vendor's website. Even in the case that the patron is on campus, however, sometimes the patron must still use the proxy server. This contingency is built into the game. During this step, users also need to confirm the patron's IP address, because it is common for patrons to think they are on-campus when really they are at a private business located in campus town.

The fourth step, if the patron is off campus—and they are in this particular scenario—is to ask if the patron is using the VPN or proxy server. If they are using the VPN, there is often an easy fix to a common issue—selecting the "Tunnel All" option when the user signs into the VPN. For the fifth step, the patron is asked to clear their browser cache or use a different browser, as these are equally common solutions to common issues blocking e-resources access. The sixth and final step in the game involves either Googling the problem or asking if the patron is getting a specific error message, as both of these actions are equally likely to solve the issue, but are less common than any of the preceding issues.

To create the game, the correct path was first written. The correct path involved proceeding through the steps listed below in the order in which they are listed. These steps are presented to the user in the final screen, with the option to click on each for further information and the rationale for its place in the preferred order.

- Make sure the patron is an authorized user of e-resources.
- Confirm that we have access to the resources or article from the library computer that you are using.
- Ask if the patron is on or off campus. Confirm their IP address.
- Ask if the patron is using the proxy server or (only if they are off campus) the VPN.
- Ask the patron to clear their cache or use a different browser.
- Google the problem, and/or ask if the patron is getting a specific error message.

The design team decided that the "right solution" to the problem in this specific scenario would be getting a specific error message: hostname error. This way the library employee would have to proceed through all of the early steps to get to the right answer, ruling out more common problems first. Then alternate scenarios were imagined with the steps out of the correct order. Many of the "wrong" paths resulted in the game ending early because the player either jumps to the last step, solving the problem without first ruling out more common problems, or because they get a misleading answer. An example would be accepting what the patron says when they say they are on-campus instead of investigating further and looking at their IP address.

Finally, SFX issues are also a possibility during the troubleshooting process, where the information about the subscription is wrong. So the authors built an SFX error into the game, asking the user to identify the correct type of ticket to fill out.

After many alternate paths were imagined and written, with four possible answers per scenario, the different paths were checked for consistency and to make sure they each made sense. The game was tested by a variety of library faculty, staff, and graduate assistants.

Twine

After exploring possible options and tools to gamify the training process Twine was selected because of its simple and user-friendly interface, variety of features, and active support community. Originally created in 2007 by Chris Kilmas, Twine's current version (2.0.10) was released on November 20, 2015 ("Twine Information" 2015). It is available as both a downloadable desktop software and a browser-based application. As a browser-based application, Twine stories are stored directly in the browser's local storage, are not available in other browsers, and are deleted if the browser's history is deleted ("Where

78 Part II. Teaching Staff to Teach Patrons

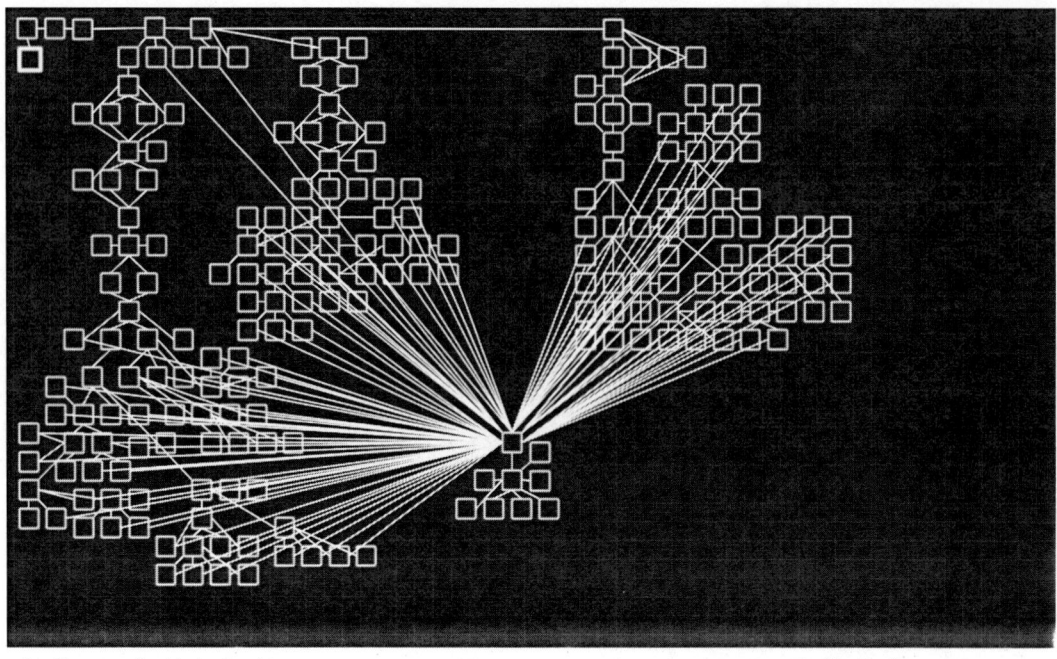

Full Twine Story Map Displaying the Various Paths Within the Game

Your Stories Are Saved" 2015). Because of this, the desktop version of Twine was chosen for its stability. The software and browser-based versions make collaboration difficult; stories must be exported and then imported each time edits are made if multiple editors wish to work on the same story. While collaboration is possible by passing versions of the file between editors, simultaneous editing is not possible. Twine stories are published to .html files, making them easy to host on a website and access from any computer with an Internet connection.

Twine features a very user-friendly and intuitive interface. Once within a story, the entire story map is displayed, making it easy to visualize and keep track of the various paths, or storylines (see Figure 1). This made the transfer of the narrative from XMind to Twine smooth. It also features three built-in story formats that control the appearance and behavior of the story during play, and stories can easily be switched between formats. These do not affect the interface when editing content. The appearance of the story during play can further be adapted and personalized by creating a stylesheet and utilizing CSS code.

In Twine, stories are written by creating passages. A passage is a unit of narrative that players navigate through by clicking on underlined hyperlinked text ("Passages" 2014). A passage can be created by simply clicking on the "+ Passage" button (see Figure 1). They can also be created while editing a previous passage by marking a link with the appropriate syntax and assigning an unused passage title. For example, in Figure 2, a new passage was created in the Intro passage by linking the text "Play the game" to a new passage titled "Welcome." Two square brackets are used to create a link, and the pipe symbol is used to separate the displayed text from the title of the linked passage. In general, the syntax in Twine is straightforward and easy to use.

"Macros" can be used in passages to create specific desired effects, such as altering

```
Intro                                                                    ✕

+ Tag

Welcome to //Adventures in Access//! This game is designed to simulate the types
of e-resources access issue questions that are often asked at the various
reference desks. Although this game occurs in a chat setting, the process you will
go through is still applicable to troubleshooting over the phone, via e-mail, and
even in person and text message (although, let's be honest, highly unlikely).

As you play, you will select one of the hyperlinked options. Your choices will set
you down your troubleshooting path, so choose wisely! (You //can// use the back
button on your browser, but keep in mind that you can't use it in real life.) At
some points in the game, you will find additional links out to more related
information on the library's webpages. Please feel free to explore these as you
play!

[[Play the game|Welcome!]].
```

View of a Passage While Editing Content: Examples of Twine Syntax

how text is displayed. In Twine, a macro is "a piece of code that is inserted into passage text" ("Macro" 2014). For example, if one passage provides a player two choices, but both choices lead to the same final passage, the "if" macro can be used to control the text that the player sees in the final passage, allowing it to be customized to their original choice. Other features, such as "expressions" and "variables" allow for more complex personalization. Twine also supports various functions that make editing the narrative easier, such as a search and replace function, which allows an author to search for specific text within a story and replace it with another word or phrase, similar to many word processors. Additional features include tags that allow authors to add information to passages that is not visible to players, formatting text, and adding images and other media files.

Implementing some of the available features in Twine allowed the design team for *Adventures in Access!* to create a personalized experience for players that was as close to the real situation as possible. Macros, expressions, and variables were used. Adding a point system to the game was also discussed, but was decided against because of the subjective nature of choices within the various paths. Several different paths can lead to a positive outcome, even though there is still a "correct" or preferred path.

Testing and User Feedback

The game first went through multiple rounds of revision within the design team. The team developed the game by clarifying language, adding specific examples, and ensuring that the options and choices represented were true to the comparable lived experience. Once a workable draft of the game was completed it was distributed to library faculty, staff, and graduate assistants for feedback. The game code was embedded within a library web page to ensure quick and easy access from any computer with an Internet connection. Faculty and staff from the Research and Information Services unit at Illinois were asked to play the game and send written feedback. Graduate assistants were asked to participate in an observed session of the game and then discuss feedback afterwards. Participants were asked to reflect and comment on the game as a whole experience, the mechanics and flow of the simulation in Twine, the believability of the scenario, the efficacy and utility of the game as a training tool, and the implementation of the game. The participants were also asked to reflect on the possible inclusion of a scoring system that would assign points to each of their decisions as they played the game and give them a score and/or rank at the end of the simulation.

The feedback from library faculty, staff, and graduate assistants was overwhelmingly positive. All participants stated that the game was an effective, useful tool for simulating the experience of electronic resource troubleshooting with a patron. All participants enjoyed the game as presented in Twine and found the mechanics and flow to be intuitive. All participants stated that the game scenario was very realistic, even with multiple simulated problems and issues occurring within the same session. Multiple participants commented that they had experienced very similar situations in real life and that the scenario in the game would have helped them feel more prepared for such complicated and lengthy troubleshooting interactions. Multiple participants gave helpful feedback on functionality details, wording clarity, and sequencing. All of the participants expressed that the game would be most helpful if introduced during the annual e-resources troubleshooting training that occurs at the beginning of every fall semester. All agreed that the game should be introduced during the training, sent out shortly thereafter as a refresher, and linked to on internal pages and wikis for continual self-improvement purposes. One participant suggested that the link be e-mailed out to all reference staff in the library system at the beginning of every semester as a chance for new and returning employees to maintain their skills. The game could be updated to reflect changes in library policy and/or procedure. None of the participants thought that the addition of a scoring system would enhance the simulation experience. Some said that scoring would be confusing while others said that it would make the simulation too stressful. Multiple participants suggested additional potential features, including a variety of different scenarios and a side-by-side comparison of a user's chosen path with the most desirable path. One participant suggested that multiple different scenarios could enable a badge system wherein users earned badges for completing each scenario. These features may be incorporated into future iterations of the game. Multiple participants suggested changes to existing e-resources troubleshooting resources and web pages; playing the game and exploring the linked content inspired them to suggest changes to make our preexisting resources more clear and effective.

Conclusion

The feedback from library faculty, staff, and graduate assistants was used to update and improve the game, which is now posted and available online. It is linked to from all library staff web pages and wiki pages about electronic resources troubleshooting. It is also now being incorporated into the annual electronic resources troubleshooting training; this training is mandatory for all faculty, staff, and graduate assistants who provide reference services at the main service points within the library system. A link to the game and other electronic resources troubleshooting resources is e-mailed out to the reference staff listserv near the beginning of every semester. New graduate assistants are strongly encouraged to use the game to practice their troubleshooting skills, as electronic resources troubleshooting becomes a necessary skill within the first few weeks on the reference desk.

The development and implementation of *Adventures in Access!* serves as a model for using Twine to create interactive games for training and instructional purposes in a variety of library settings. Twine offers a user-friendly way to create memorable simulations that are specific to the policies and context of individual institutions. Library staff can implement games within regular training schedules to ensure excellent customer service and increased access for all.

REFERENCES

"Adventures in Access." *University Library, University of Illinois at Urbana-Champaign*. Accessed February 29. http://www.library.illinois.edu/rex/staff/eResourcesTroubleshootingAdventure.html.

Green, Melanie C., and Keenan M. Jenkins. 2014. "Interactive Narratives: Processes and Outcomes in User-Directed Stories." *Journal of Communication*. 64: 479–500. doi: 10.1111/jcom.12093.

Farber, Matthew. 2015. "Interactive Fiction in the Classroom." *edutopia (What Works in the Classroom, George Lucas Educational Foundation)*. Accessed February 19, 2016. http://www.edutopia.org/blog/interactitve-fiction-in-the-classroom-matthew-farber.

Kim, Bohyun. 2015. "Gamification: Examples, Definitions, and Related Concepts." *Library Technology Reports* 51(2): 10–16.

Landers, Richard N. 2014. "Developing a Theory of Gamified Learning: Linking Serious Games and Gamification of Learning." *Simulation and Gaming* 45(6): 752–768. doi: 10.1177/1046878114563660.

"Macro." *Twine Wiki*. Last modified September 20, 2014. http://twinery.org/wiki/macro.

"Passages." *Twine Wiki*. Last modified September 18, 2014. http://twinery.org/wiki/passage.

Seaborn, Katie, and Deborah I. Fels. 2015. "Gamification in Theory and Action: A Survey." *International Journal of Human-Computer Studies* 74: 14–31. doi: 10.1016/j.ijhcs.2014.09.006.

Szurmak, Joanna, and Mindy Thuna. 2013. "Tell Me a Story: The Use of Narrative as a Tool for Instruction." Presentation at the ACRL 2013 Conference, Indianapolis, April 10–13, 2013.

Twine. Accessed February 18, 2016. https://twinery.org/.

"Twine Information." *Twine Wiki*. Last modified November 20, 2015. http://twinery.org/wiki/start.

"Where Your Stories Are Saved." *Twine Wiki*. Last modified May 15, 2015. http://twinery.org/wiki/twine2:where_your_stories_are_saved.

On-Demand Tech Training for Students, Faculty and Staff

Ashley J. Cole, Heather Beirne *and* Brad Marcum

For years, tech-savvy staff have relied on technology to serve users both in person and at a distance, helping users navigate not just library databases but the Internet as a whole. Library staff guide users in advanced Google searching for various personal and research purposes and needs, assist patrons with understanding the nuances of using social media, help them write resumes in a difficult job market, and on and on. With the advent of 3-D printing and with the increasingly fast pace of technological innovations, makerspaces are becoming more common in libraries, particularly in K–12 and university settings. However, providing access to the technology is not enough; in academic libraries where student learning is the mission, librarians are not only teachers and facilitators of information literacy, but of all the 21st century skills and literacies that tie in with it (technological, digital, media, and visual literacies, just to name a few, and the critical thinking and learning skills to navigate and synthesize it all) for students as well as for university faculty and staff, who must keep up with new technology in order to impart these skills to students within the context of their disciplines. Recent educational initiatives such as the ACRL Framework for Information Literacy for Higher Education emphasize this mission (Association of College and Research Libraries 2015).

This essay, informed by the experiences of three Eastern Kentucky University librarians, will relate our experience building EKU Libraries' ColonelSmart program, an on-demand, a la carte, technology-based series of information literacy workshops being offered to students, faculty, and staff of the university based on their particular needs. ColonelSmart explores technology-based information literacy topics relevant to research, academic success, and teaching and learning through informal pop-ups and on-demand requestable workshops. The essay will cover the ins and outs of setting up a successful on-demand workshop program designed to teach information literacy skills around particular technology topics at your academic library.

Background

Eastern Kentucky University (EKU) is a mid-sized, regional, comprehensive public university located in Richmond Kentucky. EKU offers a variety of undergraduate and graduate degrees, taught at the main campus, several regional campuses and centers, as well as online. EKU also offers doctoral degrees in Education, Nursing Practice, Occupational Therapy and Psychology. Total enrollment is 16,874 with 2,536 of that number being graduate students. 2,962 of the total enrollment is made up of online students with 1,644 being undergraduate and 1,218 being graduate students (Office of Institutional Research 2015).

ColonelSmart: Beginnings

EKU Libraries has a long history of providing student services that are normally outside the traditional purview of libraries, such as dog-assisted therapy initiatives to help students cope with the stress of college, student art exhibits, and a Welcome Back series which includes an opportunity for homesick students to send a postcard home or cool down with a snow-cone. In the vein of this atypical service orientation, EKU Libraries initiated a week-long professional development program for students called "Steps to Success: Career Prep Week" in November 2013. The series covered topics such as drafting professional cover letters and resumes, cultivating a professional persona, and taking advantage of career services provided by EKU. After the immense success of the program, the program coordinator saw the potential to expand the scope of this pre-existing workshop series. Initially discussions were had about creating a "Navigating the College Life" workshop series, aimed at helping students acclimate to college life as part of an effort to meet strategic direction 1.2 of EKU Libraries strategic plan, "Offer creative opportunities to engage and inspire our community," with the anticipated result of "unique, free and relevant learning and academically supportive opportunities for students throughout the academic year" (Eastern Kentucky University Libraries 2014, 3). After researching other initiatives for inspiration, EKU librarians adapted elements of the "Savvy Researcher" workshop program offered by the University of Illinois at Urbana-Champaign (Slater 2012). One element of this program that EKU Libraries found appealing and wanted to model was the idea that the library could serve as a hub for campus workshops living under one umbrella, henceforth known as ColonelSmart @ EKU Libraries. One underlying goal of the ColonelSmart series would be to promote the library as a training center of interdisciplinary, collaborative information literacy instruction where all constituents, even the session facilitators, present and/or learn, no matter the theme or presenter. In creating ColonelSmart, EKU Librarians were inspired by Head and Eisenburg, who state, "Despite their reputation of being avid computer users who are fluent with new technologies, few students [use] a growing number of Web 2.0 applications for collaborating on course research assignments" (Head and Eisenburg 2010, 3). Ultimately, this workshop series would serve as a counterpart to traditional library instruction in order to teach technology-based skills and concepts that could not be taught in a one-shot session, whether because of time limitations or lack of direct relation to the course being taught. This program was imagined as a way for EKU librarians to shed those limitations and offer useful information to the campus at large without the usual constraints being imposed on the content covered and the amount of time allotted. Therefore, a variety of times, formats and levels of complexity (advanced vs. beginner) were chosen to appeal to students with a wide variety of schedules and comfort levels.

Early on, it became clear that a committee was need to assist with the planning, design, and facilitation of workshops. The committee was not specifically and solely tasked with the creation of workshops, but would solicit volunteers to teach, arrange times and dates, and suitable classrooms and venues for the workshops. Continuing this emphasis on flexibility, the committee did not limit the presenters of the workshops to only librarians. That is, the ColonelSmart workshops would be offered by volunteers from all over campus, not just from the committee, or even librarians. Any student, librarian, School of Information Science graduate assistant, staff member, faculty member, or non-library entity was encouraged to create and present a workshop either in partnership with a librarian or alone as part of the program. By allowing non-librarians to offer sessions through ColonelSmart, EKU Libraries contributed to the culture of training on campus by providing an opportunity for faculty, staff, and students to showcase their knowledge and skills, and also for student presenters to learn valuable presentation and public speaking skills. For example, the Noel Studio for Academic Creativity, a non-library entity, collaborated closely with the library to offer several sessions by undergraduate and graduate students in need of teaching experience. These workshops covered topics ranging from technology how-to's to a primary resource-oriented workshop aimed at undergraduate history students. Additionally, faculty were identified as key participants, who would have much influence on the ultimate success or failure of the program. In fact, faculty would become excellent partners in encouraging students to take advantage of the various sessions as well as assisting librarians in planning and offering those sessions.

During its first iteration, ColonelSmart was offered on a purely on a drop-in basis. For example, early ColonelSmart sessions included the following:

- Be a Google Guru: Advanced Google Searching
- Think Before You Ink: Managing Your Digital Tattoo
- Library Boot Camp: Uncover & Discover
- Be a Google Guru: Google Scholar
- Prezi for Students
- Organizing and Managing Your Citations with Zotero
- Organize Your Digital Life with Dropbox & Google Drive
- Pre-Professional School Programs
- EKU Co-Op & Internships
- EKU Career Services: Cover Letters & Resumes
- Social Networking
- Guerilla Research
- Beyond the Basics: Google Scholar and Web of Science
- Finding Primary Sources for History
- Avoid Becoming an #EPICFAIL: Protect Your Privacy on Social Media
- SkyDrive
- On the Job Resources: Research Portals for Your Professional Life

Second Iteration: ColonelSmart On Demand

Low attendance required the ColonelSmart Committee to adopt a new approach in the second iteration of ColonelSmart. The crux of the problem was simply that up until this point, students had viewed presentation attendance as an option rather than a need.

Through discussion, the committee realized that without faculty buy-in, students would rarely choose to attend the sessions, no matter how relevant or useful they might be. Consequently, in order for ColonelSmart to succeed, the impetus to participate would need to come from faculty members, who could incentivize students with class credit and other tangible benefits.

Additionally, low attendance illustrated that the stand alone, drop-in workshops offered through ColonelSmart lacked context and therefore relevance to students. The committee decided that workshops should instead to be tied to a specific need or course while still remaining outside of the traditional one-shot library instruction paradigm as a complement or supplement to those sessions. Serendipitously, the ColonelSmart Committee happened to receive a request from a College of Education faculty member for a ColonelSmart workshop to be presented in its entirety to a specific class. This request revealed a need for ColonelSmart to shift from a scheduled, drop-in model to an a la carte, on-demand, in-class, menu-driven, faculty-requested style which would make students a captive, or least motivated audience. Because faculty were the only ones that could entice or obligate students to come, and since the material was most meaningfully presented in context, the group decided that making the workshops available by faculty request would be the best way to move forward. An added benefit of offering an on-demand menu of in-class ColonelSmart workshops was that it could be used as a "foot in the door" to some departments who had not previously requested library instruction. For a time, EKU Libraries continued to offer most ColonelSmart sessions on-demand with a sampling of workshops scheduled as drop-in sessions, but at later times in the evening, typically 8 or 9 PM. When this still did not yield higher attendance, drop-in sessions were dropped entirely and ColonelSmart became a fully on-demand, menu-based model, based on the "Savvy Researcher" series offered by the University of Illinois at Urbana-Champaign (Slater 2012).

Furthermore, based upon EKU librarians' understanding of the needs of library clientele, the menu of workshops was reduced to offer only those that addressed a needed skill within EKU's Information Literacy Core Competencies Matrix, a document (based on ACRL's 2000 Information Literacy Competency Standards for Higher Education) designed by EKU Librarians to guide best practices in library instruction and information literacy teaching. The final menu of on-demand ColonelSmart programs now (as of spring 2016) includes the following workshops for students:

- Advanced Google Searching
- Avoiding Plagiarism
- Company Research
- Google Scholar for Beginners
- Industry Research
- On the Job Resources: Research Portals for Your Professional Life
- Organizing and Managing Your Citations with Mendeley
- Organizing and Managing Your Citations with Zotero
- Think Before You Ink: Managing Your Digital Tattoo

To make the Matrix more visible to the university community, ColonelSmart workshops were arranged in the à la carte menu according to the skills goals of EKU's Information Literacy Matrix, which in turn were adapted from the ACRL Information Literacy Competency Standards for Higher Education:

- Communicate Knowledge
- Construct a Question or Problem Statement
- Evaluate Sources
- Locate and Gather Information
- Manage Information
- Use Information Ethically

Organizing the ColonelSmart menu according to EKU Information Literacy Matrix not only allows for easy navigation on the ColonelSmart website, it also lends legitimacy to library instruction by aligning our offerings with national information literacy standards, of which faculty may or may not be aware. While working through the process of aligning ColonelSmart offerings with the EKU Information Literacy Matrix and as the shift to the new ACRL Framework for Information Literacy (which emphasizes the need for faculty-librarian collaboration and the interdisciplinary contextuality of information literacy skills) began to occur, the ColonelSmart Committee became aware of the need to shift the focus of the ColonelSmart series away from teaching technology tools and more toward using the technology to teach higher-level information literacy skills that could not be covered in one-shot library instruction sessions.

A major benefit of tying the ColonelSmart menu of offerings to information literacy standards lies in the potential for collaboration with teaching faculty. As experts in information literacy and critical thinking, librarians are given the unique opportunity to "train the trainer." For this reason, the ColonelSmart committee realized the potential for technology-based workshops geared toward faculty teaching and learning skills. Thanks to a request for a ColonelSmart workshop for an EKU faculty member's department meeting, the committee recognized the benefits of offering teaching and learning workshops in a variety of formats including brown-bag, drop-in, and on-demand. By offering a menu of topics which faculty could request for their departments, the library brought awareness to teaching faculty of the multifaceted expertise of EKU librarians, where many faculty may not have previously understood the possibilities. The following Teaching & Learning workshops are offered through the ColonelSmart menu:

- Organizing and Managing Your Citations with Mendeley
- Organizing and Managing Your Citations with Zotero
- Get to Know the New Library Search
- Best Practices for Using Copyrighted Material in Teaching
- Apps for Academics: Library-Centered Tools for Academic Success
- E-books: They're Not as Bad as You Think
- Got Mobile? Library Resources On-the-Go
- Endnote
- LibX: Library Bling for Your Browser

Additionally, the new ACRL Framework for Information Literacy for Higher Education advises faculty to "partner with your IT department and librarians to develop new kinds of multimedia assignments for courses" and to "consider the knowledge practices and dispositions in each information literacy frame for possible integration into your own courses and academic program" (Association of College and Research Libraries 2015, 13). Accordingly, the ColonelSmart committee will expand teaching and learning offerings in the future so as to promote "more collaboration, more innovative course designs, and a more inclusive consideration of learning within and beyond the classroom" (Association of College and Research Libraries 2015, 13).

Reinvigorate Faculty/Librarian Relationships: ColonelSmart in the Future

ColonelSmart @ EKU Libraries is an ever evolving entity. Since its initial iteration in 2013, it has received two revitalizations with a third forthcoming. ColonelSmart has transformed from solely a technology training program to an extension of one-shot instruction which uses technology training to teach information literacy concepts. Eastern Kentucky University does not offer a credit-bearing information literacy course at this time; thus, ColonelSmart is designed to complement one-shot instruction and address its limitations. The new on-demand platform is designed around Eastern Kentucky University's Information Literacy Core Competencies Matrix, an iteration of the ACRL Information Literacy Competency Standards for Higher Education. The recently adopted ACRL Framework for Information Literacy for Higher Education signifies a shift to a conceptual, contextual approach "rather than exclusively on tools or techniques" (Beilin 2015, 2). In other words, the document moved away from standards to interconnected threshold concepts known as frames, "each consisting of a concept central to information literacy, a set of knowledge practices, and a set of dispositions" (Association of College and Research Libraries 2015, 2). At its core, despite being built around the old standards, EKU's Information Literacy Matrix does go beyond tools and techniques to push information literacy as a shared responsibility to all university stakeholders. The document itself is not solely a library document but a guide for all "in an effort to provide a shared language, spark dialogue within the broader academic community, and lay a foundation for integrating information literacy into learning opportunities" (Eastern Kentucky University Libraries 2013, 1).

These new frames require liaison librarians to construct a more meaningful relationship with university faculty and students, as the Framework for Information Literacy for Higher Education encourages collaboration and contextuality around the teaching of information literacy. The new Framework suggests the idea that these concepts are not ideas that can be taught in one course session by librarians outside of the everyday classroom, as has been done traditionally. One-shot sessions have their purpose in that they "address a particular need at a particular time" (Association of College and Research Libraries 2015, 10). The framework, however, charges us to consider information literacy as "both a disciplinary and a transdisciplinary learning agenda," to be integrated within and across the curriculum (Association of College and Research Libraries 2015, 13). The key to implementing information literacy instruction is through richer relationships with faculty. While this ideal provides a goal for which to strive and work toward, this is not something that cannot happen overnight. ColonelSmart provides a bridge, for both faculty and students, to integrate richer, more complex concepts into the curriculum that cannot be mastered in a single library instruction session. ColonelSmart @ EKU Libraries educates not only students in information literacy, but also provides faculty with workshops on integrating information literacy through technology, assignment design, scholarly communications, copyright, and research tools. In this way, ColonelSmart provides a means for the library to act as not only a technology training hub on campus, but also a space for faculty and librarians to come together in the act of teaching and learning to create students who are characterized by intellectual curiosity and creativity.

Many of the current workshops at EKU Libraries are direct reflections of the ACRL Information Literacy Competency Standards for Higher Education. In the future, ColonelSmart @ EKU Libraries will continue to work toward creating workshops more specifically geared to the Framework in an effort to not only promote its value, but also the value of information literacy to the university. In doing so, faculty will begin to recognize the value of librarians as legitimate experts in information, technology, research, and scholarship on campus.

REFERENCES

Association of College and Research Libraries. 2000. "Information Literacy Competency Standards for Higher Education." *Association of College and Research Libraries.* http://www.ala.org/acrl/sites/ala.org.acrl/files/content/standards/standards.pdf.

Association of College and Research Libraries. 2015. "Framework for Information Literacy for Higher Education." *Association of College and Research Libraries.* http://www.ala.org/acrl/sites/ala.org.acrl/files/content/issues/infolit/Framework_ILHE.pdf.

Beilin, Ian. 2015. "Beyond the Threshold: Conformity, Resistance, and the ACRL Information Literacy Framework for Higher Education." *In the Library with the Lead Pipe.* http://www.inthelibrarywiththeleadpipe.org/2015/beyond-the-threshold-conformity-resistance-and-the-aclr-information-literacy-framework-for-higher-education/.

Eastern Kentucky University Libraries. 2014. "Strategic Plan 2011–15." *Eastern Kentucky University Libraries.* http://library.eku.edu/sites/library.eku.edu/files/2015_strategic_plan_-_for_web_0.pdf.

Eastern Kentucky University Libraries. 2013. "Eastern Kentucky University Information Literacy Core Competencies." *Eastern Kentucky University Libraries.* http://library.eku.edu/eastern-kentucky-university-information-literacy-core-competencies.

Eastern Kentucky University Libraries. "ColonelSmart @ EKU Libraries." *Eastern Kentucky University Libraries,* accessed November 22, 2015. http://library.eku.edu/colonelsmart.

Head, Alison J., and Michael B. Eisenberg. 2010. *Truth Be Told: How College Students Evaluate and Use Information in the Digital Age.* Washington: Information School, University of Washington.

Office of Institutional Research. 2015. "Enrollment Report, Fall 2015: 08/24/2015." Unpublished Report. Eastern Kentucky University.

Slater, Robert. 2012. "Savvy Researcher." *University Library, University of Illinois at Urbana-Champaign.* http://www.library.illinois.edu/sc/services/savvy_researcher.html.

Facing Change Together
Overcoming Differing Comfort Levels with Technology in Librarian and Library Staff Training

Christine Elliott, Dongmei Cao *and* Christa E. Poparad

When contemplating technology training for library personnel, numerous factors make it difficult for many institutions to provide the resources for effective training. Whether it is due to lack of funding, lack of personnel, or trainees with limited availability, many must resort solely to using a company or product's "canned" online training modules to get the instruction they need. Strictly online, general training for a new system or program that affects an entire library is problematic because of the diverse comfort levels of library trainees: self-driven, online training may not meet the learning style of certain individuals. Many existing online learning opportunities also lack the personalization needed to frame how new technologies affect a specific institution. At the same time, finding published examples of technology training programs are difficult to locate (Moorefield-Lang 2015).

Therefore, it is important to develop training that specifically targets each library's unique needs. Local conventions and requirements must be included. Knowing the audience allows trainers to consider the learning styles of their local participants. The timing of the training needs to coordinate with the project schedule. For these reasons, the College of Charleston Libraries in Charleston, South Carolina, identified a need for specialized training during a successful transition from LibGuides 1 (LG1) to LibGuides 2 (LG2) in the summer of 2015.

This essay will outline the process and instructional methods utilized by the College of Charleston Libraries to instruct our library personnel on an upgraded library system. Our processes are presented in the following sections:

- Background
    - o Making the initial decision to adopt an updated system

- Training
    - o Pre-training, which included introductory presentations for personnel, and training/decision making done by the administrative body
    - o Generating training materials

- Hybrid training workshops
  - Observations
- Discussion
  - Continuing Education

While this essay is very specific to a Springshare platform, the methods and procedures we executed at the College of Charleston can be applied to numerous situations, regardless of library type or training purpose. Specifics are outlined for the months before, during, and after our migration to provide a detailed scope of communication dates and purposes, meetings, plans, and technical aspects, which can be easily modified. Training can be as involved or general as an institution requires, and we hope that our methods can inspire the creation of training opportunities for librarians, staff, and student employees.

Background

Springshare provides online webinars and recordings for learning the LibGuides 2 platform. These webinars and online recordings were useful to our trainers, administrators, and those involved in the migration process, but it was decided that these sources were inefficient in meeting all the training needs of our LibGuide creators. Effective training is essential so that everyone in our diverse training population of 63 individuals is knowledgeable enough (Enis 2015) to both utilize LibGuides and assist patrons in navigating them.

A hybrid training approach was developed for our library, and the methods outlined in this essay can be adjusted and applied to various types of libraries or any number of training topics. Awareness and sensitivity of employee abilities and comfort levels with technology guided us in generating effective training sessions and materials that will continue to grow and improve as we revisit in-house teaching techniques for the future.

LibGuides 1 to LibGuides 2

As in many libraries, College of Charleston (CofC) Libraries uses LibGuides to share knowledge regarding library resources and services with our users. We use LibGuides to present subject related resources in one coherent virtual space (http://libguides.library.cofc.edu/subject_english), to instruct students in course related assignments (http://libguides.library.cofc.edu/htmt488), to inform patron groups of available services (http://libguides.library.cofc.edu/undergraduatestudentservices), and to promote library offerings and events (http://libguides.library.cofc.edu/FreedomSummer). Like many other institutions, we also use it as an internal intranet to provide a central location for information (such as how to use classroom technology, or library marketing procedures). With LibGuide creators across multiple departments and campuses throughout the Libraries, migration from LG1 to LG2 needed to be carefully orchestrated to include training in multiple modalities throughout the process. In June 2014, Springshare created our LG2 beta site, an initial experimental site to allow us to configure our new guides behind the scenes while our users continued using the LG1 site. In addition, the beta site allowed us to begin training those who would be configuring the new system and to introduce the new system to the LibGuide creators.

Training

Pre-Training

To better inform LibGuide creators what to expect during the system migration and in the final LG2 platform, the coordinator of the migration project gave a very detailed PowerPoint presentation in June 2014, which included these segments:

- What's new in LG2
- Overall timeline for migration and implementation
- Accessing the LG2 Beta site
- Training and support

To better demo the new features and functionalities of LG2, screenshot examples from the LibGuide sites of other libraries were included; we also did a live demo to show the flexibility of LG2. This was a great opportunity to get our personnel to start looking at LG2 with a critical eye and to ask initial questions.

Before and after the presentation, e-mails were sent to the library wide listserv to notify the LibGuide creators of this important presentation, to follow up with presentation slides, and to inform individuals what was expected next in the migration process. LibGuide creators were encouraged to take live training sessions or recorded webinars online from Springshare where basic LibGuide 2 functionalities were outlined and demonstrated. The project coordinator and other group members attended the offered webinars and sessions to learn about the new system, new features and functionalities, the migration process, and what needed to be done from the admin side as well as the individual LibGuide creator side.

A generic LibApps username and password was created in our LG2 beta site for everyone to play and learn the new features. Within this LG2 sandbox, they were encouraged to create individual test guides (e.g. Jared's Media Test Guide) in the new system and begin generating experimental content such as links to books in the catalog, embedded tabbed boxes, and widgets. As the single LibApps login was a new feature in LG2, questions from confused LibGuides creators were received and answered.

To better coordinate the migration process among the various departments and across campuses, the LibGuides 2 Group, an interdepartmental advisory committee composed of seven members from four departments, was established. The committee met regularly before and throughout the migration process to discuss the look of the new system, CofC Libraries' conventions, and any rising issues. The group also worked collaboratively to create the "LibGuide 2: Getting Started Guide" which consisted of information covering some of the following topics: LibApps Dashboard, LibGuides Dashboard, CofC Libraries Conventions, etc. In all, this guide consisted of ten informative tabs to instruct LibGuides creators on how to navigate around the new system through the various dashboards and how to create new content. The majority of LibGuides creators at CofC Libraries were familiar with the LG1 system, so the step by step tutorials included in the "LibGuide 2: Getting Started Guide" gave them a reference point at their individual time of need.

E-mails were sent throughout the migration process informing all LibGuide creators of any updates and what actions needed to be done on their end. For example, in the December 9, 2014, e-mail, creators were given three specific tasks to complete before the migration (which was scheduled March 9, 2015) and also attached the updated timeline up to Summer 2015. A detailed LG2 Plan/ Outline was created by the coordinator with the approval of the Associate Dean, with objective/tasks, responsible party, due dates, and notes. This document was instrumental in keeping us on target and successfully finishing the post-migration clean up and going live on July 1st, 2015. With the help of the Head of Research & Instruction, two part-time librarians carried out the post-migration clean up tasks in the LG2 Plan (A-Z database cleanup, subject association, etc.).

Training Materials

After the go-live date of July 1, a hybrid introductory training program was planned and executed. In many publications addressing library staff instruction, a survey is usually sent out preceding the planning of a training session to get a feel of what trainees expect from instructional sessions and to get a better understanding of individual learning styles (Koep and Felkar 2015, Koerber 2015, Moorefield-Lang 2015). Prior to generating our training program, our focus had been on the correct implementation of LG2, administrator and trainer education, and providing basic LibGuides information to our creators. Many of our library staff and librarians were busy with summer projects or away on vacation, so regular e-mails with updates and inquiries for questions helped us plan the training. It was very important that the applicable librarians and staff members who would be creating and maintaining guides for the fast approaching fall semester received the information they needed as soon as possible. Due to our tight timeline, a pre-training survey was not considered.

Based on unique job descriptions and responsibilities, we were aware that librarians and staff at CofC Libraries have a wide range of technological and LibGuide experience, so providing both an online and face-to-face component enabled everyone to gain access to the information needed at their own pace. The online components included the following.

- A training page, attached to the "LibGuide 2: Getting Started Guide."
- Prezi presentation (http://prezi.com/4wjwo8jm03cj/?utm_campaign=share&utm_medium=copy).
- LibGuides 2 Cheat Sheet (https://drive.google.com/file/d/0Bzq8k4gK1rfdaFFHY3o0b2FscDA/view?usp=sharing).

The training page served as a central location for all training materials, including contact information for those who needed further training or had questions. Embedded in this page is the introductory Prezi presentation and a downloadable cheat sheet. The Prezi provided a simple overview of both LG2 and the established conventions for creating and maintaining the updated guides. The presentation is very simple by design: it does not go into detail on everything LG2 can do for us, but instead educates librarians and staff of the comparative differences between the two systems. We found that this was the best way to make the transition to a new content management system less overwhelming.

The cheat sheet served a dual purpose: as an introduction to more specific LG2 concepts and a post-training reference sheet that users could keep on hand. The cheat sheet was designed much like the reference cards Microsoft publishes for individual programs in the Microsoft Suite (http://www.customguide.com/cheat_sheets/word-2013-cheat-sheet.pdf). A sample of what this sheet highlighted includes

- uniform tab structure;
- definition of the new guide types;
- basic widget know-hows; and
- how to utilize the built in A-Z Database.

The purpose of the sheet was to focus only on new LG2 components. This was to aid our librarians and staff in learning the new processes and be able to distinguish the differences between LG1 and LG2.

Training

In order to meet the technological needs and expertise of a variety of individuals, a one-hour training session was planned. After planning the session, a poll was sent out to all library staff and faculty to determine interest in the session and what dates were best suited for their schedules. A majority of respondents replied and two training dates were scheduled (the second date was provided for those who could not make the first training session). An e-mail invitation to the sessions was sent out via Outlook with information on the session, what would be covered, and links to the training materials.

Both training sessions took place in a library computer lab. The first 15 minutes provided very broad information, which included the similarities and differences between LG1 and LG2, and some of the basic functions of LG2 such as where the new navigation and working buttons were located, and the new conventions that should be followed when generating new content. The next 15 minutes were dedicated to specific functionalities. Those attending the session were invited to follow along with the presenter as we each built a trial guide from scratch. We produced the following content items step by step:

- Creating a new guide (making a title, selecting a guide type, selecting subjects, and adding tags).
- Adding a box that contains multiple types of content.
    - o Example: one box with a book from the catalog, an external link, and a database.
- Using the Widgets tool within LG2 to create a subject specific database widget.

Moving from very basic information to more complicated tasks, kept the audience engaged through the 30-minute session. Understanding the basics of a new system is essential to getting a better grasp of more complicated tasks, and we used this particular model to frame and organize our training session.

The final 30 minutes of the session was left for open experimentation. Trainees were able to create other boxes and play with different components while the instructor was readily available to provide support or reiterate certain LG2 processes.

Once the hour of training was completed, all attendees were invited to contact the trainers for more specific training or additional support. We also asked if they were interested in additional training for more complicated procedures in LibGuides 2, such as embedding certain items, incorporating LibSurvey or other Springshare services we subscribe to, etc.

Observations

Training opportunities were provided to all of our LibGuides creators throughout the migration, implementation, and go-live processes. During the Summer months, we found that despite regular, informative (and often repetitive) e-mails to librarians and staff at CofC Libraries, very few responded to these progress reports. Links to Springshare training sessions and webinars were sent out, but there was no way to track how many of our LibGuide creators utilized these sources. Regular e-mails asking CofC librarians and staff if they had any questions went unanswered. We could only assume that either the Springshare training materials were adequate for our creators, or they were not being used due to the time of year, other responsibilities, discomfort with fully online training, or lack of interest.

The face to face training gave us a better grasp of what our creators knew about LG2. The majority of our LibGuides creators attended the first training session, where they were able to get comfortable with the new system in a supportive environment. Attendees expressed appreciation of the training opportunity and the supportive training materials. Many attendees also took the opportunity to ask subject specific questions that applied to their specific department liaison duties. Making the session both instructional and interactive allowed LibGuide users to explore more unfamiliar tools within the system with their fellow peers nearby and a familiar instructor within easy access.

A majority of the questions were not about LG2 itself, but the effects the migration from LG1 to LG2 had on their existing guides. Our new guide convention was different from LG1, which meant that many guides had to undergo name and formatting changes. This gave us an opportunity to pull up an existing guide (our example was a guide on Primary Resources), and going step by step on how the title of the guide should be changed, and how to resize boxes that were warped by the migration. This was very revealing to us since this information had been provide in initial e-mails at the beginning of the migration period.

In addition, an opportunity to differentiate between asset links and in text hyperlinks helped the trainers have a better understanding of the specific needs our trainees needed that were not mentioned in all previous e-mails. Trainers were able to take this as an opportunity to make note of any additional items that needed to be added to the reference materials and the "LibGuide 2: Getting Started Guide."

Both training sessions ended with an invitation for one-on-one training or follow up learning opportunities. Most LibGuide creators expressed their comfort with the new system and appreciated the offer.

Conclusion

Any new technology or program implemented at a library is susceptible to regular upgrades and changes throughout the academic year. We are confident that the introductory training provided to CofC Libraries LibGuide creators during Summer 2015 has established a foundational understanding of LG2 basics. As Springshare continues to add new abilities to the LG2 system, we will provide informational e-mails and annual training opportunities for more complicated content creation. This will aid us in continuing a "culture of learning" where our librarians and staff members can progressively learn new ways to provide innovative services to the College of Charleston community (Real, Bertot, Jaeger 2014). For our relatively large library, we will continue to provide training workshops during our summer months, where it is easier for us to work with librarian and staff schedules. Throughout the school year, we send out e-mail updates, and raise any necessary updates during library wide meetings.

In the meantime, LibGuide administrators at CofC Libraries strive to stay up-to-date on the products we subscribe to and rely on Springshare's weekly webinars for our own training. LG2 is such an essential tool in promoting awareness of library services, events, and course resources that it is important for our administrators to stay on top of these products. The training model we designed for LibGuides can easily be adjusted for training on LibAnswers, LibSurveys, and other library services/programs, which will make future training and workshop sessions easy to organize and implement.

REFERENCES

Enis, Matt. 2015. "CSL Expands Online Training Site: Content Developed from In-Person Workshops." *Library Journal* 140 (13): 16.
Koep, Deborah Hutchinson, and Sarah Felkar. 2015. "Take our Data-Driven Approach to Staff Technology Training." *Computers in Libraries* 35 (1): 18–22.
Koerber, Jennifer. 2015. "Manage the Device Deluge." *Library Journal* 140 (9): 28–31.
Moorefield-Lang, Heather. 2015. "Change in the Making: Makerspaces and the Ever-Changing Landscape of Libraries." *TechTrends: For Leaders in Education & Training* 59 (3): 107–112.
Real, Brian, John Carlo Bertot, and Paul T. Jaeger. 2014. "Rural Public Libraries and Digital Inclusion: Issues and Challenges." *Information Technology & Libraries* 33 (1): 6–24.

Technology Instruction as a Cycle of Instructional Coaching

Sarah Frey

In many schools, librarians are the "go-to" people for technology questions and concerns. Synthesizing statements from the American Association of School Librarians, International Society for Technology in Education and National Board for Professional Teaching Standards, Melissa Johnston explains "school librarians are in a unique position to serve as leaders in technology integration efforts within their schools" (Johnston 2015). The remarks and reports that call for librarians to be leaders are inspiring but lack details on what leadership with technology involves.

Librarians, with their knowledge and skills with technology, teaching experience, and strong relationships with colleagues, may be the solution to the biggest problem with technology integration: professional development. Technology can only be effective in the classroom if the teacher can use it. Librarians can provide teachers with instruction and support that traditional professional development lacks.

Elements of Effective Technology Professional Development

Imagine sitting in a large room, squinting to see a projector screen in the distance, listening to a stranger point out all the features "you're going to love" in the new software being adopted by your institution. This scenario has all the markings of ineffective technology professional development, yet it represents standard practice. In K–12 education alone, $18 billion is spent annually on professional development but is not meeting the needs of participants. When asked what would make professional development effective, teachers described it as being interactive, relevant to their individual jobs and sustained over time (The Bill & Melinda Gates Foundation 2014). We can contrast effective and ineffective technology professional development using these descriptors. First, consider the structure of professional development for technology instruction. Just as athletes cannot improve their performance by only watching someone else play the game, teachers cannot become proficient in using new technology by attending a presentation. When technology instruction is not interactive, teachers lose focus and may not remember features and procedures.

Technology professional development that is hands-on development is not effective professional development by default; participants must recognize the instruction as relevant to their work. Technology professional development is often led by vendor representatives or IT professionals, people with a lot of technical knowledge but little in pedagogy (Dysart and Weckerle 2015). As a result, the professional development focuses only on the technology with little regards to how it supports teachers' curricula, individual teaching styles and comfort levels with technology. Without relevancy, it is difficult for teachers to integrate the technology into their practices in authentic ways.

The most distinguishing feature of traditional professional development for technology instruction is that it is confined to a period of time. One session, whether one hour or a whole day, does not provide participants with enough time to practice new skills or support after the session ends. Mastery requires continuous effort and perseverance. A study from the Center for Public Education reveals only 10 percent of teachers can transfer skills learned through professional development into practice while 95 percent can transfer skills learned with coaching (Gulamhussein 2014). Multiple exposures and opportunities to apply new learning characterize ongoing professional learning. The International Society for Technology in Education's lists ongoing professional learning as one of its essential conditions for leveraging technology, stating that educators "need to carve out time in their busy schedules to assimilate their new knowledge, practice new skills, learn from each other and work together" (ISTE 2016).

This shift in thinking about technology professional development extends beyond K–12 education. In "Professional Development in Higher Education: A Model for Meaningful Technology Integration," Dysart and Weckerle write that "professional development opportunities should go beyond individual workshops where technology experts introduce a new tool or where pedagogy experts introduce a new teaching strategy to instructors, in isolation of one another" (Dysart and Weckerle 2015). Technology professional development in any organization must be interactive, relevant and on-going to be successful.

Revisit the scenario mentioned earlier: You are sitting in a large room, squinting to see a projector screen in the distance, listening to a stranger point out all the features "you're going to love" in a new app. You may be thinking about these questions.

- What does this have to do with me or my job?
- How am I supposed to do this on my own?
- Who is going to check my work today?

The answers would be clear if instead of participating in that professional development session, you were provided ongoing professional learning through coaching.

- You are in charge of your learning.
- The coach will support you every step of the way.
- You will not be evaluated on your learning, and it will not end today.

"Coaching is the purposeful and skillful effort by one individual to help another achieve specific performance goals. The coach facilitates the player's attainment of the player's goals" (Metz 2010). Coaching is an effective form of technology instruction because it is relevant, interactive and sustained over time.

The Coaching Model

Instructional coaching, at all levels and in all content areas, consists of the instructional coach supporting colleagues in planning, implementing, and reflecting on instructional practices, otherwise known as the Before, During, After (BDA) cycle of coaching (Eisenberg 2015).

- In the Before meeting, the teacher and coach plan for implementation of the tool or strategy.
- In the During meeting, implementation of the new tool or strategy occurs. The coach may be an active co-leader or serve as a non-evaluative observer, collecting data and notes for the teacher to reflect upon later.
- In the After meeting, the coach facilitates the teacher's reflection on the During. The teacher and coach then plan for the next Before meeting.

I use the BDA model in coaching approximately one hundred staff members in my building. How do I keep meeting with every teacher, over and over? I don't. Coaching is completely participant-driven; there is no prescribed agenda and no expectations that all teachers will be involved in coaching. Coaching occurs when teachers decide they are ready to try something new.

While the BDA cycle of coaching allows the coach to work with teachers one-on-one according to their interests and readiness levels, there are instances when small group instruction is appropriate because of participants' commonalities:

- Similar need but with various readiness levels
    - Teachers from the same content, working with the same tool or strategy to create similar instructional activities, e.g. four science teachers all working to incorporate the same simulation app into instruction
- Similar needs and readiness levels
    - Teachers of various content areas, working with the same tool or strategy for application in different learning activities, e.g. one math teacher, one science teacher and one physical education teacher, all interested in creating "flipped instruction" lessons with interactive videos

Typically, participants meet as a group only for the before sessions. After practicing with a tool or strategy, a teacher will then want to do the during and after sessions with the coach, one-on-one.

The Librarian, Coaching

In pursuit of improving his professional practices, surgeon and author Atul Gawande researched and interviewed educational, athletic and even medical coaches. Gawande adopted a new mindset for his own learning, believing that "you're never going to learn unless you have a coach all the way" (Gawande 2015). This stance differs with the view of adult learning as a responsibility of the individual. Professional growth is the same for teachers and surgeons—it requires support. Coaching may seem overwhelming, but consider how a librarian can embrace the role, drawing from these elements.

Skill

Librarians have a unique skill set that combines technology know-how with teaching experience. An ideal instructional coach knows what it is like to teach; librarians can empathize with teachers because they are certified teachers (The Bill & Melinda Gates Foundation 2014). In addition to their library credentials, many librarians hold certification in other content areas. When not leading classes of their own, librarians teach with other teachers, a practice that has proven to have a positive impact on student achievement (Loertscher 2014). The relationship between a teacher and a librarian is one of congenial respect and trust, allowing teachers to collaborate with a librarian/coach without the fear of being evaluated. Adopting the BDA instructional coaching model could further increase the gains made through these partnerships.

Librarians also teach teachers. By transforming traditional professional development into coaching, teachers can "go deep and wide" into their learning (Aguilar 2014). For instance, a librarian working with teachers who are new to using tablets in their classroom can provide a limited amount of instruction in a one-hour session held before the school year begins. The session could become the first meeting in a coaching relationship, enabling the librarian to support the teachers as they continue to learn ways of using the tablets in instructional activities.

Schedule

Librarians with "flexible scheduling," meaning they do not have a set daily schedule, can manage the library program and coach without scheduling conflicts. The librarian's availability also allows teachers, whose schedules are much more rigid, more choices in determining BDA meeting dates and times. Additionally, as coaching is one-on-one, there is no issue of identifying a single time that works for everyone in a group, as is the case in a professional development session. In my coaching, B and A meetings take place during the teacher's preparation period, and the D meeting happens during an instructional period. As my school operates on an 80-minute block period, I can attend multiple meetings each block, if necessary.

Space

With the recent emergence of learning commons and makerspaces, libraries are being transformed from book repositories into active learning spaces. As such, one of the perks of being a librarian/coach is the ease of accessing welcoming, practical workspaces for coaching. Libraries are redesigning spaces to accommodate engaging activities and provide access to innovative technology.

The physical layout of my school library has multiple areas, allowing for combinations of large and small groups to meet simultaneously. I can facilitate a small group coaching session in one area of the library without disturbing other classes and activities taking place at the same time.

The library is also the unofficial location for adopting new technology in my school. Before purchasing new projectors and document cameras for classrooms, the technology department at my school set up different models for tests and demonstrations in the library. The chosen models remained in the library so I could become familiar with them and host coaching sessions with teachers so they would be comfortable with their new devices. Newly acquired software is typically installed on devices in the library for the same reason.

Support

For coaching to be effective, you need your administration's complete support. They must value what you do and promote it. I know I have my principal's support: He introduces me at the first staff meeting of the year, reminding my colleagues of my role. He includes me in the planning of professional development opportunities. When teachers approach him with ideas about technology he encourages them to meet with me.

To maintain the trust of the administration, you must communicate with them regarding areas of growth and need. Teachers' feedback, whether provided via e-mail or a structured anonymous survey, can be used in planning for professional learning opportunities. Records of coaching are also informative. I use a Google Form to log the time I spend in coaching, noting with whom I am collaborating, at what time we are together, and the focus of our meeting. After collating the data in a spreadsheet and removing any personal information, I share it with my principal to illustrate what topics or strategies teachers are most interested in and to what extent coaching is affecting instruction in a department or across the building.

What's in a Name?

At the time of my hiring, the idea of a librarian also serving as a coach was new to the school and district, and we struggled to develop an accurate name for who I was to become. It is now nearly impossible for me to squeeze my official title onto a form and it's a tongue-twister for my colleagues. It is rare that I use the official title of "instructional media specialist/librarian and technology integration coach" as it is more important that my colleagues know that they can call on me rather than what they should call me. For everyone's sake, the term librarian/coach is typically used.

Snapshots of Coaching

A social studies teacher was hired in the middle of the school year, missing out on the week-long program for new teachers that takes place each summer. After the head teacher of the department had introduced us, we began working together through the coaching cycle. First, we tackled the basics such as how to access the school's Bring Your Own Device (BYOD) wireless network, establishing classes in the learning management system and of course, how to find relevant resources from the library's digital catalog. Then we began collaborating in instructional planning; incorporating specific applications and library resources into lessons. Our partnership continued to grow as he became more confident in using technology in his lessons.

An application for checking students' work for authenticity in language arts classes merged into the school's learning management system. After testing it with one teacher, I met with the others in the department to discuss the procedures for enabling it. I was in the classroom to provide support when teachers introduced it to their students. After the classes, I met with each teacher to review the success of the deployment. The cycle continued, with us moving onto different features of the learning management system, based on the teacher's interests.

A secretary asked for assistance streamlining the procedures for signing up for an annual event. She described what problems she encountered with handling hardcopy forms and we scheduled a time to work together to develop an online tool for collecting and sorting data. She asked to meet again after she collected the data, to discuss ways the tool could be modified and used for other procedures.

A math teacher was interested in incorporating different types of formative assessments into instructional activities. During our first meeting, we discussed a few applications, and she chose one to try out in class. I guided her in creating questions and visited the class for her first attempt at using app with students. We had a conversation after class about how it went and possibilities for trying another app for different uses in the near future.

Coaching in Other Libraries

Academic Libraries

The idea of instructional coaching in higher education is gaining attention. Dysart and Weckerle call for instructors to receive support "while designing instruction; while teaching a course; and beyond teaching, while reflecting upon and improving practices" (Dysart and Weckerle 2015). This is synonymous with the cyclical BDA process in K–12 education.

A professor at a local university recently asked me about issues he was having with the interactive projection software he used during classes. I was unable to visit the lecture hall but provided as much assistance as possible through an exchange of e-mails. I did not think of reaching out to the librarians on campus and now wonder how they would have responded if I had called. Similar to school librarian/coaches, academic librarians/coaches have the unique ability to see things from two perspectives, the instructional and technical implications of technology. By working with technology, roll-outs of new hardware and software could go much more smoothly, and the faculty may be more confident in trying new things, knowing they have support.

Public Libraries

A librarian/coach is equally valuable in a public library. In *Coaching in the Library: A Management Strategy for Achieving Excellence*, Metz writes "people who work in libraries are not only constantly faced with knowledge gaps in changing technology, but also with how to manage the integration of the technology into their ongoing work" (Metz 2010). If a librarian/coach provides support through small group or one-on-one coaching, the library may save time and money previously allocated to professional development sessions facilitated by vendor representatives. Individuals may challenge themselves to learn more, knowing that there is someone they can depend on when they have new ideas or encounter challenges. These changes may close the gap between staff members who are and are not confident and proficient in using technology in their work.

Technology is in the back offices, on the shelves and at the circulation desks of public libraries and is becoming more prevalent in the interactions public library staff members have with patrons. Public libraries are increasing website, mobile app and live streaming services, and are circulating more tablets, video game consoles, e-book readers and laptops (*Public Libraries* 2014). Public library staff, regardless of their background and interests in technology are tasked with promoting and supporting these resources but cannot do so without receiving instruction and support at their level of readiness.

Becoming a Librarian/Coach

Coaching builds on the partnerships you have with your colleagues so whether you have the official title or not, you can adopt the mindset and strategies of coaching. Are you the first person people reach out to when they have a question about technology? How can you be more mindful of interactions in which you are supporting a colleague using technology so that you may develop relationships that foster learning?

If you are ready to become a librarian/coach, reach out to your administration and provide evidence that supports how coaching is already a part of you work or make the case for transitioning into coaching with current or upcoming initiatives. Coaching "nourishes workplace resiliency" and "supports the new work and constant learning" in libraries (Metz 2010). Serving as a librarian/coach is a rewarding commitment to your organization and personal growth.

References

Aguilar, Elena. 2014. "Effective Coaching by Design." *Professional Learning: Reimagined* 71:8. http://www.ascd.org/publications/educational-leadership/may14/vol71/num08/Effective-Coaching-by-Design.aspx.
Dysart, Sarah, and Carl Weckerle. 2015. "Professional Development in Higher Education: A Model for Meaningful Technology Integration." *Journal of Information Technology Education: Innovations in Practice* 14: 255–265. http://www.jite.org/documents/Vol14/JITEv14IIPp255-265Dysart2106.pdf.
Eisenberg, Ellen. 2015. "The Coaching Cycle: Before, During, and After." *International Literacy Association.* March 18. http://www.literacyworldwide.org/blog/literacy-daily/2015/03/18/the-coaching-cycle-before-during-and-after.
"Essential Conditions: Ongoing Professional Learning." 2016. International Society for Technology in Education. http://www.iste.org/standards/essential-conditions/ongoing-professional-learning.
Gawande, Atul. 2014. "Atul Gawande on Getting a Coach." Lillian Cunningham, *Washington Post*, October 15. http://www.washingtonpost.com/posttv/national/on-leadership/atul-gawande-on-getting-a-coach—on-leadership/2014/10/16/78cb94bc-5539-11e4-b86d-184ac281388d_video.html.
Gulamhussein, Allison. 2014. "What Will It Take to Change?" *Professional Learning: Reimagined* 71:8. http://www.ascd.org/publications/educational-leadership/may14/vol71/num08/Double-Take.aspx.
Johnston, Melissa. 2015. "Blurred Lines: The School Librarian and the Instructional Technology Specialist." *TechTrends: Linking Research & Practice to Improve Learning* 59, no. 3: 17–26.
Loertscher, David V. 2014. "Collaboration and Coteaching." *Teacher Librarian* 42, no. 2: 8–19.
Metz, Ruth F. 2010. *Coaching in the Library: A Management Strategy for Achieving Excellence*, 2d ed. Chicago: American Library Association.
Teachers Know Best: Teachers' Views on Professional Development. 2014. The Bill & Melinda Gates Foundation. http://k12education.gatesfoundation.org/wp-content/uploads/2015/04/Gates-PDMarketResearch-Dec5.pdf.
"The 2013 Public Library Data Service Statistical Report: Characteristics and Trends." 2014. *Public Library* March/April 53:2.

PART III
Hardware, Software and Code

Is That Code?
Using Google in Undergraduate Math and Computer Science Research

AARON J. BLODGETT *and* JENNIFER L. DEAN

Google is useful in undergraduate research, particularly for projects requiring information and tools not typically found in library databases. Using Google to find these resources maximizes time for both professor and student and may minimize feelings of doubt that can inhibit a student's confidence in starting a project. This case study will illustrate the use of Google for a math and computer science project and how faculty and librarians can work together to facilitate student success. The authors will offer implications for research and practice.

Technology instruction in academic libraries ranges from complex tasks using specialized programs to more simple tasks involving web search. The authors of this essay advocate for starting simply, and meeting students and faculty where they are. In this case study report, a faculty member used Google to assist a student with a research project. Initially, he did not involve a librarian in the process. However, as the faculty member continued to engage undergraduate students in research, the faculty member discussed the student's project with a librarian. The results of this discussion offered insight into the teaching and learning process that may prove useful to academic librarians who work closely with faculty. Readers will note that many of the insights offered in this essay are peripheral to the technology, but are instrumental nonetheless. More importantly, they help librarians and faculty develop relationships that provide a foundation for student success.

Understanding Faculty

Academic librarians, whether they hold faculty status or not, may feel frustration when they are unsuccessful in connecting with members of the teaching faculty in meaningful ways (Moniz, Henry and Eshleman 2014). This disconnect may be debilitating if left unexamined, but provides an opportunity for librarians to talk amongst themselves, with their administration, and with faculty at the local level. Librarians can choose to channel these frustrations into meaningful opportunities for interaction with teaching faculty members. Teaching faculty tend to perceive librarians as helpful and experts in their disciplines, but may not have an understanding of the role an engaged librarian can play in student research. Librarians must take the lead in building this relationship (Henry and Slutzky 2016).

An examination of the workload of teaching faculty may help librarians develop a base of understanding on which to develop their plans for faculty outreach. Teaching faculty members who are tenured or on the tenure track often carry a heavy workload, including time spent preparing for class, teaching class, communicating with students, and grading. In primarily undergraduate serving institutions, time spent in teaching activities is high. However, additional responsibilities include time teaching faculty spend on research projects and in service to their institution, profession, or community (Milton 2015). Given the varying demands of this trio of activities, especially during the fall and winter semesters, these faculty members may find themselves on call at all hours. For faculty engaged in online instruction, which may be offered throughout the year, or those in need of additional compensation, even traditional summer and holiday breaks may be minimized or nonexistent.

In recent years, the focus on undergraduate research has increased (Free, Griffith and Spellman 2015), resulting in a further increase in workload for all faculty, not only those who work primarily with graduate students. Undergraduate research requires additional hours spent in mentoring student researchers through the research process and helping the student connect to opportunities to disseminate their research findings.

Adjunct teaching faculty members face a different set of challenges. The number of these faculty members engaged directly in teaching to undergraduates is increasing (Kezar and Gehrke 2015), and these faculty members must balance a heavy load. In many institutions, adjunct faculty receive little to no orientation to their employing institution and its services (Kezar and Sam 2013). As a result, adjunct faculty may not be aware of services their institution's library and librarians can provide. Adjuncts serve under a variety of contracts, but a significant population only work part-time, and may be serving in an adjunct role in more than one institution, requiring them to move quickly from one location to another throughout the day (Kezar and Sam 2013).

Given the workload faculty of all classifications are shouldering, it is little wonder that many do not make time to reach out to librarians. Librarians must take this opportunity to reach out to faculty. Armed with an understanding of faculty work, librarians can choose how to best tailor their services to teaching faculty members, whether tenure-track or adjunct. As librarians continue to adapt to a changing environment and student population, they have an opportunity to examine their traditional practices and consider new ways of reaching out to and working with faculty members.

Understanding Students

The average college or university student is no less busy. However, in addition to a full class schedule, students are engaged in a myriad of activities, many of which may not seem academic on the surface, but which are of immense importance in helping the student adjust to the college experience, engage both socially and academically, and make connections that help increase their chances of persistence to graduation. In particular, academic engagement and support, both in and out of the classroom, are critical (Kuh and Gonyea 2015). Librarians may play a key role in increasing academic engagement outside of the classroom, especially when they are working closely with teaching faculty. Project Information Literacy (PIL) research (Head 2013) indicates that even brief encounters with a librarian, particularly when offered at the right time and place, can have a tremendous impact on whether a student develops a relationship with the library and the people and resources it offers, improving their chances of academic success and offering an opportunity to engage academically and socially. However, most students look first to their professor for guidance and resources, emphasizing the importance of faculty-librarian relationships.

Students are also extremely likely to go to the web for resources. Many students believe they will find just about anything using Google (Head 2013), and will spend an inordinate amount of time searching the web for something that has already been done on their topic. Librarians and faculty members may use this reliance on Google to their advantage, as it offers an entry point for librarians to work collaboratively with both students and faculty, meeting them where they are. Consider these points:

- Google is familiar and easy to use, available anywhere the Internet is, and requires no special logins or permission.
- Students and faculty alike may be reticent to admit their reliance on Google. This gives librarians an opportunity to reassure these groups about the utility of using Google, and reaffirm the librarian's role as a non-judgmental partner in the teaching, learning, and research process.
- The average user may not know to take advantage of advanced searching strategies—such as using quotations for phrases or limiting to specific domains—or that Google offers specialized versions—such as Google Scholar—that may simplify their search process.
- Many of the search strategies students and faculty use in Google may be transferred to searching library databases, offering the librarian an opportunity to use Google to introduce additional resources.
- The ease of using Google may allow librarians to focus their instruction on the research process, rather than simply offering a how-to session on a particular database.

The following case study, in which a faculty member advised an undergraduate student in her research, illustrates these concepts. Although the faculty member was aware of the library's databases and used these to some extent, the nature of the student's research did not lend itself to typical database searching. Given his workload and familiarity with Internet searching, the faculty member turned to the search engine Google to help the student get a start on her research. As the case study outlines, the faculty member and student were able to find several useful resources using Google, enough for the student to move ahead with her research.

Case Study

The faculty member in this case study advised a student on a math and computer science research project. A member of the math faculty at a mid-sized private institution in the Midwest, this faculty member was relatively early in his career. He was juggling his teaching load with service responsibilities, both on campus and statewide, and his own research. He was also working toward tenure.

The faculty member was working with a student in researching a cryptography algorithm that had been in existence for some time. Previous methods of attacking this algorithm depended on letter frequencies. The student's research question asked whether using texting-style language would affect the letter frequencies and render the known methods of attacking the algorithm obsolete.

Due to both the faculty member's and the student's schedule, the two researchers generally met in the faculty member's office, where the faculty member had access to his own resources as he worked with the student. The student and faculty member met weekly for 30 to 60 minutes each meeting. The faculty member prepared beforehand by assisting the student in doing preliminary research using his office computer. The faculty member discovered early on that the library had few databases that were useful in the student's research, and turned to Google. Using basic search strategies in the original Google search engine, the faculty member was able to find a few papers and several useful websites. Some of these useful sites mentioned above were sites that included, for example,

- a site that could calculate the letter frequencies of a body of text;
- sites that contained portions of C++ code that would be useful to the student when she was writing her own code;
- a large compilation of actual texts—texts sent from one person to another by phone or other texting device; and
- papers on the encryption algorithm and Internet lingo.

Using a combination of C++ code she found online and some that she wrote herself, the student was able to complete her research project, though not to the full extent possible. The faculty member explained that although this project represented a good first start in research, in only attempting one case the project was less robust than it might have been if she had explored multiple cases. In talking with a librarian, the faculty member wondered whether more efficient and precise initial research might have helped the student discover other cases. Had the student considered other cases, her work may have resulted in a better overall project.

The student presented her research twice, and the faculty member judged the student's research project to be successful. However, the faculty member wondered about how collaboration with a librarian might have affected the student's research. In particular, the faculty member wondered whether he had missed resources, either those that could be found using Google or any that would be in the library's databases. He also posed the question about finding pieces of code online that students could use: Would a librarian be able to assist in locating code for a specific algorithm and programing language, preferably code that was well commented and documented? Although the student in this case study had completed he research, the faculty member was preparing to work on additional student research projects similar to this one, and hoped to build on this work.

Further, the faculty member had doubts about the appropriateness of the Internet resources, as well as their status in terms of copyright. Some of the sites he found consisted of data compiled for other, more substantial research projects. The faculty member was unsure of whether or not it was appropriate to use these sources, and had no idea of how to begin determining this.

Lastly, the faculty member was uncertain on how to advise the student in properly citing these online resources, although he was aware that different methods of citing sources, particularly online resources, existed. However, for a small, undergraduate research project, he didn't consider the formalities of the syntax of citing to be of huge importance.

The faculty member thought all of these questions and issues could potentially be resolved by a knowledgeable librarian. However, it had not occurred to him to seek this assistance until he was immersed in the project.

Discussion

As outlined in the case study, the librarian's role does not need to be confined to the initial search for resources—in fact, the student and faculty member were able to move quickly into the experimentation and writing phase of the project due to the ease with which they were able to locate appropriate resources using Google during the faculty member's regular office hours. However, the librarian may have been able to find additional resources, and been able to put those resources in context—for example, verify that the library did not have access to any more conventional databases or resources, and that the resources available on the web were valid and appropriate to use for research. The librarian may have also been able to help save time for the student and professor in terms of searching library resources, or simply by assisting in using Google more efficiently. Finally, the librarian could have been especially helpful in assisting the student in pulling together her final project, ensuring the student had properly cited the various online resources she used.

Implications for Practice and Research

Although case study research is necessarily subjective, and the results may not be generalizable to a larger population, the results are valuable due to their ability to contextualize the findings of previous research and increase understanding. Although additional research is needed, existing research indicates a disconnect exists between librarians and teaching faculty members (Moniz, Henry and Eshleman 2014). As a result, they may feel frustrated and unappreciated when students and faculty members seemingly bypass the library in favor of resources found online. As illustrated in the case study above, the faculty member noted that he had not considered contacting a librarian for assistance in the initial phase of the research, but realized later that library assistance must have been available. However, as this case study indicates, regardless of the faculty member's level of busyness, some research subjects do not lend themselves to typical databases searches. Librarians should consider making time for dialogue with faculty members about the research they and their students are doing in order to find out what they need. In some cases, librarians may need to turn to the web, vetting and providing context for resources that may only be found on the open web. Librarians have the opportunity to consider the information they make available online to students and faculty members, using online resources as well as library databases resources in their guides and teaching documents. Many librarians already do this. But, without an understanding of the work that faculty members are engaged in, and the communication efforts needed to engage these faculty members, the work librarians do may go unappreciated. Creating useful and relevant resources is an ongoing process, and library administrators must consider this when evaluating librarian workload—librarians may need to be released from their traditional duties in order to focus on developing relationships and communicating with faculty members.

Faculty would provide a service to their students by taking time to communicate with librarians when the library's collection does not seem to be meeting their needs. In some cases, the faculty member may be overlooking a database in the library's collection, but it may also be the case that no databases exist to match the type of research the faculty member is involved in. When librarians are aware of shortcomings in their database collection, they can determine whether this shortcoming is due to the library's inability to provide access to more advanced tools, or whether the information is simply not available in a traditional library database. This helps ensure the work librarians do in creating specialized research guides and webliographies will be relevant and useful, and may assist others engaged in similar research.

Overall, more research is needed to examine the understanding that teaching faculty members, whether tenured, tenure-track, or adjunct, and librarians have of one another. The more these two important members of the academic community understand one another, the better they will be able to serve their students.

Conclusion

Although online information is plentiful and easy to find, the library and librarians have a vital role to play in faculty and student research. Students and faculty are busier than ever, putting the onus on librarians to ensure they are engaged as partners in the research process. The Internet and search tools like Google offer an alternative to the traditional library search, but librarians do not need to be threatened by this, or discourage the campus community from using these tools. Projects like the one outlined in this case study offer an opportunity to examine the library's collection, thoughtfully determine whether library tools exist to assist with the project, and consider how best to serve students and faculty who have successfully navigated the early research steps in the process.

REFERENCES

Free, Rhona, Suzanne Griffith, and Bill Spellman. 2015. "Faculty Workload Issues Connected to Undergraduate Research." *New Directions for Higher Education* no. 169: 51–60. doi: 10.1002/he.20122

Head, Alison J. 2013. "Project Information Literacy: What Can Be Learned about the Information-Seeking Behavior of Today's College Students?" *Association of College and Research Libraries (ACRL) Proceedings 2013*. Chicago: American Library Association.

Henry, Jo, and Howard Slutzky. 2016. "Building Mindful Relationships with Faculty." In *The Mindful Librarian: Connecting the Practice of Mindfulness to Librarianship* by Richard Moniz, Joe Eshleman, Jo Henry, Howard Slutzky, and Lisa Moniz, 137–156. Amsterdam: Elsevier.

Kezar, Adrianna, and Sean Gehrke. 2014. "Why Are We Hiring so Many Non-Tenure-Track Faculty?" *Liberal Education* 100, no. 1: 44–51.

Kezar, Adrianna, and Cecile Sam. 2013. "Institutionalizing Equitable Policies and Practices for Contingent Faculty." *The Journal of Higher Education* 84, no. 1: 56–87, doi: 10.1353/jhe.2013.0002.

Kuh, George D., and Robert M. Gonyea. 2015. "The Role of the Academic Library in Promoting Student Engagement in Learning." *College & Research Libraries* 76, no. 3: 359–385, doi: 10.5860/crl.64.4.256.

Milton, Constance L. 2015. "Ethics and Academic Integrity." *Nursing Science Quarterly* 28, no. 1: 18–20, doi: 10.1177/089431841455862.

Moniz, Richard, Jo Henry, and Joe Eshleman. 2014. "Communication with Faculty." In *Fundamentals for the Academic Liaison,* 35–51. New York: ALA Neal-Schuman.

Rise or Fall of a Library Intranet
Best Practices, Tips and Hints

JOSHUA K. JOHNSON

This essay is intended to guide those curious about getting announcements, training, policy and procedure, and other information to or from library staff without thousands of e-mails per year. I suggest you reflect on the following questions and resources as you consider implementing an Intranet in your library.

What Is an Intranet?

Intranets are basically the same in design and function as websites build for the Internet, except that they are a closed system available only internally to an organization. This means that the same information and collaborative techniques available on regular Internet websites are also potentially available for use in-house with an Intranet.

Where Do I Start?

Let's assume you have decided to implement an Intranet. There are a variety of questions you could ask yourself about your organization including who will create it, and what you hope it will do for your library. You would do well to consider the following topics as you begin thinking about how your organization would best use an Intranet.

What Type of Intranet Would Best Suit my Library?

It may sound strange, but there are many different types of Intranet structure. Let me explain by borrowing terminology used to describe the Internet. The terms Web 1.0 and Web 2.0 have become commonly used to describe two overarching themes or eras of web development. Web 1.0 generally describes websites created to disseminate information to users without a lot of input from users. In contrast, Web 2.0 sites are designed both to disseminate information provided by the site creators and encourage participation, and content creation from users.

Intranet design can be described in much the same way. If your library is really only interested in providing easy access to organizational information like policies or directories, that type of Intranet is essentially Intranet 1.0. If your organization is considering using blog posts with comments, wikis, document sharing, or forums, then the structure that best fits your plans would be more like Intranet 2.0.

There is nothing inherently wrong with using an Intranet primarily as a tool for dissemination, in fact it may be that the Intranet you design acts as an institutional repository at point-of-need access. There is also nothing particularly right about an Intranet that allows users to generate content, such as an internal blog; it is just a different set of design preferences. What really matters is that you consider what type of Intranet would best meet your library's goals or needs, and design accordingly.

What Types of Tools Can an Intranet Offer Library Employees?

When considering all that you might want or need in an Intranet, it is easy to become overwhelmed by the many and varied tools you might incorporate. Below is a list of some of the more prevalent options, but it is certainly not exhaustive. The Intranet you develop is truly limited only by your imagination, ingenuity, and perhaps your budget.

- Online and Paperless Forms
- Document & File Sharing
- Wikis and Forums
- Audio and Video Content
- Blogs, Chat, Instant Messaging

Who Will Build Our Intranet?

Once you discover the features and possibilities that best suit your library staff and organization, the next logical step is finding someone to build it for you. Really, there are only two options-either find someone already on staff with the necessary skills or hire someone from the outside to design it.

Internal Technology Staff

It is likely that finding someone already employed by the library will be the simplest solution. In fact, if you are fortunate, you already have a department or an employee who takes care of your web presence and online catalog. Since, as we previously mentioned, an Intranet uses the same structure as the Internet, the employees in charge of your website probably already have the skill set needed to create an Intranet. If this person is already overburdened, you may be surprised to find that there are other employees who know or can be taught the basics of web design. Having the employee that takes care of your web presence create the initial page layouts and structure of your site; then allowing the novice to fill in content and functionality can be an excellent way of recruiting talent within your organization and building interest in the project.

It is important to include them in the process early on, before designing and conceptualizing-especially if you choose a content management system (CMS) as a platform for the Intranet that is different from your library's Internet presence. For those unfamiliar with the term, a content management system is software that allows the creation and ongoing management of a website without detailed knowledge of how to program a website. It will be necessary to give your designers time to explore options and a CMS that would best suit your needs. They will also need time to become familiar with how the CMS functions so that they can act as a resource the during conceptualizing and design phases of development. If you need shopping suggestions, below is a list of common CMS platforms and a link to online information about them.

Sharepoint, https://products.office.com/en-us/sharepoint/collaboration
WordPress, https://wordpress.com/
Drupal, https://www.drupal.org/
Joomla, https://www.joomla.org/
Sitefinity, http://www.sitefinity.com/
Google Search Appliance, https://www.google.com/work/search/products/gsa.html
ExpressionEngine, https://ellislab.com/expressionengine

External Technology Resources

If you do not have someone on staff with the skill set needed for designing an Intranet, you may still have other options. Perhaps you fortunate enough that you can call on an Information Systems or Information Technology department to aid you in design and setup. For example, I am currently involved in an Intranet project where I am in charge of content for the organization, but our county's computer department takes care of much of the design and CMS infrastructure. It saves me a lot of the heavy lifting inherent in keeping up the design, but gives our organization a lot of control over pages and content.

Even if you don't have the option of leaning on another department or agency with professionally trained web designers, you still have the option of contracting with a web design professional for the original design, or even for ongoing work; costs may be prohibitive. However, the professional you hire will likely be equipped to make suggestions or decisions regarding the CMS for your Intranet.

How Do I Get My Staff Invested in the Process?

There is evidence that the most important factors in the success of a library Intranet rests with how invested staff are in its process and implementation. One particular piece of research, based on Intranet adoption at a university in Norway, indicates that one of the most important indicators of successful Intranet adoptions were the number of "ambassadors" active within the organization. These ambassadors were employees trained as early adopters that understood the capabilities of the Intranet, received initial training so as to become mentors and trainers to coworkers, and who helped pioneer use of the Intranet in their sphere of influence and championed its use during staff adoption (Hustad, Kydland, and Aakre 2014).

Below are some suggestions for implementing an Intranet in your library organization, including ways to cultivate the types of "ambassadors" described in the study and related suggestions.

Who Will Use the Intranet?

The preceding information and discussion has probably already given you a good idea about some of the more attractive features that would be beneficial to your library. As you design and implement it in your library, consider the following questions about your users.

- What types of users are most likely to benefit from the ways your Intranet functions?
- What tasks will the Intranet make easier? Who performs those tasks?
- Are there different levels of potential Intranet use? Managers? Line Supervisors? Clerks? Committees?
- How do your employees actually accomplish tasks?
- In what ways will the Intranet make these tasks easier?
- How could the Intranet integrate with these individual's workflow?
- Which natural workgroups exist in your organization that would benefit from using the Intranet?
- How do these groups prefer to interact? What ways can the Intranet integrate into their workflow?
- Which groups or employees are most likely to ignore the new tools available via the Intranet?
- What are some of the largest organizational obstacles to implementing a new Intranet?
- What are some ways that the Intranet might alter your workplace culture? How will it alter communication between employees and workgroups?

After developing answers to these questions it will be instructive if you develop user scenarios based on your answers. For example, technical processing clerks who label materials and clean discs, but do not have a computer at their desks, would not be excellent early adopters or ambassadors, because their workflow is outside the direct influence of Intranet tools.

However, a Youth Services Librarian who works at the reference desk and collaborates with a Youth Services committee may be a very good candidate, since she might benefit both from the top-down information dissemination for information regarding public services policy and procedure as well as from various Intranet options for collaboration with colleagues on the committee with which she often communicates.

Involve Key Staff

Let me make two suggestions concerning which employees should be involved in designing and building the Intranet: select those you feel will benefit the most from Intranet features, and their supervisors. This gives you a built-in group of "ambassadors" as mentioned above, but also gives you a core set of invested users to draw on when testing for usability and who are vested in the new system because they helped bring it to life.

Promote the Intranet

At a certain point in the development of an Intranet project that included much of the same sort of planning discussed above, I discovered that only a handful of staff were using the carefully crafted Intranet. After some informal polling of coworkers at various branches, the main reason no one used it was because no one remembered it existed. It just wasn't part of their workflow and didn't figure into their decision-making.

Promotion is the only way that an Intranet becomes viable-if people don't know about it, they can't adopt it as part of their daily work. If they don't make it part of their daily work, then all of the time, money, and effort put into building an Intranet is wasted. Here are some suggestions for promotion.

- Revisit the list made above and meet with individuals and groups that would most benefit from the Intranet-discuss the ways they will directly benefit from the new system.
- Make the Intranet the home page of every staff computer.
- Send e-mails to employees explaining features and how they might incorporate them into their work.
- Create a flyer or ad that markets some of the most important or useful features of the Intranet and post it for employees to see.

Make Sure You Train Staff

Training staff to use the Intranet goes hand in hand with promotion. They need not, and really should not, be considered separate activities. Those who have been trained to use the Intranet are automatically aware of it, and capable of using it-two of the most important factors concerning whether or not they will adopt it as a daily tool to better accomplish tasks. Then, as these trained, early adopters interact with coworkers, they naturally communicate their (hopefully) positive experiences implementing and using the Intranet. They become the ambassadors so necessary to successful implementation in your library.

Really, the first thing you need to do is train the trainers. Training a small group to use the Intranet, then tasking them with the training of the larger group allows them to mentor others *and* cement their understanding of the Intranet in the process. Using the initial training group to train the rest of your staff will free up the Intranet Administrator to continue developing and maintaining the Intranet without getting bogged down in minor questions and issues. However, trainers should be instructed to pass suggestions for improvement on to the Administrator so that appropriate adjustments may be made to the Intranet's design and content.

Maintain Relevance

Thus far, suggestions and tips have been made with the assumption that the Intranet designed and implemented by your library organization is actually better than the processes and tools it is replacing in some meaningful way. However, there are some problems that may creep into the project that could make it seem like the previous ways of working are more effective or efficient.

For example, if information is organized poorly or if content is not updated regularly (e.g., phone numbers become incorrect, or procedures become out of date), then the Intranet's usefulness wanes, and it is discarded in favor of some other way of doing things that delivers relevant or accurate information in a more reliable way. Here are some areas to consider updating frequently:

- Directories
- Procedures and Policies
- Calendar Items
- Reports

Test for Usability

If you want employees to use the Intranet, usability testing is second in importance only to promotion. First, they need to know the Intranet exists, *then* it needs to be organized and function in a way that allows them to adopt it without a lot of frustration. To use another example from my experience, when I polled Intranet users, another very common reason staff members weren't using the Intranet was that it took too long to load.

As with all web design, intranets should be user-based. Regular communication and testing with users is the best way to make certain the Intranet is a viable, worthwhile tool. For those baffled by usability testing, I highly recommend Steve Krug's *Don't Make Me Think* (2014). He gives a good, brief overview of the process and why it is needed.

Consider Organizational Culture

It seems only natural that an Intranet will lead to change in workplace culture. If you are nervous about your organization's ability to adapt, consider another finding from the Norwegian study discussed earlier. It seems that some work environments were more conducive to implementing a new method for communication and collaboration than others. Fortunately, these predispositions were less important, overall, than the presence of ambassadors who were well trained, and enthusiastic about the positive implications of an Intranet. Departments that had difficulty adopting the Intranet struggled because they failed to train employees, and failed to adequately promote Intranet use as suggested above (Hustad, Kydland, and Aakre 2014).

What Happens the Intranet Administrator Moves On?

While it will be less of a problem for a library that relies on a separate department or an outside vendor or specialist to build and maintain an Intranet-at some point, the person or group who designed and implemented your library's Intranet will get another job, move up in the organization, or retire. What can you do ahead of time to make sure that the transition between administrators goes smoothly?

Think Sustainably

Really, it boils down to making sure that the administrator manages processes, rather than content. For example, if your Intranet administrator is in charge of updating staff directories as well as maintaining the wikis and forums-he or she will be more difficult to replace, and your directories may not be updated as quickly because they are not as high on a site administrators' list of importance as they would be for a group leader or supervisor. The tasks, while similar looking, require different skill sets.

A more sustainable way to handle this situation would be to have the Intranet Administrator take care of processes and structure, and allow content experts like supervisors to generate and maintain content in a timely manner. Most content management systems have the flexibility to allow multiple levels of access (i.e., administrators, editors, and general users), which would allow for content specialists to make some changes without endangering the system. The same process can be used to make sure other content is created and maintained more sustainably. Examples might include calendar events, procedures, and any other relevant or timely content on the Intranet.

Make Documentation a Priority

There *is* at least one form of content that needs to be written and maintained by the Intranet Administrator-process documentation. Process documentation, at its most basic level, is like a "how-to" manual describing how to manage the CMS and any other parts of the Intranet. This may include how to create a new page on the site, who is in charge of creating which content, descriptions of bugs or quirks in the system, how to upgrade the CMS, relevant contact information for vendors-anything that explains the system to an outsider. This last part is critical-it is important that the documentation be detailed enough that someone coming to the system with little or no experience with the system will understand the basics of how to maintain the Intranet.

Good documentation generally includes detailed written instructions with appropriate screenshots and other images to provide clarity. It need not be written on the level of a novice, but could be depending upon the needs of the organization. Good documentation of processes, as in the examples above, adds dramatically to the sustainability of your library's Intranet.

Where Can I Go for More Information?

This essay is intended to provide basic information related to understanding, implementing and designing an Intranet. Accordingly, the following suggested reading list is not intended to be exhaustive. However, it should give interested individuals a start toward understanding what an Intranet is, what it can do for an organization, and how to go about attempting to implement one in their library.

Suggested Reading

Hustad, Eli, Fredrik Kydland, and Marit Aakre. "Knowledge Management in an Academic Context: A Framework for Successful Intranet 2.0 Implementation." *Proceedings of the European Conference on Knowledge Management*, vol. 2, p. 444. Academic Conferences International Limited.

Johnson, C. D. 2014. "Cultivating a Grapevine: Building an Intranet Using WordPress." *Tennessee Libraries* 64, no. 1.

Krug, Steve. 2014. *Don't Make Me Think, Revisited: A Common Sense Approach to Web Usability*, 3-D ed. San Francisco: New Riders, Peachpit, Pearson Education.

McHale, N. 2014. *Designing and Developing Library Intranets*. London: Routledge.

Norton, A. 2014. "'Where Do I Find That?' Creating a Central Shared Documentation System for Publishing Staff Using Google Tools at the University of Michigan Library." *Library Hi Tech News* 31:10, 6–9.

Riemke-Gurzki, T. 2015. "Developing Intranet Strategy: An Interdisciplinary Building Block Model." *icom* 14, no. 1, pp. 97–99.

References

Hustad, Eli, Fredrik Kydland, and Marit Aakre. 2014. "Knowledge Management in an Academic Context: A Framework for Successful Intranet 2.0 Implementation." *Proceedings of the European Conference on Knowledge Management* 2 (May): 444–454. http://libaccess.sjlibrary.org/login?url=http://search.ebscohost.com/login.aspx?direct=true&db=lih&AN=99225208&site=ehost-live.

Krug, Steve. 2014. *Don't Make Me Think, Revisited: A Common Sense Approach to Web Usability* 3-D. ed. San Francisco: New Riders, Peachpit, Pearson Education.

Starting a Device Club

Deloris J. Foxworth

In 2015, the Pew Research Center reported that 68 percent of adults have a smart phone and tablet ownership has reached 45 percent for adults (Anderson 2015). This has presented a set of challenges for libraries as much borrowing and information seeking has moved to an online or digital platforms. To stay relevant, libraries must secure funding for digital resources, increase training for staff, and develop new programs to get patrons into the library. This essay proposes device clubs as a programming option libraries can use to engage a growing population of mobile users.

Becoming Mobile

An increase in device ownership means patrons expect libraries, like many other organizations, to become more mobile. In many cases, libraries have stepped up to the mobile challenge with support from various vendors. For example, Boopsie is a vendor that offers customizable apps for libraries on all major operating systems including Android, Blackberry, iOS, Windows, etc. (Boopsie.com 2016a). Through Boopsie, libraries can elect to integrate the online catalog, calendar of events, social media feeds (Twitter, Facebook, YouTube or blog posts), and even third party services into this single app branded for their library (Boopsie.com 2016b). Boopsie currently supports 39 integrated library systems including multiple products from Innovative, SirsiDynix, and The Library Corporation (TLC). Encore, Millennium, Polaris, and Sierra are the four Innovative systems supported. The SirsiDynix supported ILS versions include Horizon, iBistro, Symphony, Unicorn, and SirsiEnterprise. Boopsie supports Carl.X, TLC Library.Solution, and TLC LS2 on the TLC platform. In addition to ILS systems, Boopsie supports 19 third party services including eBook and audio books readers, database and platform integrations, reviews and recommendations, and other platforms (Boopsie.com 2016a). Overdrive and One Click Digital are two popular eBook/audiobook readers Boopsie supports. Overdrive reported distributing more than 120 million eBooks and audiobooks to borrowers during the first nine months of 2015 (Burleigh 2015). Tutor.com is one of the database and platform integrations Boopsie supports. It provides access to experts in 25 subject areas through live tutoring services for K–12 students (Tutor 2016). Goodreads, a site designed to record reading behaviors and discover new books for reading (Goodreads.com 2016), is one of the reviews and recommendations services Boopsie supports. Other platforms include things like Mango Languages and Evanced Solutions. Mango Languages teaches over 60 conversational languages through interactive lessons (Mango Languages 2016). Evanced Solutions is a Demco Company that provides room booking solutions, reading tracking products, and event calendar management (Evancedsolutions.com 2016). While these partnerships between Boopsie, various third party vendors, and the library can increase convenience for patrons and likability for the library, these partnerships may also present challenges for libraries with populations unaware of the capabilities of their mobile devices.

Review of Current Programs

In an effort to educate users, many libraries offer digital literacy training. According to the 2014 Digital Inclusion Survey by the Institute of Museum and Library Services almost 90 percent of libraries offer some type of digital literacy training and 62 percent "support training related to new technology devices" (Gravatt 2015). Libraries provide this support in various ways. For example, the Scott County Public Library in Georgetown, Kentucky, offers free online instructional videos through Atomic Training (Scott County Public Library 2015). Atomic Training gives patrons access to thousands of "online, on-demand video training tutorials on the most popular software and devices including Microsoft® Office®, Adobe® Creative Suite®, Google™ Docs, iPad®, and more" (Atomiclearning.com 2016). In addition, the library offers in-person workshops in a computer lab and one-on-one consultations (Scott County Public Library 2015).

While many public libraries offer similar types of technology trainings, these are often seen as impersonal and generic to patrons and expensive for libraries. Online trainings allow libraries to provide technology training on complex topics its staff may not be equipped to teach and allows patrons to take trainings when convenient for them. However, for libraries these conveniences come at a hefty price tag and sometimes with little usage from reluctant patrons seeking staff participation. In-person workshops, a popular method for teaching technology, limit the range of topics to the library staff's expertise and the available equipment, meaning the topics are not always what patrons want. One-on-one consultations typically satisfy the patron, but demands a lot of the library in terms of staff time and library space. However, there is another alternative that may be more satisfying to both the patron and the library: starting a device club. A device club can accommodate the patron's need for personal attention and current topics while reducing the commitment by the library.

Definition of a Device Club

A device club is similar to a book club; however instead of meeting to discuss a book, the patrons meet to learn about their devices. The library can choose to focus on type of device, operating system, or particular apps. No matter which method chosen, the key is to combine formal instruction with participant testimony and demonstration. Clubs organized around device type offer the most specific type of instruction as everyone's device would be exactly alike. This type of club should be used only if there is a large number of patrons with the same device.

Clubs centered around the type of operating system may offer the best benefit for patrons and the club leader. For example, iPads and Android devices use different operating systems so the standard features and how to access different apps may be different. However, a patron that has a Samsung Galaxy Note and a patron that has a Samsung Galaxy S4 phone would have access to similar apps and features on their devices. While the devices are not exactly the same, they are similar enough to demonstrate many of the device's features along with digital library services. From a leader perspective a club based on device type of operating system means the leader has to only be familiar with one operating system. If needed, a different leader could lead a club using a different operating system.

The other option is to focus on demonstrating library apps instead of the type of device. This can sometimes be easier for the leader as they only have to be knowledgeable about a particular app and not the overall functions of a device. However, the leader will likely have to be slightly familiar with all devices and operating systems or at least comfortable enough with technology to adapt to different devices. This method seems like an effective way to promote and teach the library's digital services, but it may be challenging to generate interest in only a library services device club.

In addition to teaching patrons new skills, device club can also be used to create a sense of community among its members. The first key element in creating a sense of community is to host the device club at regular intervals (monthly, biweekly, quarterly, etc.). This helps create relationships among the participants as well as reinforce concepts taught. Another key element in creating a sense of community is participant involvement. A device club should not be a normal lecture/demonstration-based workshop. While having a formal instruction component can be essential in demonstrating how to use a particular feature, it is also important to invite the participants to share experiences with the devices. This can be done with different instructional approaches. One approach has the leader conducting a formal demonstration of the device and then opening up to the participants to ask questions and/or share experiences. Another way would be to elect a participant to conduct the formal demonstration at each meeting. This approach may give the participants more ownership, but can sometimes make patrons reluctant to participate if they feel unknowledgeable about the device.

These are just some of the ways to approach a device club. Each library should choose the appropriate type of device club for its particular population. The best way to do this is to collect statistics about the library users.

Collecting Statistics about Device Usage

A library considering a device club should start by determining the most popular device among its patrons and/or in the community. To find information about patron populations, libraries can count statistics, either informally or formally. Informal statistics can be gathered from employees who help patrons or observe patrons with devices. Formal statistics can be gathered from surveys during training sessions or device statistics from the libraries technology tools. For example, the Scott County Public Library uses Meraki MR18 WAPS, manufactured by Cisco, to disperse the wireless signal throughout the library. Meraki systems collect statistics about users, including the types of devices that connect (Schweiss 2014). This information can be used to determine popular devices used inside the library. Libraries may also be able to collect device statistics through online services offered by the library. For example, Overdrive allows libraries to collect statistics about the types of downloads (audio, eBook, music, video) and the type of device used.

The data collected can reveal valuable information about uses of devices, but before initiating a device club or clubs, it may be useful to collect some qualitative information from users. Again this can be formal or informal. Formal methods may include surveys distributed during workshops, at the circulation desk, or even on the website. Informal methods may include suggestion or topics boxes, on-the-fly interviews with patrons using their devices, or during device help sessions. Topics to explore in either formal or informal polls may include comfort level with device, apps used, apps curious about, interest in learning more, or potential participation in a club.

Resources for a Club

Once a need is established, the library should evaluate resources. The library will need a staff member or volunteer; access to a conference room or other inviting setting; a device for use and training; and a web cam, computer, and projector to display the lesson. In addition, the library should devote resources to the promotion of the club.

Staffing the Club

For the club to be successful a library should find an employee or volunteer willing to coordinate the event. The time commitment would be based on how often the club met. The person should attend the event and plan a short lesson or list of topics to cover at each meeting. Possible topics besides library services include downloading apps, system updates, connecting to Wi-Fi, taking and viewing pictures and video, setting up security on the device, and much more. During the meeting, the leader would present the lesson or introduce each topic. The leader would also guide the discussion of the group by facilitating the use of the equipment for demonstration. Due to the nature of the leadership role, the employee or volunteer would need to have prior knowledge of the device, seek training, or be comfortable with self-exploration to learn the device.

Location for the Club

After staffing, the next big commitment from the library is space. A successful device club will meet regularly requiring the library to devote dedicate space. The space should be a small conference room or other inviting meeting space. The library should avoid using a classroom or lecture-based setup. Instead, the library should select a room with chairs around a table, a conference room for example, or simply an area where chairs can be set up facing each other. Either of these environments would facilitate discussion.

Equipment for the Club

Equipment can be minimal if necessary. First, the library may need a device matching the patron's device. There are multiple ways a library can gain access to a device. Libraries can purchase the device if unowned. Employees can volunteer to use their own personal device (not recommended). Or libraries can seek a volunteer willing to lend/donate a device to the library or lead the club. If none of these options are feasible a library may still implement a device club, but will rely on participant devices and demonstrations during the meetings.

If purchasing a device, libraries do not need to buy the most recent device. The library should concentrate on the most popular versions of a device based on collected data. If the library needs access to an older device and cannot find an employee or community member that is willing to lead or lend/donate the device, the library can use services like Amazon or eBay to seek an older version of a device. The library may also be able to contact the manufacturer to purchase an older model.

Besides the device, the library also needs to secure a webcam, projector or large display monitor, and a computer. New equipment does not need to be purchased if the library already owns these. The equipment just needs to be available and portable or located in the room of the meeting. The webcam is used in conjunction with the computer and projector or large display monitor to display, step-by-step, each process. A free standing webcam, not built into the computer, would be best. This makes positioning the camera to capture both the device screen and the device users' hand movements easier. The webcam should be connected to a computer that is connected to the projector or large display monitor. This allows demonstrations to be easily seen by all participants. By being connected to a computer, the session can also be recorded if the webcam software or another software allows.

Promoting the Club

Once the library has acquired all the necessary resources and is ready to start the club, the library needs to promote the club as a regularly occurring meeting for device owners or those interested in the device. How the promotion occurs can be flexible, but should follow promotion for similar events at the library. This may include promotion through social media, online and paper library and/or community calendars, the library website, signage in the library, bookmarks, etc. Most of this will be of minimal cost to the library. If resources allow the library could consider additional promotion in local television, radio, newspapers, or other medias attractive to the target population.

Benefits of a Device Club

Libraries that successfully start and maintain one or more device clubs may see several benefits. First, a device club promotes a core value of many libraries, supporting lifelong learning. Another important benefit for many libraries is new patrons. A device club can be a great service to offer to reach new patrons. With potential new patrons and/or current patrons in a regular program it is a great time to promote additional library products and services. For example, a library can promote and demonstrate e-book services like Overdrive or Freading, Library Ideas' affordable, pay-per-use eBook service of over 50,000 titles (Libraryideas.com 2016). Finally, the device club helps build a sense of community among its participants. This can result in more sharing of library resources, community resources, etc.

Combating Challenges When Starting a Club

Libraries may also experience some issues or notice limitations with device clubs. One of the biggest issues is scheduling. Some administrators may not be open to scheduling a room, equipment, and personnel monthly or more frequently to a new program. Programmers can combat this problem by sharing statistics and feedback collected from patrons and other library services. Another big issue for some libraries may be access to devices and training for staff. Many devices can be purchased for under $500 and may be able to improve other library programming. For example, an iPad can easily be integrated into story times and other children's programming. Almost any web-enabled mobile device can be used at any event for registration using Google Forms. Google Forms can be easily set up to collect participant's name, contact information, and other desired information. After collecting this data, Google makes it easy to sort and use the information to customize future promotion. Employee training could be an issue, but many electronic stores, like the Apple or Verizon store, may be willing to send an employee to train library staff on their devices.

A big hurdle many libraries may face in implementing a device club is building a sense of community. What keeps patrons coming back after they learn about the one feature they need? This is where ownership in the group plays a role. By engaging patrons with the technology and inviting them to share their successes and failures with the device, patrons are likely to return and use library services.

Variations to a Device Club

Being a relatively new idea, device clubs are not common in libraries; however, there is a lot of potential with this type of club. Just as many libraries offer book clubs for different populations, the library could offer different device clubs for different populations. For example, there are over 75,000 education apps through the Apple's App Store (Apple 2016). Libraries could create a device club specifically for preschool age children and their parents. The library could use this forum to introduce parents to safe and educational apps for their children. There could be a mix of library services and other apps presented in the club. Another variation to the device club could be a teen club similar to a study group. The purpose would be to introduce teens to more academic-based apps. This type of device club could demonstrate tutoring apps, research/database apps, and other apps offered by the library or other vendors.

An alternate approach to starting a device club could be integrating devices and digital library products into existing programs. Instead of asking patrons to commit to a new program, incorporate device training into current programs. For example, many libraries offer some type of genealogy program. This would be a great opportunity to introduce patrons to any genealogy apps or databases the library offers. Writing or memoir groups are another potential audience for device clubs. These groups could benefit from learning about some of library digital services as well as recording features on various devices.

Summary

There is no perfect formula for a successful device club. However, a library chooses to implement a device club, it is important for the library to make the club its own. This essay is meant to be a guide that, used in conjunction with the library staff's knowledge, can create another programming option to meet patron's needs while meeting the library's goals.

REFERENCES

Anderson, M. 2015. "Technology Device Ownership: 2015." *Pew Research Center*. Last accessed February 15, 2016, http://www.pewInternet.org/2015/10/29/technology-device-ownership-2015/.

Apple Inc. 2016. "iPad in Education." Last accessed, February 15, 2015, http://www.apple.com/au/education/ipad/apps-books-and-more/.

Atomiclearning.com. 2016. "Online Library Training Solution—Atomic Training." Last accessed February 21, 2016, https://www.atomiclearning.com/training/library-patron-training.

Boopsie.com. 2016a. "Boopsie Customer FAQ | Mobile Apps for Libraries." Last accessed February 16, 2016, http://www.boopsie.com/frequently-asked-questions/#library-mobile-strategy.

Boopsie.com. 2016b. "Mobile Apps for Libraries | Library Mobile Apps." Last accessed February 16, 2016, http://www.boopsie.com/.

Burleigh, D. 2015. "Public Libraries Evolving to Meet Readers' Needs in the Digital Age." *Overdrive*. Last accessed, February 20, 2016, http://company.overdrive.com/news/press-releases/public-libraries-evolving-to-meet-readers-needs-in-the-digital-age/.

Evancedsolutions.com. 2016. "Evanced Solutions." Last accessed, February 21, 2016. http://evancedsolutions.com/.

Goodreads.com. 2016. "About Goodreads." Last accessed, February 21, 2016, http://www.goodreads.com/about/us.

Gravatt, N. 2015. "2014 Digital Inclusion Survey Results Released." *American Library Association*. Last accessed, February 15, 2016, http://digitalinclusion.umd.edu/content/2014-digital-inclusion-survey-results-released.

Libraryideas.com. 2016. "Freading." Last accessed, February 21, 2016, http://www.libraryideas.com/freading.html.

Mango Languages. 2016. "#1 Language-Learning Resource in Public Libraries." Last accessed, February 21, 2016, http://www.mangolanguages.com/libraries/.

Scott County Public Library. 2015. "Computer Help." Last accessed, February 15, 2016, http://www.scottpublib.org/computer_help.php.

Schweiss, J., D. Foxworth, D., and W. Smith. 2014. "Tracking Wi-Fi: Demonstrating the Impact of Wireless Access." Presentation at Kentucky Library Association 2014 Spring Conference. http://kpla.pbworks.com/w/file/fetch/78769961/Tracking%20Wi-Fi.pdf.

How to Design a New Software Class

JULIA J. DAHM

You may develop a new technology class for a variety of reasons. Sometimes a software package, such as Microsoft Office programs, is heavily used, and you want to offer either a beginner or advanced workshop for those who use it every day. Other times, a new program, such as Prezi for designing presentations, gets a lot of buzz, and your audience is interested in seeing what it's all about.

This essay contains step-by-step instructions for creating a new software class, based on my technology instruction experience at the Health Sciences Library System at the University of Pittsburgh. The main focus is on productivity and creativity software, incorporating some of the programs that are used in a variety of academic and public settings by a broad audience.

Teaching software skills requires a different instructional style than an information session or lecture. To use the software more easily, your users must practice those skills. Many people turn to online video tutorials or step-by-step instructions for help on any number of subjects, but your target audience is probably looking for a more personalized approach where they can leave a class with a new set of acquired skills. For this reason, hands-on instruction is optimal for mastering new software. In this format, the instructor can demonstrate a set of instructions in front of the class, and each student can duplicate what the instructor does on his or her own computer. The following steps are aimed to provide a start-to-finish guide for creating a new hands-on software class.

When creating a new software class, start with setting up a production timeline. This is useful to allow enough time to plan and implement the class. Consider these steps when planning.

- Determining class session logistics.
- Developing class lessons and examples.
- Writing the handout.
- Practice sessions.
- Scheduling, advertising, and registration.
- Developing a class evaluation.
- Day-of-class preparation.
- Conducting the instruction.
- Changes for subsequent classes.

Determining Class Session Logistics

Before preparing the class, it's important to first identify the class logistics. Consider the following.

- Audience: Who will be attending? Will there be limits based on their experience with the software? Are they required to attend for their academic program or employer?
- Environment: Will the class be taught in the library or off-site? How many computers will be available? Will you have access to the computers prior to the class session?
- Duration: What timeframe is available, or can you set your own class duration? What duration would work best for your audience?

The content of the class should be adjusted for your audience. If it's open to the public, you should plan to describe the experience level (beginner, advanced) or address certain skills that will be covered in the class. If the class will be required for school or work, talk to the coordinator to see what type of skills they hope to be taught and if the class is related to a particular project. This will help you to develop examples.

The class environment will be most important for your practice sessions and day-of preparation. If the class will be taught in the library, you can more easily check that the correct version of the software is installed and practice the session as your audience will experience it. Because computers are configured differently, they may behave differently from when you develop the class on your office or personal computer. Practicing in advance will help you to plan your lessons and examples accordingly.

The duration of the class will help you to determine how much content can be covered. Since the class will be hands-on, and not lecture-based, the attention span and engagement of your audience will be somewhat longer. If your desired class content will take longer than the desired time, you may consider breaking up the class into multiple sessions.

Developing Class Lessons and Examples

In preparing to teach software for the first time, the best way to get started is to immerse yourself in the new software program. Your knowledge of the software will help you to better prepare the class and answer questions from the class attendees. If you see a menu option or button that is unfamiliar, click on it and see what happens. Start using the software for everyday tasks. For example, if you are drafting an agenda for a meeting, try typing it in the new software instead. Seeking online tutorials or other in-person workshops will also be useful. Seeing how someone else teaches the program tools will give you more ideas on how to teach it yourself.

Once you feel comfortable with the software program, you are ready to begin developing the class. Mapping out the flow of the class is important, since some skills will build upon themselves throughout the session. The class should conclude with a finished product. Start with a blank canvas or a partially developed document, and think of the steps you would need to take to end up with a final version.

In this type of scenario-based session, having examples will help guide your class. Sometimes examples are easy to identify from your audience, for example, if you have a group of students who are developing a presentation on cancer research. Other times, you will be looking for something more generic. A good fallback is to use the software itself as your example. For instance, if I am teaching a Prezi class, I will have the attendees design a presentation about Prezi, including a text bubble on signing up for a Prezi account, a PDF that advertises the library as place to get Prezi help, and a YouTube video on how to use the zoom feature in Prezi.

In teaching productivity software, usually more than one type of element is used, including text, images, graphics, and multimedia. To generate these types of files, you have the option of creating them yourself or finding examples elsewhere. You may be less restricted on how the files are used and distributed if you create them yourself, but you may have more options if you can identify files online that come with the proper usage rights. In the example of the Prezi class, I created a PDF by designing a document titled "Help with Prezi," including basic contact information, formatted it with a few different colors, and saved it as a PDF. This is a very simple way to create a new media item that I can safely distribute.

Writing the Handout

Handouts are very useful tools for hands-on software instruction. Handouts show the main tasks to be learned at a glance, and can help attendees get on track if they fall behind or work ahead. They also serve as a resource for the students after the class when the instructor is not there to guide them through the steps.

Start by creating a new document in Microsoft Word. Word has built-in formatting that makes it easy to create headings and a table of contents. Each lesson should have a title. Highlight the lesson title and click on Heading 1 from the Styles menu on the Home tab. Following the title, you may have some subtitle text that introduces the lessons or explains any items not covered in the steps that follow. Highlight the subtitle text and select Subtitle from the Styles menu. After that, number each step of the lesson. Since these are instructions, use concise, command language. Make sure that the words you use to describe items on the screen are spelled and capitalized exactly how they appear in the program. Each numbered item should start with a capitalized letter and end with a period. At the end of the numbered list, you may want to add an additional tip, which you can format using Subtle Emphasis. The following is an example lesson from Microsoft PowerPoint.

LESSON 5: CREATING SMARTART GRAPHICS

SmartArt Graphics provide shapes for text to represent lists, processes, hierarchies, relationships, and more.

1. Go to Slide 9: Graphic Options.
2. Right-click on the body text and select Convert to SmartArt.
3. Select More SmartArt Graphics to see the gallery of graphics.
4. Select a graphic from the list.
5. Change the look of your SmartArt Graphic by going to the SmartArt Tools-Design tab.

SmartArt Graphics can also be added by going to the Insert tab and selecting SmartArt.

Page numbers should also be added so that you can quickly reference where each lesson begins. From the Insert tab, click on the Page Number menu. Choose your preference for placing the number at the bottom or top of your pages.

Next, design a title page. Go to Page 1 and type the title of your class. Including your name and e-mail address is beneficial for attendees who wish to contact you with questions after the class. On this page, you can insert a table of contents from the References tab. If you have formatted your lesson titles as headings, they will automatically appear in the table of contents, along with a page number of where the lesson begins. When editing, the table of contents won't be updated automatically; instead, you must right-click on it to refresh data. You'll be given two options. Select Update Entire Table if you have changed or rearranged the headings, or select Update Page Numbers Only if you have just edited the steps of the lessons but have not rearranged them.

Practice Sessions

Reviewing your class materials will be an iterative process to improve the clarity and flow of your class content. Once your handout is complete, follow the lessons you wrote while performing it in the software. Make sure all the instructions are correct and make sense the way they are ordered. If possible, you should do this in the same environment you will be teaching in, using the student computers. Adjust your handout and instructions according to any differences you encounter.

Practicing in front of colleagues can also be very beneficial. You will rehearse how you will teach the lessons, and your colleagues can act as a student attending the class. Your colleague can provide feedback on your pace and clarity, as well as notify you of anything notable from the student perspective. Taking into account this feedback, you may update your lessons and examples again, until you are comfortable with a class session that will provide the maximum impact for your audience.

Scheduling, Advertising and Registration

The content of your class will greatly impact how long the class will last. Extra time may also be needed if your audience is more engaged or asks many questions. For roughly ten to 18 lessons, the class could take around two hours. A shorter class would be less in-depth, and could only cover a few key aspects of the software. A longer class can explore more lessons or work through multiple examples. A class longer than two hours may get tiresome for your audience, so consider breaking it up with a new activity or a midpoint break. Another option is to hold separate sessions on the same software, with the second building from the first.

The duration of the class should be estimated for scheduling purposes, though plan for the class to run up to 15 minutes past the scheduled time, allowing you some wiggle room if needed. To schedule the date and time, keep in mind your audience: is there a certain free slot in their weekly schedule, perhaps during lunch, or before or after class or normal work hours? If you are catering to a broad audience with varying schedules, it may be less clear what times will be best. Consider scheduling multiple sessions of the same class to accommodate a larger group.

Your class session will need a title. If possible, the title should target your audience with a brief description of what the class will accomplish, or for whom the class is intended. Using the words "Advanced," "Beginner," "Introduction," or "Basics," will help identify your audience. Also include the software title, and how the software will be used. Some examples are

- Adobe Photoshop for beginners;
- Advanced PowerPoint for presentations;
- PowerPoint for conference posters; and
- Prezi for presentations.

The class description should further clarify what the session will accomplish. Providing an accurate description is essential so your audience can determine how the class will benefit them. You may choose to list your lessons, or for a briefer version, describe what the finished document will include. Here is an example description:

ADVANCED POWERPOINT FOR PRESENTATIONS
Does your audience find your slides plain and boring? This hands-on workshop demonstrates ways to incorporate design, images, videos, and transitions into your PowerPoint presentations. We will discuss effective presentation tips and customizing handouts for your audience.

Your title and description are indispensable information for advertising your class. Timing the advertisement is important as well. Leave plenty of time before the class so that more people will hear about it and plan to attend before their schedules fill up. For a class that doesn't require registration, your audience may not decide until closer to the time whether they want to attend. This is a good reason to also advertise more widely during the week before the class.

When advertising, you should indicate if registration is required. Requiring registration is most helpful for the instructor to plan ahead for the amount of students. This also confirms for the attendee that they will have a seat reserved. But for an audience that has many commitments, requiring registration may discourage attendance. You can always appeal to both by encouraging prior registration but also allowing walk-ins if seats are available.

Developing a Class Evaluation

To further develop your topic and your teaching ability, ask for audience feedback with an evaluation form. Some questions should focus on the class itself, like the difficulty or quality of the skills learned, and some can reflect on your teaching style, such as your clarity or how you paced the material. You may ask about what they liked best or liked least for some new suggestions or areas that you can skip next time.

An evaluation form can also help with your advertising or future scheduling of the same class by asking about their day of the week or time of day availability. Evaluation feedback can be easily collected from online survey tools or by a paper form.

Day-of-Class Preparation

You are scheduled to teach a new software class, and now it's time to prepare yourself and your environment. Following this timeline will guide you to the typical setup steps.

- Earlier in the day or week:
    o Print and staple handouts.
    o Print a sign-in sheet or registration list.
    o Print evaluation forms.
    o Prepare an introduction presentation with the class name, date, time, your name, and your contact information.
- 15–30 minutes prior to the class:
    o Bring any necessary items to the classroom, including handouts, a sign in sheet or registration list, evaluation forms, and examples files that are being used in the class, if not already loaded onto the computers.
    o Load any files you need onto your instructor computer and to the student computers. If you plan to visit websites during the class, having them already loaded in the browser can come in handy.
    o Pull up the first slide of your introductory presentation. This will help them know they are in the right place when they arrive.
- 5–15 minutes prior to the class:
    o Have your attendees sign in or check their name on a registration sheet.
    o Pass out handouts or leave a stack for them to pick up.
    o Greet attendees and answer any questions they may have prior to the class beginning.
- 0–5 minutes prior to the class:
    o Set the lights to dim.
    o Place handouts and sign-in sheet near the door for anyone arriving late.
    o Announce that the class will start in a few minutes.

Conducting the Instruction

When the class begins, make sure to introduce yourself and the class session. It's important to let your audience know what to expect from the session. This is also a good time to talk about the class duration, which you may be able to estimate a little more accurately based on attendance at that time. The audience will be more accepting of a class running late if you mention that possibility before the class begins. You may also notify your audience of the class evaluation at this time; if they decide to leave the class early, they will then know to fill out the evaluation before they leave.

For the hands-on portion of your class, follow the lessons as you rehearsed. You will need to go slower than you think for the audience to see your motions on the screen and to duplicate them on their own computers. Describe your motions, such as where you are clicking or if you are holding down a key. Give directions in relation to the screen, for example, if an option is in the top right corner or third button from the left. Repeat your steps at pivotal points, and ask for questions between lessons. It may seem like a long silence, but waiting ten seconds for questions will allow them the time needed to formulate a question.

As you can imagine, the class may not always go as rehearsed. Sometimes you have late arrivals, people who get lost, computer problems, or students who start exploring on their own. How do you manage all of this as an instructor? One of the main decisions you'll need to make is when to step away from the front of the class to attend to a student. For a small class, this is less interruptive and usually well tolerated by the class as a whole. A larger class may become more impatient if you need to step away often. Each situation is different, but many times you can get a lost or late student back on track by pointing out where you are in the handout. Since the handout has step-by-step directions, they can follow by reading to catch up with the class.

Sometimes a student will have a question that you can't replicate from your computer. You may decide to look at their computer to remedy the issue or answer the question. For bigger computer issues, like if the program crashes, having them switch seats is a good option. They may also look at another computer. For any of these situations, aim for a good balance. A struggling student will value some individual help as needed, but the class as a whole should still receive the majority of your attention.

Upon finishing the class, take questions. Ask if there's anything that they had hoped to learn in the class that you didn't cover. Not everyone will think of questions right away, and some may prefer not to ask in front of the group, so make sure you restate your contact information for those who wish to ask questions later. Encourage your audience to fill out the evaluation form by letting them know that their feedback will help improve future classes.

Changes for Subsequent Classes

Now that you've taught your first class, you will have a good idea of what went well and where improvements could be made. This is time to plan any future sessions of the class. As you plan your next class, consider your audience feedback when you revisit your lessons. Even after you make adjustments from feedback, you must also practice your class before each session. Computers and software programs are moving targets-there is always something changing, and you might find that a change has a significant impact on your class structure. When you go through your lessons, take note of any change in labels and menus, and practice inserting or downloading files to make sure everything acts as you would expect. If you are using websites as resources, take note of any recent changes. For online software, like Prezi, you may see updates much more often than software that is run locally from the desktop.

In this essay, you learned the steps to take to prepare, practice, and conduct a software instruction session using a hands-on method. With each class you teach, you'll learn more about the software and how to respond to the needs of your audience. You'll also experience how rewarding it is to see your audience practicing new skills in a personal setting and becoming independent technology users.

How to Design a Non-Traditional Software Class
PowerPoint for Conference Posters

JULIA J. DAHM

Software packages like Microsoft PowerPoint commonly serve a specific purpose, such as creating slides and displaying presentations. With a wide array of tools, the software can sometimes serve many purposes. Instruction that shows a user how to think outside the box with a software package can demonstrate how tools that normally serve one purpose can be expanded to fulfill different technology needs.

This essay will give you step-by-step instructions on how to teach a software package for non-traditional use. Microsoft PowerPoint is a commonly-used program for making slides, but it can also be used to make a variety of other purposes, including posters. While the example of PowerPoint for poster design is used throughout the essay, this information can also be useful for anyone who plans to teach a software class with a particular product in mind, whether it is a common or unique product of that software.

The following steps are based on a class titled PowerPoint for Conference Posters, which I teach to interested students, staff, and faculty at the University of Pittsburgh Health Sciences Library System. In a two-hour session, the attendees learn about poster design principles in a lecture format, and then create a poster from their computer by following the instructor and using example files. A current version of Microsoft PowerPoint is used to design the poster, but the class incorporates the use of Microsoft Word, Microsoft Excel, PDFs, and image files, keeping in mind that attendees will be using a variety of programs and file types to pull together their information for a poster.

Choosing Microsoft PowerPoint as the software for a poster project is a good way to teach a novice user how to bridge from slide design to poster design. The ability to move text boxes and objects freely on a slide, and the option to scale a slide to a much bigger proportion, allows your user to create layouts and designs easily.

To design your own class that teaches how to produce a conference poster in PowerPoint, follow these main steps.

- Determine the audience.
- Discuss design strategies.
- Discuss program limitations.
- Work with sample files.

- Practice with layouts.
- Edit existing content.
- Create new content.
- Discuss printing process.

Determine the Audience

The targeted attendees are those who are planning to present a topic at a conference poster session. These individuals could be associated with a number of disciplines in the arts, humanities, and sciences. Some topics are focused heavily on research while others may be project descriptions or broad overviews of programs and services. The audience should have a basic understanding of PowerPoint, with prior experience using the program to create slides.

In the PowerPoint for Conference Posters class, the main focus is on how to use PowerPoint to create a well-designed conference poster. Your audience should already know, or plan to discuss in other forums, considerations such as selecting a topic, narrowing information, or applying for acceptance into a conference. Focusing exclusively on design topics in this class allows your audience to walk away having practiced the different tools and skills they will need for creating their own poster.

Discuss Design Strategies

PowerPoint presentations are created digitally and generally viewed digitally as well while posters are created digitally but are primarily viewed in their printed physical form. Therefore, becoming knowledgeable on how a digital format translates to printed format will be pivotal information to share with your students. For instance, establish guidelines for font sizes so that they can be read from a few feet away. This will give your audience some perspective on how the size of what they see on the screen relates to a much larger printed poster.

In this age of infographics and highly visual information, posters must convey data, research, and detailed information in a way that is easy to understand and pleasing to view. Discuss how to balance the three main elements of a poster: text, graphics, and blank space. Graphics, such as charts, tables, and pictures, help to draw in a viewer and convey complex information in a short amount of time. Text should be concise and essential to the topic. Blank space is necessary to make the poster appear uncluttered and easy to follow.

Color selection is another important topic to discuss. Colors build visual interest, tie together a look and feel, and also display clarity between content and background. Multiple colors should be encouraged to create an aesthetically pleasing poster; however, too many different colors can be distracting. Additionally, the color of text should have a high amount of contrast with the background, such as black text on a light background, or white text on a dark background. Backgrounds can be colorful, but a background that is too colorful or too busy is discouraged. Instruct your audience on selecting a few different types of backgrounds that are interesting but do not take attention away from the important content that will be displayed on the poster.

One of the bigger challenges to the audience is how to get started organizing their content into a layout. Some people don't feel creative enough to come up with an eye-catching design like posters they have seen elsewhere. Discuss using templates: where you can find them and how to customize them while applying the design principles established in the class. Also, share a variety of examples with your audience. Having one or two printed posters on display is ideal, but could be cost-prohibitive if you don't already own them. Look for and share examples of posters online to help your audience brainstorm ways to turn their topic into a well-designed poster.

Discuss Program Limitations

Another important topic for your audience is a review of software limitations. When you use a software package for an alternate purpose, you may find that you can't exactly do everything you want. Talk about work-arounds for these types of limitations. For instance, the maximum size of a PowerPoint slide is 56 inches tall by 56 inches wide. To create posters of greater sizes, explain how a poster can be enlarged in a later step, such as after it has been saved as a PDF or by the printing service.

Additionally, PowerPoint will not be the only program used to gather and assimilate the content of the poster. Brainstorm the types of files and programs that may be used, such as Microsoft Excel, images from the web, statistical analysis exports, and works cited lists. Be prepared to demonstrate the best way to work with these files and programs. You should give an overview of intellectual property rights and provide resources for further information. For instance, students should walk away knowing that they cannot download any image they find on Google and print it on the poster, but you could also provide information about how to find free images on the web that can be used with proper attribution and replication.

Work with Sample Files

In the PowerPoint for Conference Posters class, the discussion on design elements is followed by step-by-step instructions. Providing sample files for your audience will provide a scenario similar to their own before creating the poster. A good place to get started is to create a sample poster yourself. Perhaps you have designed a poster in the past, or you can research different topics for ideas that are familiar to your audience. Try to include a variety of content as to give many examples to your attendees to maneuver. Your poster may include

- title and subtitle;
- author names and institutions;
- introduction;
- objectives;
- results;
- tables;
- charts/graphs;
- pictures;

- SmartArt Graphics;
- shapes;
- logos;
- conclusion;
- references;
- acknowledgements; and
- contact information.

Your audience may be developing their files outside of PowerPoint, or creating content primarily within PowerPoint. Plan to practice both; identify some files from other programs that can be copied or imported to the poster, and others that can be created from within PowerPoint. Sample text and table data will need to be supplied to your audience, since it would take too long to type out during the class.

Practice with Layouts

In the hands-on section of your class, instruct your students to take the samples files and combine them to achieve a finished poster. Start by designing the poster size and style. By default, PowerPoint will start a blank presentation with a slide sized for standard screen or widescreen display; demonstrate how to change the dimensions to that of a poster by using the Design tab. Other design features, such as using theme colors, fonts, and background styles should be addressed.

Prepare to organize the poster content by designing a layout. A layout is a guide to where the content should go, showing the borders between content and blank space. This can be done by adding rectangles to achieve visual borders: one for a title, and one for each section or column. For more advanced users, you may set up layouts using Slide Master and PowerPoint's built in content boxes. It is important to extensively explore the size and position of shapes, as well as alignment tools. Since posters will appear much larger than the computer screen, show your attendees how to ensure that all columns are exactly the same height and width, and that the edges all line up precisely to each other. The Format Shape pane, which may not be commonly used in PowerPoint slide design, is an important tool to show your audience for these tasks. Alignment commands, such as Align Left and Distribute Horizontally, can be found on the Drawing Tools Format tab or under the Arrange menu from the Home tab.

Edit Existing Content

With a layout in place, you will now begin to organize your existing content. For text editing, refer to the design principles discussed at the beginning on the class. Demonstrate how to select appropriate text size, color, and paragraph spacing. Paragraph text that is too small or too close together will look cluttered, so extra text may need to be eliminated, or reformatted into shorter phrases or bullet points.

Data in tables should also be optimized. Look at cell spacing, text size, and shading that is colorful but subtle. Talk about chart data in Office format, and how it can be customized to match the poster. Sometimes chart or graph data is exported from other programs. If the exported file is an image, it may not match your poster design or display at a high enough quality. For these reasons, you can suggest adding a new chart from the Insert tab, and retyping the data into the Office formatted chart.

Picture files can also be formatted in new ways to add visual interest to your poster. The coloration of an image can be easily manipulated, made brighter or darker, high or low contrast, or recolored in any of the theme colors. An image can also be scaled and cropped, but advise the audience not to enlarge a picture too much: doing so may create a pixilated image when printed in a large format.

Create New Content

After you have incorporated existing files and content into the poster, show the audience how to add new content from within PowerPoint. One of PowerPoint's hidden gems is the SmartArt Graphic: this is a way to display bulleted text in a graphical format. It can simply show a list with each phrase as its own shape; it can be as complex as showing an organizational chart to display how different objects or ideas are connected to each other.

A SmartArt Graphic is especially useful in posters that may have a lot of text and not a lot of applicable graphics. By placing your text in a SmartArt Graphic, it will be perceived as an illustration while still conveying information. SmartArt Graphics can be designed with colors and effects to match the poster theme.

A screenshot is an image file that can be produced from a computer screen to capture what a desktop application or website looks like. A screenshot may be useful for a poster that is explaining a program or orienting others to a web resource. Screenshots can be inserted from within PowerPoint from the Insert tab. The clarity of a screenshot will vary depending on your computer monitor resolution and the size of the text and graphics on the screen. A helpful tip for your audience is to increase a web page size by using the Zoom In feature on most browsers. To check that the screenshot will not be blurry, use the Zoom control from the status bar in Microsoft PowerPoint to preview it at a much larger size.

A poster is often an opportunity to discuss your research or program with other interested individuals in your field. This collaboration can be facilitated by adding some supplementary information to your poster, such as a link to your school program, or a QR code for mobile users to save your e-mail address to their phone or tablet. Instruct students to add a text box in an unused part of their poster with such information. QR codes can be generated and downloaded from a variety of Web sites.

Discuss Printing Process

After leading the class through the creation of a poster, discuss their last step in moving from digital to print format, which is having their poster printed. Many business stores and online printing services are available for this part of the process, so the logistics will vary depending on the service they choose. Be sure to mention any necessary steps from a software perspective, which will include saving the poster in PowerPoint. Show your audience how to save as a PowerPoint file (.pptx) so that it can be edited, and how to save their final version as a PDF, which may be the preferred format for the printer. Advise the audience to look at the different paper and size options, and to request a proof before having the poster printed at full size. Printing a poster can be costly, so it is important to ensure that their poster is in the optimal format before achieving its final form.

The size of the poster you design in PowerPoint may not be the size of poster you would like to be printed. Explain to your audience how they should address this in their design and how to discuss this with the printing company. The process is simplest when designing within the constraints of PowerPoint slide sizes. For example, if you want a poster that is four feet wide by three feet tall, you would set your PowerPoint slide size to 48 inches wide by 36 inches tall. This poster would be printed at 100 percent, or full size. However, you may want a poster that is five feet wide by four feet tall, but you cannot set your slide size to over 56 inches wide. In this case, you would need to determine a smaller size to use for designing in PowerPoint. Set your dimensions as large as possible without going above the maximum, or decide on a percentage, like 125 percent larger, that you can communicate to the printer. Here is how both scenarios would be calculated to get the proportions right for a five foot (60-inch) by four foot (48-inch) poster.

SCENARIO 1: USING THE MAXIMUM DIMENSIONS IN POWERPOINT TO DETERMINE THE SIZE
- In PowerPoint, set the slide width to 56-inch maximum. The height will need to be in the right proportion. Find the percentage:
    o 56 (actual) divided by 60 (desired) is 93.333 percent
- Multiply the percentage by the desired height to get the actual height:
    o 0.93333 (percent) multiplied by 48 (desired) is 44.8 inches

In Scenario 1, your poster will be 56 inches wide by 44.8 inches tall in PowerPoint, and you will ask the printer to enlarge it to 60 inches wide by 48 inches tall.

SCENARIO 2: USING A PERCENTAGE TO DETERMINE THE DIMENSIONS IN POWERPOINT
- Determine a percentage you want to increase, such as 125 percent
- Divide your width and height by that percentage to receive your PowerPoint dimensions:
    o 60 inches (desired) divided by 1.25 (percent) is 48 inches
    o 48 inches (desired) divided by 1.25 (percent) is 38.4 inches

In Scenario 2, your poster will be 48 inches wide by 38.4 inches tall in PowerPoint, and you will ask the printer to enlarge the poster by 125 percent, or to a dimension of 60 inches wide by 48 inches tall.

Though it takes proper planning to have the poster sized correctly, it's a very important step. A poster that is enlarged too much may display blurry graphics. Sometimes the blurry graphics can't be detected from a proof, since it is much smaller than the actual poster size. If the sizes are not to proportion, then the poster may look like it is stretched too far wide or squeezed on the correct size. To help with your explanation of correct sizing, you may come up with a guide of commonly used sizes that your audience can choose from.

Once your session has ended, your audience should have gained the basic building blocks for poster design, and how to use the tools in PowerPoint to create a poster from start to finish. The class combines a lecture portion to introduce design topics, and a hands-on portion to practice with the software. In addition, you can enhance your poster design session by a few preparation steps prior to the class.

- Prepare a printed handout with the design guidelines, step-by-step instructions for creating the sample poster, a mock-up of the poster to be designed in the class, and links for templates and intellectual property guidelines.
- Load example files on the student computers prior to class and test the computer for accuracy with your step-by-step instructions.
- Mount sample posters in the classroom or on portable bulletin boards so the audience can see the size and look of a printed poster.

The instructions in this essay are geared towards poster design, but they can be applied to other types of projects using PowerPoint. For instance, users who are looking to add new skill sets to creating presentations will find it useful to learn about SmartArt Graphics, choosing backgrounds, and understanding the Format Shape pane. Flyers and handouts are also designed commonly in a wide variety of disciplines; you can teach how to scale a PowerPoint slide to be the size of a flyer, and discuss how to incorporate a variety of file and content types onto one sheet.

In this essay, you learned how to teach your own class on using PowerPoint to create conference posters. With this advice, you can introduce your patron base to a unique product of a software program that is commonly used for another purpose. You may find a niche audience that highly values this instruction, or you can apply some of the ideas towards another class that looks at products of software packages that are outside the box.

Ways to Use Digital Badges in the Library
They're Not Just for Students Anymore

Laura Bohuski

Digital badges are a growing part of the new and innovative ways that educators and librarians are motivating students to learn. This learning is happening in universities, in elementary schools, in a person's home, and in libraries. But digital badges do not need to be confined to any one area of learning, they do not even have to be used by teachers to encourage students to learn and grow in interesting ways. Badges could be used to display the level of competency a person has achieved outside of academia, to train a new or current employee, to enhance collaboration, and in many other ways. This essay will look at new and varied uses for digital badges and how they could be implemented within the library. First though, we must look at what digital badges are and what pros and cons we might encounter when using them.

What Are Digital Badges?

The MacArthur Foundation (an independent organization that supports learning, creativity, and human rights) describes digital badges as a credentialing and assessment instrument housed online that could validate formal and informal learning and change where and how learning is valued (MacArthur Foundation 2014). This description, while correct, does not tell you what a digital badge, here after referred to as "badge," really is or how it works.

Badges are a combination of a clearly identifiable image or logo and embedded metadata that defines the scope of the achievement the badge is being used to represent. What this actually means is that whoever is issuing the badge (a university, a community college, an online workshop, a school or public library, or any other entity) designs a logo or an image to represent themselves and the achievement they are awarding. For example, an academic library might use its school logo as the background image with a banner or text in the foreground proclaiming the title of the achievement, like "Research Expert." This image is saved in .PNG format, a common extension for an image file similar to a .JPEG or .GIF, and becomes the public and visual representation of a badge earner's achievement.

The other half of the badge is embedded, invisibly, in the .PNG image. This embedded information is textual data that is, in badge vocabulary, "baked" into the coding of the image. This textual data does not in any way change the look or design of the badge image and only by clicking on a displayed badge, which has been assigned to a specific person, could the data attached to the image be retrieved. The data for each badge is linked to that specific image and to the badge earner through an e-mail address, and could include a wealth of information.

Though a great deal of information could be stored in a badge, there are a few metadata fields that are required to make a badge valid. The required fields include

- the company or organization the issued the badge (the issuer);
- the name of the person who received the badge (the earner);
- the earner's e-mail address (so the badge could be issued to that specific person);
- the date issued;
- the name of the badge;
- the criteria required for receiving the badge; and
- any evidence, or URL links to evidence, that could prove the completion of the stated criteria.

The embedding of the metadata in the image helps to deter the duplication of the badge image to falsify credentialization. The data baked into the image is permanently linked to the institution that issued the badge and to the person who received it. When a badge is clicked on, the data embedded in the image generates a webpage for the viewer to examine the embedded metadata. If the encoding attached to the badge does not match information being requested from the server that hosts that information, the verification of the badge fails and the requested information could not be received or an error message displays.

So, a badge, at its most basic, is an image that functions similarly to a hyperlink. This image has information attached through the use of computer coding that could be read by anyone who clicks on the image. Once clicked, the badge opens a pop-up window that displays the information in an easy to read format. Badges are a quick and easy way to display information about anyone's achievements both in the classroom, in the library, and outside of academic settings.

Pros and Cons of Badges

In this age of advancing technology, we are able to attach a wealth of information to an image approximately the size of a computer icon. This image is so small it could be placed anywhere without taking up too much screen space. Badges could be added to personal webpages, electronic resumes, faculty/staff websites, or any digital forum one could imagine. The implications of badge's usefulness extend beyond the classroom; badges could be used for more than just documenting that a student or patron has successfully completed a lesson or a workshop. They could be used to highlight accomplishments such as volunteering or public speaking, they could be used to help secure a job, and they could even help craft a career path through websites such as Mozilla Discover.

Badges are similar to the teaching tool known as gamification, which is the use of common aspects of gameplay to other areas of activity. Badges could become motivational tools for students and patrons who lack the drive to accomplish achievements, either inside or outside the classroom, on their own. They could be used in the same way as trophies or achievements are used in games where completing a goal, or in this case receiving a badge, rewards them for completing that objective. Receiving the badge may also unlock the earner's ability to access and complete other badges. More levels may become available, or areas of badge earning that were previously hidden could be revealed when the first badge has been earned. Badges could not only help earners display credentials they have received through hard work, but they could be motivating tools in and of themselves.

As with every reward system though, there could also be downsides. It is not easy to duplicate a badge; the verification system embedded in the image's metadata helps to deter cheating in this manner, however, the verification only works if both parties understand how badges function. If each badge is not verified, then simply copying a badge image and pasting it onto a resume or website could be enough to falsely advertise a skill set. There are also those who figure out how to cheat the system, either through providing false evidence to receive a badge, by hacking, or through the creation of their own badge which comes with no official credentials.

In addition to cheating the system, there is the concern that students, patrons in the library, and employees could become too badge focused. Badges are a great supplement to traditional learning, and they are a fantastic way to denote professional development or a competency achieved outside of an academic setting, but they should not be relied upon as a complete assessment tool. Some educators are also worried that the use of badges might remove the drive of those who are already self-motivated, or that the use of badges may cause other students, patrons, or employees to concentrate too much on only achieving the goals related to badge completion. Similar to how schools are focusing more on teaching to the standardized tests, students would become focused on completing a badge instead of achieving badges as they learn.

Badges from the Classroom to the Library

Badges intrinsically lend themselves to use either inside an academic environment or through roles of formal learning, but this is not the limit of where and when badges could be used. Already there are many companies and organizations that are using badges as part of continuing education or professional development. Badges could become a part of training programs for employees within libraries, they could be integrated into library programming, and used by libraries to facilitate learning in an academic environment.

Badges to Promote Training in the Library

Training staff, faculty, or students in a library could often be difficult as the learning management systems and integrated library systems used in academic, school, and public libraries could be hard for new employees to understand. Without documentation of how current workflows are accomplished when any employee leaves, institutional memory could be lost. Badges could halt some of this loss through the creation of training badges. Badges are incredibly flexible in terms of the achievements they represent and, once a badge system is implemented, they could be created by anyone. The flexibility of task recognition within badge systems allows for the creation of badges that are personalized to the jobs of individual library employees. Each employee could then create a collection of badges that represents their job by creating a badge for every job task that they complete.

The author's library is currently transitioning to the use of a new integrated library system. After the transition is complete, workflows in our library will undergo major changes as the new system lends itself to creating different ways of accomplishing tasks. When these new workflows are determined and both faculty and staff are comfortable in their new positions, we could begin to document how people complete the tasks that fall under their purview. With the creation of this documentation, it will be easy to create badges for each person's job. The following paragraphs include an example of how badges might be put into effect in the author's library after the new integrated library system has been implemented.

Library employees, whether they are faculty, staff, or students, complete multiple separate tasks in the execution of their jobs. Some of these tasks are common; they are actions an employee repeats multiple times per day or week. But some tasks are of a more unusual nature and are only completed once a month or a few times a year. Each of these tasks combine to delineate specifically the steps an employee follows to accomplish their job. If each employee outlined the tasks they complete in the course of their job, then a badge could be created for all the tasks that are completed in the department. The criteria required for the verification of each badge would be the successful completion of the task with evidence provided through a screenshot or verification by a superior.

Since each job incorporates multiple tasks, and for training purposes in the case of a new employee or a student worker, each library employee would be required to complete multiple badges in order to be proclaimed proficient at their job and earn the final badge assigned to their job title. The collection of badges earned toward the final badge, would also allow new hires to come into a position having a clear set of tasks they need to learn in order to achieve a basic level of competency in their job. The breakdown of overarching, or "Job" badges, into smaller task badges would reduce the number of badges that needed to be created by applying the same badge to multiple job tracks. A benefit of breaking down each job into component tasks is that employees could then be cross trained just in a specific task, such as simple cataloging or placing book orders, and still receive recognition for completing that specific skill set.

The earning of badges does not have to be limited to an employee's current job. If any library department wished for its employees to be cross trained, the badge system is a great way to ensure that there will always be a person who could complete a needed task. Once badges have been created for a task or a job, anyone could be asked to complete a badge for any task that has a definable workflow. If earned badges are then displayed on employee webpages or on a departmental page that is used to display earned badges, a list of those employees who could accomplish the required task is easily accessible.

Badges in Professional Development

The earning of badges does not have to be a linear accomplishment, progressing in a straight line from one task to the next. Multiple badges could be earned in multiple different areas, and when this occurs new badges or tracks could be unlocked. The idea is to stack the badges together, earning new ones as new tasks are learned or mastered, and when all of the tasks associated with a specific job or project are earned, the earner unlocks, and is issued, the definitive badge for their completion. This badge could be applied to an employee or personal webpage, attached to a resume, or the employee could print out the image and display their achievements in any manner they wish.

In an academic, public or school library setting, badges could be used to track requirements for promotion or tenure. For example, as a new faculty member, it is difficult to understand everything that must be accomplished to receive tenure, especially in light of the fact that the requirements for tenure could vary between universities or even departments within the same university. The issuing of badges would in no way guarantee the conveyance of tenure, but it could be a method used to help facilitate the completion of required accomplishments. There could be a badge for publication, one for presentations, and another to document communication both within the university and outside of it. There could even be multiple levels of badges; if someone is more prolific with publications or with presenting, they could achieve a higher level badge in that year to demonstrate their extra effort. The badges could be re-issued every year, with continuance badges given once a year as milestones to acknowledge that continuance has been granted to the earner. If there are special requirements at an institution that faculty are required to meet before continuance, or tenure, could be granted, those badges could be added as well to facilitate the achievement of tenure. Tenure or promotion "badge trees" could be displayed on promotion and tenure websites or within documentation as a visual checklist for the completion of tenure.

Similar to the ideas of using task badges for cross training and the earning multiple badges to achieve an ultimate or definitive badge, the use of badges in professional development could follow the same configuration. When undertaking professional development by attending workshops or webinars or conferences, employees (faculty, staff, and students) might not receive visible recognition of having completed those tasks. Although attending these professional development opportunities may grant an employee a check mark on their next evaluation, there is not usually another recognition system in place to internally reward employees so they are motivated to continue learning. Badges could become both a reward system for library employees and a way for administrators to keep track of employee achievements, large or small.

In any library that promoted professional development for their employees, badges could either be created for each individual achievement an employee accomplishes, or badges could be linked to a series of accomplishments. For example, if a staff member watches five webinars then they could receive a "Webinar" badge to add to their evaluation forms. Or if they attended a conference they could receive a "2015 Conference X Attendee" badge. This could become a way to track events that staff, students, or faculty participate in, and it also makes the information readily available and at more than the departmental level. If desired, the badges could be incorporated into evaluations or social media to be displayed outside of the department for recognition.

Badges in the Library

Training and professional development are both ways in which to use badges in the library. So far these uses have been explained in the context of library employees, and there are other uses for badges that could engage patrons in public, academic, and school libraries. The use that almost immediately comes to mind is as a part of library instruction. This is likely the most common use for badges in libraries, but the use of badges within the library does not have to be limited to library instruction.

Badges could be used effectively in library instruction, and to develop collaboration between the library and other departments in an academic setting. The skills taught in a library instruction class improve a patron's ability to effectively use the library. Since there are many components to library skills, badges could be created for each skill being taught. For example; a badge for "Database Searching," one for "Identifying Sources," and another for "Analyzing Information" would all be badges earned during a library instruction or information literacy course. These badges could be combined together as components that unlock the receipt of a high-level badge, such as a "Researcher" badge, that students could receive at the end of their course.

Badges similar to these could also be earned through the library in conjunction with other departments on campus. Since specific research skills are needed in different departments, badges could be developed that link information literacy in the library to research methods for a specific discipline. If a professor had an assignment that requires students to conduct research in the library, a badge could be used to provide verification that the student did indeed use the library to complete their research project instead of retrieving information from the Internet. The form of assessment required to complete this badge could have the student engaging a reference librarian for help in locating resources, or have the student provide a screen shot of their database search that resulted in a source the student used in their research project. In this way badges could be used to facilitate collaboration between libraries and other disciplines.

Badges were created to help with the recognition of achievements that are not usually recognized through formal means. This is ideal for many libraries that offer courses or learning opportunities for patrons. Public, academic, and school libraries could create badges to promote the skills they are helping their patrons to learn, whether in a formal classroom setting or not. For those patrons needing to learn basic skills such as Microsoft Excel or typing to more advanced skills like Adobe Photoshop and basic Web design, these are all accomplishments that could, and should, be recognized. When learning opportunities are offered through any library, badges are excellent ways to validate a patron's accomplishments. For those patrons seeking to improve their skills for school a job, these badges could be placed on resumes, personal webpages, or social media sites, such as LinkedIn, as digital and visual representations of their skills and motivation.

Conclusion

Badges have a variety of uses both in and out of the library. They could highlight achievements and competencies that normally have no official form of recognition. These achievements could range from the successful completion of a basic Microsoft Excel course to completing training either at a new job, or within a new computer system, or for skills attained through a class or through life experience. Through the acknowledgment of these achievements, badges could motivate students and patrons within class settings, they could help patrons to increase their skills in the job market, they could motivate faculty and staff to engage in professional development, and they could facilitate both the retention of knowledge and training of workflows within the workplace. What makes badges such a good technology to implement is that users do not have to change how a class is structured or create new forms of assessment to effectively incorporate badges. Badges work with the methods that are already in place and could be used to enhance current approaches. Though there are disadvantages to the implementation of any new technology, the benefits of badges to libraries and to patrons far outweigh the disadvantages.

REFERENCES

"About Credly." *Credly*. Accessed October 6, 2015. https://credly.com/about.
"Alliance to Increase Access to Open Badges." *MacArthur Foundation*. Published June 26, 2014. https://www.macfound.org/press/from-field/alliance-increase-access-open-badges/.
"Badges." *MozillaWiki*. Last modified December 18, 2014. https://wiki.mozilla.org/Open_Badges.
"Badges/FAQ." *MozillaWiki*. Last modified March 26, 2014. https://wiki.mozilla.org/Badges/FAQs.
"Create Badges and Badge Systems." *University of Texas at Austin*. Accessed November 10, 2015. https://openbadges.coerll.utexas.edu/create-badges/.
"Digital Badges." *hastac*. Accessed October 22, 2015. https://www.hastac.org/initiatives/digital-Badges.
"Discover Open Badges." *Mozilla Discover*. Accessed November 13, 2015. http://discover.openbadges.org/.
Grant, Sheryl. 2014. *What Counts as Learning: Open Digital Badged for New Opportunities*. Irvine, CA: Digital Media and Learning Research Hub. PDF e-book.
Madda, Mary Jo. 2015. "How to Make Micro-Credentials Matter." *edSurge*. February 2. https://www.edsurge.com/news/2015–02–02-how-to-make-micro-credentials-Matter.
Meinke, Billy. 2012. "Open Badges: Want to Make Your Own Badges by Hand? Here's How." *Billy Meinke* (blog). Posted on May 24, 2012. https://billymeinke.wordpress.com/2012/05/24/open-badges-want-to-make-your-own-badges-by-hand-heres-how/.
"Open Badges." *Mozilla Open Badges*. Accessed October 17, 2015. http://openbadges.org/.

Beyond the One-Shot
Online Video Tutorials for International Students

MICHELLE EMANUEL

More often than not, a student's first experience to use a college/university library—beyond a quiet place to study or a place to get coffee between classes—is during a library instruction session held a few weeks before the due date of the first research assignment of the semester. Thankfully, due to library outreach instruction initiatives, more and more students are coming into the library with at least one of their classes during their first-year experience, rather than waiting until the second semester of their senior year. Whether a lower division or upper division course, the appointments that faculty make to bring in their students can be a whirlwind orientation for the novice user, with information specific to a particular course combined with intellectual concepts of information literacy, all within the time constraint of 50 to 75 minutes. So much rides on this "one-shot" session because it is the only time during the semester that the entire class will be in the same room with both a librarian and the professor. Though we as librarians know that the one-shot really is not sufficient to meet a student's information needs, especially in light of the recently-adopted ACRL Framework, we also know that in many cases, that is the only class time that the professor is willing to relinquish to us. Librarians have learned that it makes for a more efficient session if the students' topics have been approved in advance, but questions may still arise about the nature of the assignment (*Can we use articles from newspapers?*), or about how to access particular resources (*Why is it asking me for my password?*). If the topic has not been selected and approved in advance, the approval process can eat away at already limited time. International students, often new to an institution, to university-level studies, as well as to a particular country, must learn to use the same resources as their classmates while also interpreting the cultural cues of the library itself: where to be quiet, where to study with friends, how to access resources and even how to take them out of the building. International students do not assume that they can check out books, or go to the stacks themselves, or even ask the librarian a question; they have to be told this. Sin closely examines the information behaviors of international students (2015), and the challenges they face. But how to add cultural information to an already jam-packed one-shot session? Her study examines the use of library resources by international students, including Everyday Life Information Seeking (ELIS), and finds that "while some online sources (e.g., Web search engines) were frequently used, sources considered to be traditional (e.g., print and mass media) were also often-used" (473). One challenge is that "international students are often found to not be fully aware of the whole range of library services available to them" (467). In addition to their academic needs, international students often have difficulty "finding relevant and trustworthy daily life information" (467) on topics ranging from legal, financial, and health information to important local issues. "Scholarship as a conversation" is thereby complicated by a language barrier.

At the University of Mississippi (UM), like many American institutions of higher learning, international students must demonstrate proficiency in English before they are allowed to enroll in university-level courses. If they have not yet achieved a certain score on the Test of English as a Foreign Language (TOEFL), they can enroll in UM's Intensive English Program (IEP). Their incoming language level is assessed, and they follow a schedule of courses over multiple semesters—focusing on reading, writing, grammar, or speaking and listening—until they can successfully complete the "Advanced Plus" sequence. In their final semester in Advanced Plus, they take a course called "English for Academic Purposes," which is structured much like a standard course in an American university, and includes a research project. The student is encouraged to choose a topic in the field that s/he will be studying once admitted to UM. To successfully complete this project, the students in the English for Academic Purposes course are required to visit the library.

In the University of Mississippi Libraries (UML), subject selectors offer library instruction for both lower and upper division courses to the departments they work with. In the case of the IEP, this instruction fell to the selector for its parent department, Modern Languages. After years of working with the English for Academic Purposes class, often taught by different instructors, I found that this particular course had different needs from my regular one-shot instruction sessions for Spanish and French. These particular students were not looking for resources in language and literature, which has always been the focus of my instruction. In our library, technical services librarians with subject expertise, like me, are allowed and encouraged to participate as subject selectors. Though I have experience at a reference desk from earlier in my library career, I am not as familiar with all of the ins and outs of our current databases, as I am not teaching students how to use them on a weekly basis during a shift at a public desk. Instead, I decided, what the IEP students really needed was a reference librarian with instruction experience in multiple areas to point them in the right direction for questions about science and engineering, business, psychology, and other subjects. The instructor of the IEP course, however, did not share my enthusiasm, and was reluctant to make this change. She said that her past students had appreciated my general introduction to library services, tailored specifically to international students, because I understood that their perspectives varied from "traditional" American students. But there was still only enough time on the course syllabus for the one-shot visit. As a compromise, using TechSmith's Jing and Camtasia products, I made three short video tutorials that the IEP students could watch via Blackboard in advance of their library instruction session. Because the videos are on YouTube, and embedded into their Blackboard course site, the students can read the closed captioning or even rewind if they need something repeated. I also provided a quiz/written exercise that the students could turn in to their instructor. Rather than flipping the classroom with an online library tutorial, as surveyed by Obdradovich et al. (2015), I expanded the classroom beyond the confines of their regularly scheduled meeting.

International students have specific needs that their native speaker classmates do not encounter. In a comparison of native Chinese speakers and native English speakers at McGill University, Zhao and Mawhinney's study (2015) focused on knowledge and the use of resources and services, such as locating full-text, evaluating sources, reading, writing, and citing. Language difficulties, which also include difficulty understanding library jargon, with terms such as "interlibrary loan," not only affect student understanding of assignments but also influence their willingness to seek help (713). Both native speakers of English and international students have difficulty finding the resources that they need, but international students face additional problems "relating to search strategies" (713) such as finding the most efficient keywords to use, or in using Boolean operators when the equivalents might not exist in their native language. Cultural differences can lead to difficulties in "proper attribution of sources and seeking out help from librarians" (713) but, as they note, "they gladly make use of the library's assistance if encouraged" (714). For students who come from countries where rote learning is the standard, independent research can be a completely new concept. They found that students from these countries struggle "to know what is expected in a western academic context" (714). Most library literature has focused on "the role of the library and its services, with," until recently, "very little literature on the information needs, information seeking behavior, and library experiences of international students" (714). "Academic libraries," Sin writes, "are poised to contribute to the growth and well-being of international students by preparing them to be proficient information seekers in both academic and everyday contexts" (466). Further complicating the issue of how best to help international students: depending on their academic backgrounds in their home countries, the student may be an experienced researcher, just not in English, or a completely novice researcher both in English and his or her native language. The only way to know what the student needs is to actually ask.

Though the purpose of the videos was to extend the one-shot beyond the standard class time, I also knew that they would need to be both short and focused. Having previously made short videos for the purpose of promoting a database trial (Emanuel 2013), I had experience with using both Jing and Camtasia. Jing, a product of TechSmith, allows a user to make short videos of up to five minutes that record both audio and video of what is happening on his or her computer monitor, including toggling between browser tabs, mouse clicks, and real-time searching. The user has the option to add voice narration and/or visual annotations. Up to 2 GB of content created with Jing can be stored for free on Screencast.com, also a TechSmith product. For videos longer than five minutes, I used Camtasia, TechSmith's licensed screen recorder, which also allows editing. It has a slightly higher learning curve than Jing, but can be used for more complicated projects as well. In the interest of keeping these videos with the library's other video tutorials, they were downloaded as .swf files, edited using Camtasia, and uploaded to the library's YouTube page, where closed captioning could be added. In addition to making online content accessible to the hearing impaired, closed captioning also lends an added benefit for speakers of other languages who can read along with the narration while they are listening. To ease the process of adding closed captions, I recorded the narration from a script that I had written in Microsoft Word, which I could then upload to YouTube.

The first video, "Part A," is an introduction to the library itself, and runs just under five minutes. It emphasizes points that may seem obvious to a native speaker of English, or to someone who has grown up in the United States, to say in the first ten seconds: "You will use our website to start your research projects." From the library's homepage, the video moves to the university's homepage, which may be easier for an international student to remember, and recreates the path of finding the library's site. It then points out the features of the website's front page, using tech savvy jargon such as "tabs," "drop-down menu," or "search box," which we take for granted but that show up in the close captioning feature. Using one of the online campus maps, the introduction explains where the library is located, as well as our branch library, and explains what is (and is not) found in each location. For example, it may not be obvious from the name "Science Library," located inside the School of Pharmacy, that its collection only includes resources for chemistry and pharmacy while the rest of the sciences are actually in the "Main Library." Additional topics include finding library hours, including those of our coffee shop, using the "Ask a Librarian" chat box, browsing our subject and course guides, and using Interlibrary Loan. The "My Library Account" feature is also demonstrated, because it might not otherwise come up in an instruction session that students can remotely renew materials that have been checked out. This is among a list of standard services in an academic library that international students often do not realize are available to them for no extra charge.

The second video, "Part B," subtitled "Finding a Journal Article with Library Resources," is just under eight minutes long. Starting with a general research topic, in this case, childhood obesity, the video shows how, through the use of facets, additional keywords, and strategies, our discovery service can be manipulated to reduce the total number of hits from 313,781 to 55,576 to 9,692 and smaller. The video follows the process of clicking through a PDF link, after explaining what that means, adding an item to a folder, and e-mailing the folder's contents in a specified citation format. It also clicks through a second article, this time one that requires using the link resolver and proxy server. These are concepts that many novice users can stumble with, but especially those whose native language is not English. Technical terms are rampant in this video, but are eased with the use of captioning and on-screen annotations. Unfortunately, after we complete the implementation of our new discovery service, we will need to update the video, but that is the nature of video tutorials: they eventually lose relevancy and have to be re-recorded.

The final video, "Part C," uses the discovery service to find a book in the library's print holdings. With the example of looking for a dictionary, it shows the user how to remove the facet for "full-text articles," and limit the search to the library's physical collection. Looking at the first three hits for "Arabic English dictionary" after the search has been faceted, using on-screen annotations such as circling and underlining, I illustrate the differences among the records, pointing out the difference between building locations, how to read a Library of Congress call number (which most international students have never seen), and how to interpret an item's "status." Also explained are the types of formats available in the library, including media, and the loan periods which vary among undergraduate students, graduate students and faculty. Because I also used Camtasia to edit this video, I was able to add photographs of locations within the library, such as the DVD cabinets and the two circulation desks, in addition to the screen recording. In the last section of the video, I demonstrate searching the library's catalog for feature films, including international films, isolated from the discovery service. By searching with the subject "*Feature films—[country]*," international students can browse a list of American films in our collection, but also see if we have any films from their home country. By demonstrating how to find practical items in the library that they might not have realized we have, we encourage international students to use the library for all of their information needs, beyond the requirements of their current assignment.

For libraries with limited staff and resources, it can be daunting to commit to making "how-to" tutorials for using our website, databases, or particular services; there is no question that they will need to be updated every few years. Recent conversations among my colleagues have raised the question of do we need to make our own videos, or can our webpage just link to tutorials with higher production values at bigger schools? Does every academic library in the United States need to make its own video explaining the Library of Congress Classification System? I would say not, but there is definitely value in making locally-focused content available to students who may not know how or to whom to ask their questions. The videos I made for UM's IEP students could be accessed by any novice user to learn about the features of our library's website, how to find an article, and how to find a book or DVD. They were made to start the research conversation for those who are new to the jargon of research as well as the concept of research. In no way do the videos replace interactions with live librarians, but they can be easily embedded into course management software, such as Blackboard, as well as our LibGuides, to give the incoming students an idea of what they will be asked to do during their library visit, and to show them how their institution's library—and its librarians—are ready to help them. For some international students, knowing that there are friendly people waiting to help them when they need it is the greatest service that we can provide.

Appendix: Quiz for Library Visit (English for Academic Purposes)

1. To check out a book, you will need _____.
   a. ☐ $20 in cash c. ☐ Your passport
   b. ☐ Your Ole Miss ID card d. ☐ A letter from one of your professors
2. To read an article online, you should click "PDF Full-text" or "Find It."
   ☐ True ☐ False
3. There is only one library on campus.
   ☐ True ☐ False
4. What can you find at the library? (CHECK ALL THAT APPLY)
   a. ☐ Books c. ☐ DVDs
   b. ☐ Journals and magazines d. ☐ Robots
5. When talking about articles, "peer reviewed" and "scholarly" have the same meaning.
   ☐ True ☐ False
6. After finding an article online, you can ____. (CHECK ALL THAT APPLY)
   a. ☐ Go ahead and read it c. ☐ Send it to your e-mail inbox
   b. ☐ Save it to your computer, or USB drive d. ☐ Print it out
7. Which of the following subjects is NOT found in the J.D. Williams Library?
   a. ☐ Political science c. ☐ Astronomy
   b. ☐ Chemistry d. ☐ Education
8. To get help with a research project, a student should go to the ____ Desk in the Library.
   a. ☐ Reference c. ☐ Circulation
   b. ☐ Archives d. ☐ Interlibrary Loan
9. If a book is kept in the Reference area of the library, it cannot leave the building but can be taken to another area.
   ☐ True ☐ False

10. To find a book in the library, you need a _____.
    a. ☐ Flashlight   c. ☐ Call Number
    b. ☐ Bookmark   d. ☐ Librarian

Answers: 1. b; 2. true; 3. false; 4. a, b, c; 5. true; 6. (all); 7. b; 8. a; 9. true; 10. c

REFERENCES

Emanuel, Michelle. 2013. "Using Screencasting to Promote Database Trials and Library Resources." *Journal of Electronic Resources Librarianship* 25 (4): 277–282. doi:10.1080/1941126X.2013.847675. http://dx.doi.org.umiss.idm.oclc.org/10.1080/1941126X.2013.847675.

"Framework for Information Literacy for Higher Education." American Library Association, last modified February 9, 2015, accessed February 11, 2016, http://www.ala.org/acrl/standards/ilframework.

Obradovich, Alexandra, Robin Canuel, and Eamon P. Duffy. 2015. "A Survey of Online Library Tutorials: Guiding Instructional Video Creation to use in Flipped Classrooms." *The Journal of Academic Librarianship* 41 (6): 751–757. doi:http://dx.doi.org/10.1016/j.acalib.2015.08.006.

Sin, Sei-Ching Joanna. 2015. "Demographic Differences in International Students' Information Source Uses and Everyday Information Seeking Challenges." *The Journal of Academic Librarianship* 41 (4): 466–474. doi:http://dx.doi.org/10.1016/j.acalib.2015.04.003.

Zhao, Jennifer Congyan, and Tara Mawhinney. 2015. "Comparison of Native Chinese-Speaking and Native English-Speaking Engineering Students' Information Literacy Challenges." *The Journal of Academic Librarianship* 41 (6): 712–724. doi:http://dx.doi.org/10.1016/j.acalib.2015.09.010.

Girls Who Code in the Library
Community-Led Programming at Its Best

JENNIFER BUNTON FORGIT

Librarians understandably have difficulty keeping technology instruction up-to-date and relevant, given the speed with which technology changes. So how do libraries react when patrons demand computer skills that go beyond the training of the staff? They turn to expert community members to lead programming. When the librarian invites and recruits library users to share their knowledge with the community, everyone benefits. One example of community programming in practice today is Girls Who Code (GWC). Their programs can be hosted in public libraries, middle school and high school libraries, university libraries, or other community organizations. A host site only needs to provide computers and meeting space while GWC provides lesson plans. Classes are taught by qualified volunteer instructors. This essay shows how to host a GWC club and how librarians can apply this model to successfully implement more technology instruction by using free, widely available resources and volunteer instructors.

GWC is a national nonprofit organization working to close the gender gap in Science, Technology, Engineering and Math (STEM) fields. In middle school, 74 percent of girls express interest in STEM, but when choosing a college major, just 0.4 percent of high school girls select computer science. This disparity is alarming, given the growth in the technology field and the high number of high paying jobs available to those who have a computer science background. The industry is projected to have 1.4 million jobs by 2020 (Solomon 2015). Despite this, only 12 percent of graduates with computer science degrees are women. (Girls Who Code 2015). Girls Who Code is working to bring more women into the field by providing free computer science instruction to girls in 6th through 12th grade. Their programs "work to inspire, educate, and equip girls with the computing skills to pursue 21st century opportunities." The nonprofit was founded in 2012 by Reshma Saujani, a former U.S. Congressional candidate and advocate for women in leadership roles. Saujani has put her experience fundraising to good use. In 2014, Girls Who Code raised $7.7 million according to their annual report. Their clubs program is offered for free to students and host sites.

As of 2015, Girls Who Code has taught over 10,000 girls coding skills in over 40 states in the U.S. The organization is also working hard to make sure that their training continues by building an alumni network with major tech companies from Facebook to Microsoft with a campaign called "Hire Me" (King 2015). The clubs program has had great success in its first three years. Participants from the first summer immersion program entered college in 2014 and 2015. One hundred percent of students from the first summer immersion program choose Computer Science or Engineering as their major, despite most of these students having been undecided or planned to enter a different field before participating in the program (Saujani 2014).

Students who learned introductory coding in the 1980s and 1990s may remember BASIC coding language. Students would be given a series of commands to type out and then run the program. Debugging was a matter of going through line by line looking for typos. Now new coders can use graphical, drag and drop introductory coding programs, like Scratch, that allow students to do so much more than memorize and transcribe a series of commands. Girls Who Code uses Codesters, which uses graphical, drag-and-drop Python. This allows the student to learn the concept and understand how the code works quickly using blocks of pre-selected code.

The Girls Who Code curriculum includes more than hard concepts like variables and syntax. It recognizes that there are social barriers to the female coder. Girls can be intimated by the prevailing stereotype that coding is only for geeky guys (Golod 2015). There are a number of reasons that girls are not choosing computer science in college and as a career. One of the reasons is a difference in learning styles between girls and boys. Girls tend to be much less comfortable with failing. Coding can require a lot of trial and error. It requires you to fail repeatedly before you solve the problem. According to Saujani the most important lesson Girls Who Code teaches is that it is okay to fail. She says, "Coding is challenging, and it doesn't come right away to anybody. But I've learned in my experience that learning from your failures will make you stronger, more confident, and more resilient for whatever comes next" (King 2015). Girls also tend to favor collaborative learning environments, and want to understand how their work could make a positive impact on others. The lesson plans that GWC develops take these social factors into consideration.

Why Should I Host a Girls Who Code Club in My Library?

Anyone who has tried to teach technology in a library knows that one of the biggest challenges is working with a group of learners who have different levels of knowledge. Girls Who Code is designed for beginners and advanced coders to work side by side in the same class. Students take a pre-test to assess their skills and are placed in one of three tracks: beginner, intermediate and advanced. During the coursework, if the student finds the material too easy, they are able to take the assessment again and take on more challenging material.

Girls Who Code has been hugely successful in a number of libraries already. If your library is concerned about bringing more people into your library in general, or if you are struggling to attract teens to library programs, then a GWC club is a great way to accomplish your goals. Even in communities where attendance at teen programs is generally low, Girls Who Code clubs attract a dedicated and loyal membership. Girls Who Code is a program that uses existing resources, so it is free and it is easy to implement. A GWC club provides a way for students to test the waters of computer science before taking a class for credit, and is especially needed in school districts where coding is not yet part of the curriculum.

How Do I Host a Club in My Library?

You will need

- buy-in from staff and administration;
- computers and reliable Internet connection;
- a staff liaison (also known as Club Advisor); and
- a meeting space available two hours every week

The first thing to do is to start the application process. Clubs run during the academic year, starting in September and running through May or in the summer from June through August. Applications for host sites are accepted on a rolling basis, so check the Girls Who Code website and click on Clubs for more information. The online application explains most of the details about hosting a club, so even if you have not yet decided to apply, it is a good idea to read over the application so that you understand what you will need to provide. As a host site, you will need to get the written permission of the Decision Maker (that is, your library director or school principal). Approach your Decision Maker early in the application process. The best time to start planning is in the spring or summer before your fall launch date, but you can start any time. Your application must come from a staff member who will become your Club Advisor. (Members of the public are not allowed to submit an application listing your facility as a host site.) This person is responsible for attending club meetings or checking in frequently with the instructors to ensure the club is running smoothly. Your Club Advisor does not need to have any training in computer science.

Once you have been approved as a host site, you will be matched with a Site Manager. Your Site Manager acts as a liaison between your club and Girls Who Code. As a Club Advisor, you will check in monthly with your Site Manager who can help answer questions you or your instructors have. You will provide updates on the club's progress, such as how students are managing the coursework. Note that you must complete the application process each year.

As the club advisor, you are responsible for

- recruiting a volunteer instructor;
- advertising; and
- student registration/sign ups.

How Do I Find Volunteer Instructors?

While Girls Who Code provides the curriculum and club support, you will need to find a volunteer in your community. Depending on where you live, Girls Who Code may be able to pair you with an instructor who has already applied to volunteer, but it is more likely that you will need to do the work of recruiting a leader for your club.

Advertise

You will need at least one volunteer instructor for your club. Girls Who Code provides an attractive PDF flyer that you can print out to help recruit volunteers, but there are many ways that you can reach out to potential volunteers. Advertise the position your library's social media accounts and on your community's e-mail listservs. Contact the Computer Science department at a college near you asking for volunteers. Search online to find out if there is a local chapter of Women in Computer Science in your area, and contact them about volunteering.

Meet Your Volunteers

Invite your volunteer to meet with you in the library well ahead of your projected class. No matter how many volunteers approach you to teach the class, it is a good idea to conduct a short, informal interview to make sure that the volunteer candidate understands the commitment they are making and that you feel confident that this person has the skills required to manage a classroom full of students. In this meeting, explain that you are looking for a volunteer who is willing to have fun and take on new challenges and who will encourage their students to do the same. Ask the volunteer what days of the week and times would work best for them and try to be flexible about setting up the class meeting schedule with them. Inquire about their background in Computer Science, and ask if their employer is familiar with Girls Who Code. More and more companies are supporting Girls Who Code, and companies who are familiar with the group and their mission may be willing to flex their employee's schedule to encourage them to volunteer. If you have more than one volunteer, you may want to pair them together in the same class, especially if they are new to teaching.

Ideal Volunteer Skill Set

The idea volunteer

- has a background in computer science;
- is friendly, welcoming; and
- communicates in a clear, timely manner.

Once you have selected an instructor for your class, she will need to apply to be a volunteer instructor on the Girls Who Code website. Their application includes a test of her coding skills. She also needs to agree to a background check. In some cases, your school or library may have a policy in place that all volunteers need to pass a CORI check. If this is the case, she will need to fill out paperwork submitting to both background checks.

What Technology Do I Need to Provide?

If you are in a large public library or school library that already has its own computer lab, you have a great head start! For most libraries, finding enough computers for all of your students to use in class will be the greatest challenge.

In order to be approved as a host site, you will need to provide at least ten computers. Students are welcome and encouraged to bring their own laptops if they have them. If your library circulates laptops to the public, talk with the Library Director or Head of Technology about reserving the laptops for your GWC class. While it limits their circulation to the general public, your library may decide that the two hours a week needed to host a GWC club is worth diverting those resources.

If you are limited to a small number of desktop computers, find out if your library can add enough to host a class. A computer is a good investment for your Friends of the Library, Foundation, or local charitable group to consider. The equipment they provide to your library will not only help teach a girl to code, but for the rest of the week that computer is available to the general public. Talk with your Library Director before soliciting donations so that you are aware of your library's policy.

Students are welcome to bring their own laptops to class, but there is a higher potential for problems with equipment. Student laptops sometimes run slow, have trouble connecting to the library's wireless network, or have insufficient battery to operate without being plugged in. Though none of these problems will prevent students from participating, they will have a better experience if their equipment is in good condition. The other problem with students bringing their own devices is that more and more students have tablets and Chromebooks, but many of these devices are insufficient for the coursework in Girls Who Code clubs.

If you are using laptops there are a couple of additional tools you might consider, including

- a cart to transport the laptops;
- two or three power strips with surge protector and cords at least six feet long; and
- an extension cord

What Can I Do to Support My Instructors?

In this partnership model Girls Who Code provides all of the curriculum support and the class is taught by volunteer instructors. However, in order to ensure a successful class, there are some things you as the Club Advisor must prepare before anyone sets foot in the classroom. The work that you do in the spring and summer before your class starts will mean that your instructor will be poised for success when the class starts in the fall.

As a host site, you must be able to provide a dedicated space. Ideally your class will take place in a computer lab or community meeting room, but if that is not possible, then reserve a quiet part of the library where your class will not be interrupted and will not disturb other library users.

The lesson plans provide time for students to take breaks from the screen and typing. It is helpful to have some basic classroom supplies on hand for these analog activities, like

- computer paper;
- pencils or pens;
- colored pencils; and
- scrap paper or sticky notes

Class meeting times can be set depending on your library and your instructor's preferences. Most clubs meet in two-hour sessions, once a week. The GWC requires clubs to meet at least 8 hours per month. Clubs held in school libraries will be held after school, but public libraries have more options to choose from. If you hold your class on weeknights, it is helpful to set the time late enough that students are able to go home for dinner after school and return to the library for the evening session. An evening start time is also often convenient for instructors, who may work full time in the technology industry. Other classes choose to meet on weekends. Talk with your potential instructor and decide what will be the best fit for the library, the instructor and the students.

Beyond Girls Who Code: How to Host More Community-Led Technology Programs

Mentor-Led Programs

There are a growing number of organizations who make good partners for STEM-based technology programs in the library, and many that are specific to coding. Like Girls Who Code, there are programs that are led by mentors in the field. Some examples include FIRST whose mission is to inspire young people to be science and technology leaders using mentor based robotics and Lego programs. While FIRST does not collect fees from members, there are fees associated with starting a club. FIRST clubs are offered in 80 countries around the world (FIRST 2015).

Depending on your location, there may be more local programs aimed at teaching technology. Black Girls Code was founded in April 2011 and has chapters in the Bay Area, Atlanta, New York City, Chicago, Detroit and more (Springer 2014). Black Girls Code uses volunteer instructors and is another example of how mentor led programs are a successful model for technology instruction.

Volunteers in Your Community

High school or college students may approach your library to volunteer to teach technology in your library. These are great opportunities for students to practice their public speaking skills and to share their knowledge. Meet with the presenter well ahead of the planned program. Discuss what they plan to present, how long the presentation will be, and what they need for audiovisual equipment. In your advertising, include a brief biography of the presenter, and list their credentials. Include courses have they studied in school that apply to the topic they plan to teach and whether they belong to any after school clubs that are relevant to the topic. Students who seek out teaching opportunities like this tend to be highly motivated. Red flags would be volunteers who do not respond to phone calls or e-mails. It is a good idea to designate a staff member to be present for the class to provide support and to observe their interactions with students. Programs presented by volunteers can feel risky, because the librarian gives up some of the responsibility and control. The best way to ensure a successful program is to have a conversation in person with the instructor ahead of time and to make it clear in the advertising who the presenter is. With partnerships like this, the library and library patrons stand to gain all of the knowledge of the members of the community.

Free Online Resources

If your library is not ready to launch a club or mentor-led program, or if you are seeking a gender-neutral coding program, you might consider working with any number of free, online coding instruction websites. Some examples include Code.org, Codesters, Code Academy and Scratch. Hour of Code is a great way to introduce your patrons to code in a relaxed, fun way (Solomon 2015). These modules are designed to be self-taught. The librarian only needs to provide basic computer assistance and be able to help students work through problem by prompting them to review the information provided in the module. Often voicing the problem aloud helps students work through the problem on their own.

Conclusion

Girls Who Code is a great example of how to successfully leverage the knowledge in your community to provide quality programs to your users. Nothing compares to working with instructors who are current in their field. With this model your library can offer more frequent technology instruction at no additional cost and gain the benefits of your community's existing experience and expertise.

REFERENCES

"About Us." 2015. *Girls Who Code.* http://girlswhocode.com/about-us/#section3.
"Cost and Registration." 2015. *FIRST.* http://www.firstinspires.org/robotics/fll/cost-and-registration.
Golod, Amy. 2015. "No Boys Allowed: Tackling the Coding Gender GAP." *U.S. News and World Report.* April 22. http://www.usnews.com/news/stem-solutions/articles/2015/04/22/girls-who-code-takes-on-gender-gap-in-computer-science.
King, Leo. 2015. "Girls Who Code Has Taught Nearly 10,000 Young Women … And It's Just Getting Started." *Forbes*, October 29. http://www.forbes.com/sites/leoking/2015/10/29/girls-who-code-10000-women-hire-me-att-facebook-microsoft/.
Saujani, Reshma. 2014. "2014 in Review." *Girls Who Code.* http://girlswhocode.com/2014report/.
Solomon, Gwen. 2015. "Hours of Code: Past & Present." *Technology & Learning*, October 28.
Springen, Karen. 2014. "SisOps: New Girl-Friendly Technology Initiatives Challenge Tech's Boys-Only Culture." *School Library.*
"What We Do." 2014. *Black Girls Code.* http://www.blackgirlscode.com/what-we-do.html.

Mobile Computer Lab Services to Tent City Communities
A Case Study

Danielle M. Duvall *and* Lisa Fraser

"All we need is a piece of land and running water."—Tent City resident

While people experiencing homelessness can learn to manage on the most basic of resources, they do need more than land and water to live with dignity. They have a variety of needs that include personal growth, optimal health, meaningful work, entertainment, and involvement in a community, as do all library patrons. They also have unique challenges that present significant barriers to their use of traditional library services. This essay will provide insight into these barriers and practices that can help overcome them, based on the technology service developed for Tent City communities by author Danielle M. Duvall of King County Library System (KCLS).

According to the One Night Count, an annual event held each January by the Seattle/King County Coalition on Homelessness, 10,047 people were homeless in King County on January 23, 2015. At least 3,772 of these men, women, and children were counted without shelter on the street, an increase of 21 percent over those found without shelter the prior year. Although this event is one of the country's best-established point-in-time counts of homeless people, the published number is always assumed to be an undercount. Volunteers are not able to count every individual, particularly since many people take great care not to be visible (Seattle/King County Coalition on Homelessness 2015).

King County in Washington State has several formally-recognized encampments for people experiencing homelessness. Each "tent city" typically moves every 90 days, locating on property provided by a local church, community center or public agency. Representatives of the camp work with elected officials to determine the sites that are acceptable. They work with local law enforcement to ensure the safety of the campers and to increase comfort levels of nearby residents. Encampments are often required to pay utility expenses and city permit fees. Most encampments are governed by the residents, all of whom are required to work shifts in security, clean-up, and administration, as well as attend weekly community meetings. They are limited to 75 to 100 residents per camp, living in traditional tents with larger community tents for the kitchen, office and gathering spaces. Currently, KCLS staff visit four homeless encampments on a regular basis, usually once per month.

Early in Danielle's tenure as a Public Service Specialist in the KCLS Mobile Services Department, she identified the Tent City residents as high-needs individuals who may not make full use of library resources. People experiencing homelessness often have barriers to access, such as inadequate transportation, lack of technology skills, and limited resources that prevent them from using the library or other vital services. By building services that they can access on-site and that will move with them, Danielle could provide what might be the only opportunity for residents to use the library.

Danielle had one essential tool at her disposal—Techlab. The Techlab vehicle is a customized 36-foot Winnebago with eight PC work stations, put into service in 2006 to bring off-site digital literacy and computer skills instruction to underserved populations. Additional equipment includes a kit of eight laptops and iPads that can be used outside the vehicle. All computers have a comprehensive suite of software that includes the usual programs as well as photo editing, coding, and game design programs that allow greater depth and flexibility for curriculum development. The Techlab has an onboard wireless service that allows patrons to access the Internet from both inside and outside the vehicle. Although the KCLS service was built around Techlab, many types of technology training and support can be provided without a vehicle.

Initiating Contact with Encampments

My first attempts at contact were misguided and ineffective. Using methods that had been successful with other community partners, I emailed and called each encampment to schedule a meeting. I talked and corresponded with whomever answered, presenting an awesome opportunity to have the library bring a technology vehicle to them, where they would have the chance to utilize computers and get computer and job training. The response was unfailingly polite and always a dead end. "I will bring it up at our meeting and get back to you." Weeks went by without any further contact. I had to figure out where my approach was going wrong.—Danielle

When she hit a wall on her first contacts with homeless encampments, Danielle discovered that communication can be challenging. There is a high turn-over rate in residents and management within the Tent Cities. The people answering the phone and emails aren't always in charge or accountable for more than just taking a message. This structure is different from most community organizations with which a library might partner, so it requires a different approach for initiating contact.

To increase success when contacting an encampment,

- find out as much as possible about the structure and governance of the encampment before making contact;
- have patience with residents, who may be volunteers with changing duties; and
- be aware of the cycle of life and its impact on communication; everything may shut down during a move.

After several failed communication attempts, I decided just to show up. I walked up to the encampment and was met with a stop sign—a physical stop sign. Like most, the encampment had only one entrance point for increased safety. The perimeter of the encampment was fenced off using tarps that completely enclosed the tent area, with a walkway to indicate where foot traffic should follow. At the entrance there was a staffed office where residents were working at administrative tasks. Most visits from non-residents are donation drop-offs, so camps are set up to facilitate this quickly and privately. After an introduction, I chatted with the security guard. While we talked, residents came out, drawn by the unfamiliar voice. I introduced myself to them, shaking hands and making eye contact with each person. Once I had their attention, I asked, "Could I come by next week with my computers?" Hesitantly they said, "Yes!" Finally, I was in.—Danielle

Danielle did not realize the significance of shaking residents' hands and making formal introductions, but later understood it was a real breakthrough moment. Residents are used to people stopping by and donating but they are not accustomed to being addressed as peers. Library staff who make contacts and provide direct service need to have a clear understanding of this dynamic and their role in the relationship. Training and advice from professionals working with this population can increase staff skills, establish clear expectations, and help to avoid misunderstandings.

To increase success when visiting the encampment,

- choose library staff who are comfortable working closely with patrons who have more specialized needs;
- approach people warmly and professionally, as though you were meeting with a peer at his or her office;
- adhere to all rules of the encampment (if you are unsure of the rules, ask); and
- ask permission before entering the camp or communal spaces within it (Residents' tents are private).

Building Credibility with Encampment Residents

During one of my first visits to an encampment in late fall, one of the residents said to me, "People only come during the holidays." I listened to him and understood what he was saying. If I was going to start the service, I was going to have to offer them the respect of consistent service and not just participate in the annual "holiday giving cheer."—Danielle

Public libraries typically have high credibility in their communities, so staff do not often have to make a conscious effort to establish credibility as part of a new service. With some high-need, low-use populations, this step is essential to the service getting off the ground. During this early time, it is critical to demonstrate a commitment to the service by being there consistently, listening to the residents' needs, and adapting offerings in response.

After seeing the residents' hesitance in accepting the program choices she had described, Danielle took a different approach from her usual computer classes. She recognized that it would be vital to create and maintain a welcoming and responsive environment that encouraged residents to come in and relax. For the first few visits, when residents looked into the vehicle, they would find music or a movie playing and computers set to friendly websites. Residents first came in for the movie or the shelter, and then eventually began asking questions and using the computers. This continues to be the norm—sometimes we are there to provide a quiet warm space and other times we are working on more traditional library and technology tasks.

To increase credibility with high-need, low-use populations,

- establish trust by providing consistent and reliable service;
- create a welcoming environment in and around the vehicle;

- make residents feel respected and safe to ask for help finding information;
- bring "things"—a small browsing collection or library giveaways;
- note patron requests for materials and activities and deliver at the next opportunity;
- be prepared for residents' needs, whether it is technology tutoring or a quiet, warm space;
- adapt to changes related to the mobility of the encampment, including different physical spaces, parking changes, and disruptions to the schedule; and
- offer an open lab instead of a structured class, allowing opportunities for computer use that they may not be able to get at a branch.

Library Policy Issues

One of my residents was a 16-year-old girl who had recently moved from Texas, living in the encampment while her family waited for a permanent housing solution. Our visit gave her an opportunity to work on her homework, as most classes have an online component. She is also an avid reader, so getting a library card that enabled checkouts was essential. She relies on staff to bring her new and interesting books. This is especially impactful since most schools in her area have lost funding for libraries. Within three months she was able to find resources to help her with her education, check out books for herself and her siblings, as well as attend a Life After High School program at her local branch. She has even learned to take the bus to the nearest Seattle Public Library to maximize her borrowing potential.—Danielle

Although Techlab is not a traditional bookmobile, Danielle often received requests for books and materials to check out. In addition, residents needed online databases, eBooks, and other resources that require a library card. For Tent City residents, this can be one of the more difficult barriers to get past. Libraries run on policies and procedures, and outreach activities can sometimes challenge these. Libraries may also be subject to federal, state, or local laws that impact how and to whom services can be provided. For staff who hope to provide full library service to migratory populations, understanding this framework is essential, whether choosing to work within it or advocating for change.

Currently, KCLS policy requires proof of residential address to obtain a full privilege library card. While seemingly straightforward, the application of this policy to Tent City residents, who live within the district but do not have a residential address, is open to some interpretation. The Library has a mission directive of providing "free, open, and equal access to ideas and information to all members of the community" (King County Library System, under "About KCLS") while the *Revised Code of Washington* defines the community as "the inhabitants of the governmental unit in which it [the library] is located" (RCW 27.12.270). In response to evolving realities, KCLS is currently reviewing its policy with regards to library cards for patrons without residence to ensure we are providing equitable service while meeting our legal requirements.

To increase success when developing services for non-traditional patrons,

- in addition to your organization's policies, procedures, and guidelines, understand any federal, state or local laws that apply to your library;
- support any proposal to change library policy or procedures with relevant data;

- allow patrons with existing cards in good standing to continue to check out while policy changes are under consideration;
- if patrons are not able to check out due to prior issues or library policy, explore options for lending donated or uncatalogued items; and
- focus on incremental change, if necessary. If the residents cannot get a full-access card, try proposing a limited checkout or ebook-only card to start.

The American Library Association (ALA) notes that the term "homeless" "can become a label for people, replacing their identity, when really they are just people experiencing a particular—and hopefully temporary—condition" (American Library Association, under *Outreach Resources for Services to Poor and Homeless People*). The ALA cites many barriers to library service that are experienced by those without stable housing, including policies that require patrons to have a fixed address, prohibitive fines, limited promotion of services, limited access to library buildings due to transportation or hours, and staff who lack training in working with this population.

Legal challenges to access barriers establish the framework upon which libraries can build services to the homeless and other high-needs groups. "Legal precedent has held that public libraries, as places set aside by the government for the public's receipt of information and services, are designated public forums subject to the First Amendment. As such, individuals possess a right to access the public library that is protected by the First Amendment" (*Kreimer v. Bureau of Police*, 958 F.2d 1242, 1259 (3-D Cir. 1992). The ALA provides resources for libraries on their website under Outreach to Underserved Populations.

Access and Skills

Another resident was an out of work contractor. Staff introduced him to educational databases where he could take free online courses in Microsoft Office products and other topics that would increase his job skills. He also went online to request materials on how to start his own business. Working with residents one-on-one is essential to serving these patrons, who come from different backgrounds and have distinct interests and needs. In my experience, a pre-established curriculum and structured classes that are successful in the library do not work as well here.—Danielle

As a mobile computer lab, Techlab is set up to support classroom-style instruction. There is a teacher workstation at the front, with student computers facing it. KCLS has developed a curriculum for technology skills that is used in both libraries and Techlab. Danielle saw clues from the beginning that this structure would not meet the diverse needs of the Tent City residents. It was impossible to anticipate the skill level or technology needs in advance. More often, Danielle would adapt on the fly to respond to each patron's needs. For example, a patron's difficulty typing information into a web form could result in Danielle directing him to a basic mousing program or typing tutor website.

Tent City patrons also need instruction to learn how to use electronic devices such as smart phones and tablets. Some have acquired these devices through donation programs and are not aware of the features that are available even without data service of their own. Wireless Internet inside and outside the vehicle allows patrons to access email, job/house searching websites, library databases or downloadable content, and other resources. Libraries without a mobile lab could provide similar access by bringing hotspots and laptops or tablets.

Coordinating Across Departments and Branches

One day while working with Dan, a librarian new to the service, a patron came in. I was busy doing reader advisory with another patron so he approached Dan and asked, "So, do you want to hear my story?" Dan said, "Sure." The resident proceeded to explain from the beginning the events in their entirety that led to his experience of homelessness. Dan just sat there and listened. When the resident was done he said, "Well, thanks for listening" and walked out. Dan's reaction and response made that interaction a success. He just sat and listened without expectations or judgement. That moment wasn't directly related to service or reference but his response ensured that when the patron sees Dan again, he will know that Dan will treat him with respect and compassion.—Danielle

King County Library System has a Mobile Services department that operates separately from the system's 48 branches. Encampments move to multiple locations within a year, so it was likely that this service would impact most of our regions eventually. The logical option was to have Mobile Services and the branches work together. Partnering addressed two issues: the need for at least two staff members on the vehicle at high-needs sites, and building a connection between the encampment residents and the nearby branches. The service initiative was presented to all management teams and Adult Service Librarians. Over a few service cycles, a group of librarians from different branches who had a passion for helping with this service emerged.

Camps usually get only a few weeks' notice before a move, so having a communication system in place that quickly adapts to the changing service area is crucial. Danielle created a KCLS intranet site that included a group work space, a resources page, and a service calendar. Branch staff populated it with information such as community resources and local program opportunities. Notes about residents' materials requests were added to the calendar. When the encampment moved to a new service area, staff had the information needed to ensure a seamless transition between local teams.

In this situation, reaching out to local branch staff to participate in this service was vital for its success. In one case, a librarian wrote a letter to the staff serving the new site, outlining best practices and identifying key needs of the patrons and paving the way for an easy transition between service areas. Partnering with the branch also allowed opportunities to offer programming outside the scope of Mobile Services. For example, when we began to notice an increase in children living in the encampments, local librarians held story times in the community tents.

To help create a more seamless service during transitions,

- create shared resources on your intranet or other accessible online location (include a calendar, collaboration site or bulletin board, resource lists, specifics about the needs, requests, and details for each encampment, and communication tools—this helps rotating staff be informed about changing situations and allows them to quickly access resources and program information);
- help the staff who are involved in the service become ambassadors, sharing information and success stories with their local colleagues; and

- present information about the program to groups such as branch managers regularly.

Developing External Partnerships

In January 2015, KCLS received an email from staff at Seattle Public Library. Tent City 3, which had been residing in North Seattle, would be moving a few miles away, into the KCLS service district. SPL staff wanted to discuss how the two systems could work together to make the transition as seamless as possible for the residents. This resulted in the addition of Tent City 3 to the Techlab Service, and the transition represented a successful partnership between SPL, Mobile Services and Branch Staff.—Danielle

Two different library systems serve King County. The Seattle Public Library (SPL), a department of the City of Seattle, operates within the city limits. King County Library System, an independent library district, serves the rest of King County, with the exception of two small cities that have not annexed into the district. Patrons, especially new users, often are not fully aware that there are two different library systems until they find themselves in the "other" one. Homeless encampments are likely to move across the borders between the two library systems, creating the potential for service disruptions and inconsistencies. The initial call from SPL has grown into a valuable collaboration between staff in the two systems. In addition to sharing best practices, we have built on each other's successes. For example, SPL staff worked at a KCLS site to learn how we incorporated technology into our programming.

Social service agencies provide another opportunity for collaboration. We share our service calendar with Hopelink, a local agency that helps people access a variety of services, so that they can schedule appointments with their clients that coincide with our visit to the encampment. This allows them to use our computers and Internet access to help clients search for housing or jobs, or access other services.

- Become familiar with organizations in your area that may provide services to the residents, and ask them how your visits to the encampment might help them.
- Share service calendars, publicity, and best practices.
- Work to overcome inconsistencies and territoriality.

Defining Service Goals and Evaluating Success

I have one resident who never steps on board or participates in the service, but when I arrive he always greets me with a firm handshake. He has made it his personal job to make sure I park safely. He alerts residents to my arrival, gathers materials, and brings me a soda. He takes pride in making sure we are taken care of and feel like welcomed guests. He has taken ownership of the program and become the camp advocate making sure all residents are responsible users. It is hard to say what motivates him but I am certain the mutual respect we feel for each other is a factor. He is also an incredibly nice, thoughtful man.—Danielle

Traditional statistics do not reflect the impact of this service. On average we see about 15 to 20 residents per visit, perhaps 300 a year. Circulation is minimal but significant for those who do check out materials. Use of downloadable books has also increased as residents learn to use their devices. We can count computer usage sessions on Techlab, but not those residents using the wireless from outside the vehicle. None of these numbers is significant when compared to branch or other Mobile Outreach statistics.

Harder to measure but more important is the change in residents' skills, attitudes, and behavior as a result of this service. Where residents may start out feeling skeptical or wary, over time many feel comfortable enough to apply for library cards, look for jobs or housing, or work on their computer skills. This is the real measure of impact.

It is also important to seek input from the patrons about their satisfaction with the service. Danielle does this continually, responding to patrons' suggestions and making small adaptations to better meet their needs. Asking for feedback from partner organizations can help round out the picture.

Beyond the shift from counting heads to measuring outcomes, service to homeless encampments required a change in data-gathering methods, as well. Asking residents to provide personal information or fill out a survey the first time they step on the vehicle can make a return visit unlikely. Instead, staff may need to rely on observation to learn about changes in the residents' behavior over time. Some patrons may choose to tell their stories once trust has been established. If well-documented, this information provides valid and compelling evidence of the impact of the service.

To evaluate the impact of outreach services,

- set realistic goals that allow time for the relationship-building necessary for residents to use the service;
- use a combination of statistics, stories, and patron satisfaction to evaluate the success of the service;
- look for innovative ways to measure changes over time; and
- ask for feedback from community partners.

I was working with a patron recently and she told me about a situation that meant so much to her. "Last week someone gave me a hug. I needed that, I deserve that." We can't meet every need through our services, but we can offer opportunities that preserve the dignity of our patrons and include the human touch. It may be difficult to quantify the impact our service has had on the residents, but I can tell you my life will never be the same from the privilege of working with this group of people.—Danielle

Providing technology services and instruction in Tent City encampments helps to overcome the barriers preventing residents from accessing these resources. While having a vehicle like Techlab gives KCLS Mobile Services an added advantage, similar services can be developed with less investment. The key is to create a welcoming environment that demonstrates a commitment to relevant, patron-focused services.

REFERENCES

American Library Association. "Equity of Access Issues for People Experiencing Poverty or Homelessness." *Outreach Resources for Services to Poor and Homeless People.* http://www.ala.org/advocacy/diversity/outreachtounderservedpopulations/servicespoor.
King County Library System. 2015. "Our Mission, Vision & Values." *About KCLS.* http://www.kcls.org/about/mission.cfm.
Kreimer v. Bureau of Police, 958 F.2d 1242, 1259 (3-D Cir. 1992).
Revised Code of Washington 27.12.270.
Seattle/King County Coalition on Homelessness. 2015. "2015 Results." *What We Do.* http://www.homelessinfo.org/what_we_do/one_night_count/2015_results.php.

Part IV

Strategies, Planning and Partnerships

Marketing and Managing Technology Education in the Face of Library Anxiety

Cara Marco

Research shows that in spite of librarians' best efforts, patrons are often reluctant to ask for help. That can be sobering news for committed library professionals because when it comes to technology, research also shows that many library patrons need help wherever they can find it. How can librarians educate patrons to use technology effectively when patrons can be reluctant to even approach them, and how can librarians get those same patrons to attend an outreach event if they won't even venture to the reference desk?

Librarians may be surprised to realize the extent of the need for technology education among their patrons. The oft-discussed Millennial generation, for example, which is defined in *America's Skills Challenge: Millennials and the Future* as respondents between the ages of 16 and 34 at the time of the assessment, may have grown up with computer technology in common use, but that does not necessarily mean they are using technology skillfully (Goodman et al. 2015). When tested on PS-TRE, or "problem-solving in a technology-rich environment" (6), against students from other countries, the group of young American adults demonstrated the highest percentage of respondents who did not demonstrate proficiency among 20 participating countries (14). Lest one believe that it is only this age group that demonstrates poor skills, an earlier study was cited in the same report in which adults between the ages of 16 and 65 were tested in PS-TRE showed that the American respondents' average scores ranked 18th out of 20 participating countries (7).

While libraries and universities are a wealth of opportunities to learn "problem-solving in a technology-rich environment," library anxiety may prevent patrons from seeking those opportunities. In spite of librarians' earnest efforts, library anxiety, first labeled by Constance Mellon in her 1986 article "Library Anxiety: A Grounded Theory and Its Development," is a common experience. In Gillian Gremmels' essay "Constance Mellon's 'Library Anxiety': An Appreciation and a Critique," Gremmels recalls that Mellon came to three major conclusions during her qualitative research process: that students often described their experience with the library in terms of fear, that they were ashamed by their fear and perceived ignorance, and that asking questions was aversive because they felt it would reveal this embarrassing shortcoming (2015).

With all of that in mind, a librarian introducing a library patron to new technology has emotional obstacles to overcome before instruction even starts. Those emotional obstacles also need to be considered when marketing services to potential patrons. By understanding and directing marketing toward the accomplishment of patrons' goals while addressing patrons' fears, librarians can attract patrons to the library and educate them effectively once they arrive.

Know That Fear Often Appears in Disguise

During instructional sessions, some patrons may brag or be condescending. Others will seem tense or irritable even while they are asking for help. Given Mellon's research, it would be reasonable to assume that those behaviors are partially attributable to anxiety or insecurity with the material. If the behavior is disruptive, a librarian can use the strategy recommended by Lynne Curry in *Beating the Workplace Bully* (2016) and turn the tables with a question like "What would lead you to say that?" or "Then what brings you to this presentation?" or "What did you hope this presentation would accomplish?" which maintains control of the session while offering an opportunity to see where the student is dissatisfied and address the issue if appropriate.

Encourage Competence

In the article "Recognizing Student Fear; The Elephant in the Classroom," authors Bledsoe and Baskin write that teachers should "create a nurturing environment for your students" (2014, 37). Librarians can take practical steps to help the patron feel comfortable, competent, and confident in their surroundings. A librarian can take a moment to not only introduce him or herself by name and title, but also to provide a brief explanation of what librarians do. If a librarian is giving a formal instruction session, that librarian can start by explaining where the bathrooms are located, when the group will be taking a break, and where patrons can get a drink or a snack. When marketing events, librarians can use signage and fliers to help attendees arrive on time and to understand where they need to be, perhaps providing maps of the building, parking information, and other content that helps orient patrons in their physical space.

Foster Reasonable Expectations

Librarians may need to remind anxious patrons that they are beginners learning a new skill, and while they might learn it quickly, they also might experience frustration or weariness. Librarians can be prepared to help patrons remember that early setbacks are not necessarily a reflection of their intelligence or the level of skill they might eventually develop. Reminding patrons that this is how learning sometimes feels can encourage them not to give up or fall into self-criticism. Librarians may find it especially effective to be honest about their own early struggles to learn the technology that they are now showing patrons to use.

Carol Dweck's writing, as discussed in the *Harvard Business Review* article "Talent:

How Companies Can Benefit from a 'Growth Mindset'" (2014), is clear about the value of thinking of talent, intellect, and skills as resources that can increase with practice, rather than fixed quantities that can never change. If library patrons show the negative side of a fixed mindset by saying, "I'm no good at research" or "I'm not very book-smart," a librarian can take the initiative to reframe their challenges as being an opportunity for growth in those areas instead of a source of shame.

Additionally, a librarian may need reminders that some students will need to work hard to learn the material and may experience setbacks, and that it is not a reflection on the librarian's skill as a teacher or on the patron's ability as a student, merely a part of the learning process.

Keep the Goal in Mind

In order to focus marketing efforts, librarians can carefully consider why patrons might want to use a particular technology. Unlike librarians or early technology adopters for whom the journey of learning new technology is a reward in itself, more reluctant patrons may consider learning a new technology to be intrinsically unrewarding. When they struggle, a librarian may need to remind them why they are there and what they are going to gain. Librarians can explain what this technology is intended to accomplish and how it is commonly used, then clarify how this particular patron plans to use this technology. After the conversation or instructional session ends, librarians can remind patrons how much they have learned since they began the session, even if their gains are basic as knowing the name of a new piece of equipment. Librarians can help patrons understand what progress really looks like and celebrate it as they progress toward their goals.

Be Realistic

Librarians may find that their goals and patrons' goals are sometimes in conflict with one another.

Some common patron goals observed by librarians include the following.

- Getting a good grade in a class.
- Feeling competent and comfortable.
- Getting the work done and getting out of the library to do something fun.
- Engaging in activities that the library patron finds interesting and intrinsically rewarding.
- What are some of the common goals that librarians have?
- Attracting patrons to the library.
- Helping patrons learn.
- Encouraging patrons to ask for librarian assistance.
- Teaching patrons to use databases, books, and other library resources.
- Educating patrons to use high-quality resources, not easy, expedient, yet lower-quality resources.

The reluctant patron likely wants to get out of the library and do something perceived as more fun; the librarian probably wants the patron to use the library more often. The patron may want a good grade with the smallest possible expenditure of suffering; the librarian wants the patron to think critically. The patron probably wants to avoid betraying ignorance by talking to a librarian, and the librarian encourages the patron to ask for help. A reasonable strategy for bringing these priorities into alignment is to accept the real wants and needs of the patron and to manage patrons' wants while addressing their needs.

For example, a patron may want a good grade, but the patron probably also wants to minimize suffering and effort. A librarian who trains a group of students to use a database, for example, may be challenged by the conflict between the librarian's goals and those of the reluctant students. Reluctant students may decide that they can achieve the same goal of getting a good grade by using an online search engine. While developing research skills will benefit the students on an ongoing basis, these students will be tempted to choose the familiar and expedient over the unfamiliar and more challenging path. Therefore, librarians need to acknowledge that potential conflict while teaching library patrons the skills they need.

Accept That Short-Term Temptations Sometimes Overcome Long-Term Goals

One way a librarian instructor might react when faced with a patron who is finding the education process difficult may be to cite long-term, intrinsic goals, such as developing critical thinking skills that can be applied to future careers. While those are real and valuable motivating factors, human beings are constantly tempted to forgo long-term goals for short-term ones, so it may be wise to be prepared to address short-term goals as well. Doing so will create rapport with the patron and help make the instruction as relevant as possible.

An example would be for a librarian to remind a group of reluctant college students in a university library that their professor is requiring a variety of different sources in a paper, and that a person who knows how to use a database can find a variety of current resources with one simple search. The librarian could remind them that can save time, save energy, get a higher grade with less work, and find more resources more quickly using a database than they would with a search engine. The goal should be to show them that appropriate research methods can help them not only complete the task well, but complete it efficiently.

This is not to suggest that librarians should blindly follow patrons' every desire, only to suggest that it is beneficial to recognize human nature and acknowledge the goals of patrons so that librarians can more effectively achieve their mission.

Edit Ruthlessly

Technology instruction can benefit from deliberately omitting less important details to highlight the essentials that remain. Instead of rushing to cover a great deal of material, an alternative would be to tell patrons that only essential functions will be covered in this session and to provide them with a means to find more information. It is far preferable to explain a few essential features thoroughly than to race through every button and menu item on the screen. Once the patron has developed the confidence and sense of self-efficacy that comes with mastering a few functions, the patron may be motivated to explore other functions as needed.

The decision on what features to cover should be driven by the patron's needs, but put in terms of the patron's wants. For example, a university student may *want* to find resources in the simplest possible fashion in order to get a grade in the most painless way. That method could easily lead the student to a basic search engine or to a simple keyword search in a database and the quick selection of the first ten articles that appear. That said, the patron probably *needs* to find scholarly journals that were published within the past five years, which would lead to an academic database, in order to achieve the grade that the patron wants.

When viewing the database, the interaction can benefit from showing the patron the minimum number of features needed to achieve the desired result, such as a simple keyword search, a date limiter, and the option of adding additional keywords in order to narrow the results. If those features render the results that the patron wants, the librarian can leave Boolean searches or the dozens of other features for a later meeting.

Remind Patrons of How Much They Already Know

The same patrons who complain that research is boring may spend hours clicking from link to link, poring over a favorite musician's lyrics or a hometown baseball teams hit stats. When doing research training, librarians can consider what search terms to use to best interest patrons, and compare the results to those found in a common search engine. By showing patrons that they already have more research skills than they realize, patrons may better appreciate the practical applications of library skills.

A librarian who is teaching a new technology skill could remind patrons that there was a day they did not know how to drive a car or use a smartphone, and while there is no way to be sure that they will immediately grasp a new technology skill, their past successes probably provide adequate evidence to assume that they can master it eventually. By emphasizing the skills that patrons already possess, librarians can build rapport, connect education to patrons' goals, and help build a sense of competence.

Use Teaching Technology Effectively

Since patrons are already in an inherently uncomfortable situation and using their cognitive ability to master a new skill, librarians can benefit their patrons by anticipating problems with instructional technology and seeking to overcome those issues. If a librarian is giving a prepared presentation and plans to show a computer screen with a projector, the librarian could take care to zoom in on the area of the screen that is being discussed, move the mouse pointer slowly, and avoid too much scrolling that could cause a patron to lose track of what the librarian is demonstrating. If instruction takes place in a computer lab, librarians can enlist the help of an assistant to walk behind the computer screens and discreetly assist people who have fallen behind.

When working with PowerPoints or making a handout, librarians can use large images that can be read on-screen or easily viewed if the patron prints the presentation, perhaps recording the screen and posting brief video clips to which patrons can refer at a later time.

Push Them Out of the Nest

In order to cement developing skills and help patrons develop confidence, librarians can step away and allow patrons to try to complete a task alone, then return after some brief, pre-determined time. If patrons are successful at completing tasks, they will build self-confidence in the task that will help motivate them to continue. If they are not successful, the experience of trying the task on their own will quickly reveal the source of the failure and demonstrate whether they would benefit from additional instruction or a longer period of independent work.

Prepare for Failure

In spite of both the librarian's and the patron's best efforts, there is the possibility that the student will end the reference interaction, class, or meeting without accomplishing the task that librarian and patron attempted to complete. The patron may seem sad, frustrated, or may express the desire to try the technology again at a different time. On the other hand, the patron might vow to never attempt it again.

It can be helpful to prepare some supporting information to hand the patron after the session ends that includes the librarian's contact information and the main points of the session. To the successful student, the material will be a potentially helpful piece of supporting content, but to the less successful student, it can provide the student with the message that the librarian believes they can accomplish the task eventually, even if they did not accomplish it in this instance.

The librarian may need to consider whether it will be a valuable use of time to encourage the resistant student to continue during the session. If the librarian has a positive relationship with the patron and believes the patron just needs some additional encouragement, the librarian may decide to take a few minutes to encourage the patron to take a break and try it again instead of quitting. If the patron is unkind or rude, highly resistant, or distracts the librarian's attention from other patrons, the librarian may decide that it would be better to let that patron go and hope that the person returns in a more positive frame of mind at a later time.

Build on Success

If the patrons are successful, librarians can celebrate that success by pointing out all that they have accomplished before finishing the session by providing them with a handout offering additional information about the topic and showing them how to find out more.

Teaching new technology skills is a process of teaching practical skills and dispelling fears that can prevent students from moving forward in their academic or practical education. By accepting that library patrons' emotions can either be a motivator or a detriment to their success, librarians can best address their needs while building positive working relationships.

In Summary

- Accept that asking for help is painful for many patrons.
- Know that fear often appears in disguise.
- Encourage competence.
- Foster reasonable expectations of mastery.
- Keep the goal in mind.
- Be realistic about the patron's goals.
- Accept that short-term temptations sometimes overcome long-term goals.
- Edit information ruthlessly.
- Remind patrons how much they already know.
- Use teaching technology effectively.
- Push them out of the nest.
- Prepare for failure.
- Build on success.

REFERENCES

Bledsoe, T. Scott, and Janice J. Baskin. 2014. "Recognizing Student Fear: The Elephant in the Classroom." *College Teaching* 62, no. 1 (Winter): 32–41. doi: 10.1080/87567555.2013.831022.

Curry, Lynne. 2016. *Beating the Workplace Bully: A Tactical Guide to Taking Charge*. New York: American Management Association.

"Does Not Compute: The High Cost of Low Technology Skills in the U.S.—and What We Can Do About It." *Change the Equation.* http://changetheequation.org/does-not-compute.

Dweck, Carol. 2014. "Talent: How Companies Can Profit from a 'Growth Mindset.'" *Harvard Business Review* 92, no. 11 (November): 28–29. http://search.ebscohost.com/login.aspx?direct=true&db=bth&AN=98969494&site=ehost-live&scope=site.

Goodman, Madeline J., Anita M. Sands, Richard J. Coley, and the Educational Testing Service. 2015. *America's Skills Challenge: Millennials and the Future.* Princeton: Educational Testing Service. http://www.ets.org/s/research/30079/asc-millennials-and-the-future.pdf .

Gremmels, Gillian. S. 2015. "Constance Mellon's 'Library Anxiety': An Appreciation and a Critique." *College & Research Libraries* 76, no. 3: 268–275. doi:10.5860/crl.76.3.268.

Partnering to Teach Technology
Planning a Library-Based Workshop Series

KATHRYN M. HOUK *and* JORDAN M. NIELSEN

In this essay we will discuss how two faculty members at the San Diego State University (SDSU) Library presented a workshop series focused on tools and information revolving around digital scholarship, and leveraged relationships throughout the library and campus to do so. We will provide a succinct overview of pertinent trends in pedagogy, present a brief overview of the landscape for libraries teaching technological skills, and then present the current climate at SDSU that led to the authors' decisions to create a workshop series. The rest of the essay will be focused on how the authors designed, implemented and assessed the Digital Scholarship Workshop Series.

21st Century Skills and the Library

At about the turn of the millennium, educational leaders across the country and world were recognizing the tremendous impact the rapid advances in technology were having on how students learn and the work environment they'd have in the future. In 2002, the Partnership for 21st Century Skills was created (Partnership for 21st Century Learning 2015a), and has been working on developing a comprehensive skills framework revolving around digital literacy, information literacy, media literacy, core competencies and work/life coping skills. A comprehensive framework was released in May 2015 (Partnership for 21st Century Learning 2015b) includes the following learning frames: Key Subjects & 21st Century Themes; Learning and Innovation Skills; Life and Career Skills; and Information, Media and Technology Skills. Learning and Innovation Skills include the abilities to think creatively, solve problems, communicate clearly and act on innovations. Information, Media and Technology Skills include the abilities to access, use, and manage information; create media products; and use technology effectively. Life and Career Skills include the abilities to adapt, be flexible, manage time, be self-directed in learning, manage products and produce results.

Media centers and libraries of all levels are uniquely placed to be leaders in these three 21st century learning frames. Our ability to democratize access to expensive technologies and software and the buildings' often coveted placement near the physical center of campus, leads to a third space of learning that brings together a wonderful hodgepodge of talents and interests from across campus and the disciplines. This can be seen in the explosion of spaces such as digital humanities labs, data visualization labs, and makerspaces in the past decade in campus libraries across the United States (Ayers 2013). However, these spaces rarely discuss "21st Century Skills," and instead prefer to discuss how they support digital scholarship. This likely reflects the shift from creating learning products in grade school to an expectation of producing informed and well-argued scholarship at the undergraduate level and beyond. Digital Scholarship is often defined as "the use of digital evidence and method, digital authoring, digital publishing, digital curation and preservation, and digital use and reuse of scholarship" (Rumsey 2011). The authors took a very broad interpretation of "publishing" and "scholarship" to include an array of media models—not just the traditional academic paper or poster. Though the push to communicate research in new formats, outside of the traditional published article, has existed for more than a decade (Ayers 2013; Koh 2012), it has been slow to gain traction. The authors hope that by combining teaching digital tools and discussions of ethical and theoretical issues that have arisen from their use, faculty will feel more confident to experiment and push the traditional boundaries of scholarship.

San Diego State University and Its Library

The demographics of the state of California and the student profile at SDSU also heavily influenced our beliefs that the library is the ideal place to be teaching these workshops. In 2012, 50 percent of children under the age of 18 in California were living in or near poverty (Bohn, Danielson, and Bandy 2015). Eighty-two percent of SDSU's enrollment is composed of California residents, 60 percent of students identify as a minority, and 62 percent of our campus receives financial aid (Forbes 2015; SDSU Analytic Studies & Institutional Research 2015). These figures, along with anecdotal evidence, point to our students struggling financially, often choosing between textbooks or meals for the month. The demographic makeup suggests that our students may never have been exposed to advanced and costly software applications that are typical of academic environments. The library, by virtue of our purchasing and bargaining power, has some of the most technology- and software-rich spaces on campus. The ability of the library to democratize access to advanced computing and provide it for free to students and faculty makes it the ideal place on campus to teach unique tools that would aid students in expressing their learning.

Outside of the classroom and their homes, the SDSU Library hosts thousands of students a day wishing to study alone or in groups. The campus is comprised of approximately 86 percent commuter students (U.S. News & World Report 2015), many of them commuting across the border, where they wait for hours to leave Mexico. Obviously, for a majority of our students, going home between classes is not a feasible option. In order to take advantage of their time, students will often come to the library between classes to study or work on assignments. The high gate counts mean that the Library can market fairly easily to a wide audience, within the library space itself. It also means that at any given time we choose to schedule workshops during the day, there is likely to be more than enough audience to choose from.

There is also a favorable campus and library climate for teaching digital tools. The SDSU Strategic Plan was released in 2010 and states that providing diverse educational opportunities that expand the scope of student scholarship is a priority for campus (San Diego State University 2013). It also states that it will support faculty scholarship and research by creating and supporting Areas of Excellence, which focus on interdisciplinary research topics (San Diego State University 2013). One of the most recently approved clusters focuses on digital humanities, which we interpret as a clear indication that SDSU is committed to promoting the connection between digital tools, scholarly pursuits, and teaching. The goal of the library's Digital Scholarship Workshop Series (DSWS) was to provide the opportunity for all levels of students to not only interact with digital tools that they could apply directly to their class projects, but also learn about issues surrounding digital products, such as ethical use, proper etiquette on the web, and learning about how digital publishing has spawned the Open Access movement.

Developing the Workshop Series

We began planning the workshop series six months before the first session was offered in order to have plenty of time to settle on tools, request help from possible collaborators, and design each session. Goals for the DSWS were to include multiple instructors, cover a variety of freely available tools, discuss issues arising from new models of scholarship, and make the classes as hands-on as possible. Our initial development discussions revolved around the skills and tools that we would like to be covered in the series. The finalized list of free tools and issues were grouped into weekly themes with two classes related to each theme. The individual tools and issues covered over the four-week DSWS included

- infographics;
- designing research posters;
- digital maps;
- 3-D modeling;
- Creative Commons;
- Open Access;
- ePortfolios; and
- social media etiquette and branding.

Presenting the Workshops

Week 1: Visual Storytelling

The first week of the DSWS was organized around the theme of visual storytelling. The workshops held during this week were called "Creating Infographics" and "Designing Research Posters." In the "Creating Infographics" workshop, participants were given the opportunity to use the free version of the Piktochart infographic creator. The participants were also shown how to find data in the Library's CountryWatch database, and they were asked to pull out at least one economic, geographic, and political data point that could be included in the infographic. In "Designing Research Posters," participants were taught how to use Microsoft PowerPoint to create research posters. This workshop included discussion about basic visual design principles used to organize sections of a poster in order to draw attention to the most important points. It also presented free online tools for ensuring posters—online and off—were visually accessible to those with color vision impairment.

Week 2: Maps and Modeling

The second week of the DSWS was organized around the theme of digital maps and models. These two workshops had the most interest from students because they were introductions to ArcGIS and how to get started designing something to 3-D print from the library's own printers. The "Digital Mapping" workshop focused on ArcGIS and was taught by a staff member from the Department of Geography's computer lab. The workshop went over the basics: what GIS can be used for, where to find educational and training videos, and a brief tour of the interface. The "3-D Modeling" workshop was taught by our engineering and math librarian and went over how to set up an account and use a free online tool called TinkerCAD to design object to 3-D print. The attendees spent most of the time creating a nametag design that they saved and sent to the Library's 3-D printer in our BuildIT makerspace.

Week 3: Open Access

The third week of the DSWS occurred during Open Access Week, so instead of teaching just tools, we also focused a bit on some current issues in digital scholarship. The first workshop was "Creative Commons Licensing" and focused on copyright and reuse issues for items found on the web—particularly images. Led by the engineering and math librarian, this workshop presented Creative Commons as a means to license an individual's work and to find works that give permission to reuse and remix the content. The "Open Access Publishing" workshop gave an overview of the state of traditional academic scholarship and publishing and informed attendees of the reasoning behind the Open Access movement. Whenever librarians get to speak about the cost of our resources, it always leads to a sudden and shocked interest in the nuances of academic publishing, which was no different in this DSWS session.

Week 4: Professional Web Identity

The final week of the DSWS focused on creating and maintaining a professional web identity via webpages and social media. The first workshop was called "Developing ePortfolios" and was taught by the library's staff web designer. Attendees of the workshop were introduced to the free website builder, Wix, and had the opportunity to use creative commons when looking for images to develop a practice website. The final presentation, "Social Media Professionalism," was presented by a staff member from the Career Services Center and was the most highly attended workshop. Participants discussed privacy settings, building a personal brand throughout multiple social media platforms, and the importance of professionals in the 21st century having a presence on various platforms.

Collaborate or Die

A key element of this technology-based workshop series was collaboration. From the beginning, we knew we wanted to focus on leveraging the skills available throughout the university. After choosing the topics and technologies, it was crucial to identify instructors who could lead the workshops, as well as make the experience as seamless for them as possible. Most elements of the workshops were planned before potential collaborators were contacted. The workshop dates, times and rooms were already scheduled, as well as the assessments created and the presence of at least one of the DSWS coordinators assured. Collaborators were presented with one of two dates within the theme week to present, and the request that they prepare approximately 45 minutes of content on their workshop's topic. The workshops on infographics, research poster design, and open access publishing were led by us (the DSWS coordinators), as we had experience and interest in those areas; which left us with five workshops to place instructors.

The initial step taken to identify instructors was to look at library faculty and staff who had the technological and instructional skills needed for this series. E-mails were sent to the library as a whole to solicit interest in leading workshops. After reaching out, instructors were identified for the sessions covering 3-D Modeling, Creative Commons Publishing, and ePortfolio Creation. After identifying instructors for six sessions, two sessions remained without instructors. At this point, we identified the campus Career Center as a source for an instructor on Social Media Professionalism and the Department of Geography as a source for the Digital Mapping session. Both areas were contacted multiple times to eventually schedule an instructor.

Getting the Word Out

In order to increase awareness of the DSWS, multiple promotional strategies were implemented. These strategies included the use of the Library's website, digital signs throughout the library, a research guide, print signs/posters/flyers, social media, campus media, and outreach to various groups on campus.

Visual and Digital Marketing

The Library utilizes multiple social media platforms, including Facebook, Twitter, and Instagram. All of these platforms were used to promote the DSWS with content created specifically for each social media platform. The hashtag #AztecScholar was created to encourage series-specific communication, and it was used in all social media posts. The hashtag was based on SDSU's mascot plus a theme from the workshop series, that of scholarship. All social media platforms utilized by the library were featured on the print and digital signage created for the DSWS, and the #AztecScholar hashtag was displayed on all signage. There was also visual continuity with all signage and social media advertising, utilizing the same color scheme and reusing a DSWS "mascot" of a cartoon brain.

Along with reaching out via social media, we utilized the library website's status as a portal to all of the resources, services, and events within the library to promote the Digital Scholarship Workshop Series through the use of scrolling banners, and an entry on the Library's online events calendar. The banner for the DSWS cycled with four other banners, so it was prominently displayed in the two weeks leading up to the DSWS, with individual banners for each session posted the day before and of the workshop.

We also leveraged the LibGuides platform to create a dynamic landing page for anyone interested in the DSWS. This LibGuide was broken into sections, with each section including a page dedicated to one week of the DSWS. On each of these pages, a link to the registration form for that DSWS session was included, as were additional links related to the topic of that week's session. Links to the LibGuide were included on almost all marketing materials. Print signs were created using the same visual style as the online marketing materials. These print materials took the form of flyers and posters. The flyers were posted in various spots throughout the library, and across the SDSU campus. The posters were mounted in frames and displayed in the main entrance of the Library two weeks before the events started and during the month of October while the DSWS were in session.

External Library Promotion

Working with campus or local media outlets can also be beneficial for promoting a technology-based workshop series in the Library. In this instance, we gave an interview to "The Daily Aztec," the student newspaper, in order to promote the workshop series. This interview provided an opportunity for us to describe the workshops in more detail. The origin of the workshop series and the collaborative spirit of the series were also highlighted. This interview appeared online and in print a week before the workshop series began, providing marketing outside of the library's own social media and web accounts.

The SDSU Library uses a subject specialist model, with departments assigned to specific librarians. A librarian assigned to most of the centers, offices, and academic units on campus means access to various listservs for announcements regarding the library. A form letter e-mail was drafted by the DSWS coordinators and sent to the subject specialist librarians three weeks prior to the start of the workshop series. This e-mail could be personalized for each unit/office/center the librarian sent the e-mail message to and the DSWS coordinators requested their colleagues to forward the announcements. This allowed for the direct promotion of the series to potentially interested groups via a network within the library.

SDSU has a center devoted to promoting pedagogical innovation known as the Center for Teaching and Learning. The CTL often organizes meetings and "lunch and learn" events where participants are shown new tools and techniques that can be used to teach students. The DSWS fits nicely with the programming the CTL offers, and they were contacted about promoting the DSWS, and they ultimately shared information about the DSWS at their events, on their website, and their e-mail lists.

Lessons Learned/Challenges

One of the biggest challenges that came with organizing a workshop series such as this was identifying collaborators to lead workshop sessions. It was much easier to identify collaborators within the library due to the already-established relationships between the session leaders and the workshop coordinators. It proved much more difficult to identify external collaborators across a campus with a vast array of disciplines and research interests. After identifying collaborators, the hardest part was then convincing them to lead a workshop session. In particular, the session on digital mapping swapped instructors multiple times due to scheduling conflicts and lack of sufficient incentive for faculty.

In terms of individual sessions, covering the topic/tool thoroughly enough in the short period of time designated was a challenge. Each session was essentially limited to 45 to 50 minutes, and most workshops involved hands-on elements that took up much of the session. It was difficult finding time to introduce the topic and administer the assessment while giving enough time for participants to interact with the tool/technology in a meaningful way. This was particularly true of the ArcGIS workshop. The complexity and detail of the software really made it impractical for a brief workshop to even begin to introduce the tool. Most of the time with any of the more interactive tools was spent learning the organization and purpose of the various buttons and menus.

However, the greatest challenge faced by the DSWS was attendance. Registration was high, indicating an interest in the topics and tools, but attendance was significantly lower. Even with all of the marketing we attempted, it is clearly too easy to walk away from a free and voluntary library session. Incentivizing with food, prize drawings, or other methods were not options available to us due to our lack of budget for such things. It is a challenge we are looking to address by exploring completely changing the structure and method of how we teach these tools and technologies.

The Future of Digital Scholarship @ SDSU and Beyond

The DSWS served as an opportunity to promote 21st century skills to a large student population. While it did prove challenging to identify collaborators who were willing and able to highlight specific tools and techniques, it resulted in new relationships being formed between the library and other units on campus. These relationships can be leveraged in future iterations of the DSWS. The reaction to this series was largely positive, but the challenges have inspired us to think about new ways to offer these, and similar, workshops in the future. One idea is to offer pop-up workshops that can be offered informally. These workshops could be offered in a heavily trafficked area of the Library to attract casual passers-by. This could give exposure to a technology tool/topic in a way that is less intimidating.

While the DSWS at SDSU covered a wide range of topics and tools, the digital scholarship landscape is expanding and evolving. Tools for text mining, 3-D printing, and creating information visualizations are trending right now, but there are new tools emerging at a breakneck speed. Libraries can respond to this evolution by regularly embracing new tools and topics and encouraging their users to embrace them as well. By offering users the ability to explore and use new technologies, libraries are promoting digital scholarship and supporting their users' quest to acquire 21st century skills.

References

Ayers, Edward L. 2013. "Does Digital Scholarship Have a Future?" *EDUCAUSE Review* 48 (4): 24–34. http://er.educause.edu/~/media/files/article-downloads/erm1343.pdf.
Bohn, Sarah, Caroline Danielson, and Monica Bandy. 2015. *Child Poverty in California. Just the Facts*. San Francisco. http://www.ppic.org/content/pubs/jtf/JTF_ChildPovertyJTF.pdf.

Forbes. 2015. "San Diego State University." *Forbes America's Top Colleges.* http://www.forbes.com/colleges/san-diego-state-university/.

Koh, Adeline. 2012. "The Challenges of Digital Scholarship." *The Chronicle of Higher Education.* http://chronicle.com/blogs/profhacker/the-challenges-of-digital-scholarship/38103.

Partnership for 21st Century Learning. 2015a. "Partnership for 21st Century Learning: Our History." *p21.org.* http://www.p21.org/about-us/our-history.

Partnership for 21st Century Learning. 2015b. "P21 Framework Definitions." *p21.org.* http://www.p21.org/storage/documents/docs/P21_Framework_Definitions_New_Logo_2015.pdf.

Rumsey, Abby Smith. 2011. *New-Model Scholarly Communication: Road Map for Change. Scholarly Communication Institute 9.* Charlottesville. http://www.uvasci.org/institutes-2003–2011/SCI-9-Road-Map-for-Change.pdf.

San Diego State University. 2013. *Building on Excellence: A Strategic Plan for San Diego State University 2013–2018.* http://go.sdsu.edu/strategicplan/images/finalstrategicplan.pdf.

SDSU Analytic Studies & Institutional Research. 2015. "At A Glance: San Diego State University." *SDSU In Numbers.* https://asir.sdsu.edu/.

U.S. News & World Report. 2015. "San Diego State University Student Life." *America's Best Colleges.* http://colleges.usnews.rankingsandreviews.com/best-colleges/sdsu-1151/student-life.

Balancing Technology Education with Reference and Instruction

Elizabeth Nelson

Reference and public services staff in libraries, in addition to myriad other responsibilities, are charged with assisting patrons and answering questions related to research, library resources, and a variety of other topics. Many librarians and library staff also have responsibility for teaching library users in a more formal setting on topics from information literacy and research skills to overviews on genealogy resources and research, and even computer and technology classes. Technology and technological fluency have an ever-increasing impact on our lives, and teaching these skills can be an important role for the library. But what happens when these technology questions spill over from more formal instruction into the day-to-day questions encountered at the reference desk or other service point? Some librarians don't necessarily see their role as including technology instruction in the reference environment, or may even question the value of providing technology-based reference as opposed to more traditional reference services.

Libraries in a Technological World

Traditional reference and instruction was based on fulfilling information needs. Library users had questions that could only be answered by accessing information–information that was much scarcer than it is today. There is no lack of articles or presentations that point to a decline in reference transactions, as it is traditionally conceived. There are declining visits to the reference desk and a corresponding decline in the number of questions being asked at the reference desk or other service points. As information has become more accessible, the needs of many library users has shifted from finding information to applying information and "doing things" (Kenney 2015). At the same time that information has become more ubiquitous, it has also become more unwieldy for library users to navigate on their own. So while there may be fewer in-person ready reference requests, some libraries are seeing big changes in how they interact with their users, including remotely, as well as shifts in the types of questions and requests they field (Saunders, Rozakus and Abels 2015). The shift to electronic has not only affected how information is created and stored, but also how people interact and work. An increased emphasis on information literacy helps library users develop the skills to interact effectively and efficiently with the world of information at their fingertips. But the speed at which technology, and the way information is accessed, has required librarians to develop new models for what it means to be information literate in a technological world. For example, the *Framework for Information Literacy for Higher Education* provides six concepts in information literacy. These frames give librarians a flexible way to look at and work with information literacy. While these were created for higher education, information literacy is a life skill and librarians in all settings help library users gain understanding and competence in these areas. But information literacy is not enough if users can only apply it in an analog world. In order to take advantage of all the information that is available to them, library users have to be able to navigate the technology required to access it.

In order to facilitate access to information and provide a needed service to their communities, libraries have taken on the task of technology instruction. It is clear that these types of services are here to stay, as addressing patrons' technology needs is a valuable service. In addition to fulfilling an immediate need for the library user to better understand a piece of software or how to perform basic computer or online-based tasks, a level of technological literacy can give library users the tools they need to improve their information literacy or help them reach other job-related, educational, or lifelong learning goals. Seen in this light it becomes clear why those struggling with technology, or just looking to learn newest tools, have turned to the library and librarians to help them reach this goal.

Technology Instruction

Technology instruction is a category of question that continues to increase, even as technology has reduced the number of ready reference questions encountered. But even in light of the oft repeated statistics that demonstrate a decline in reference questions, librarians and other library staff have not seen a corresponding decrease in workload. While technology has reduced some types of questions, it has increased others. Technology has opened up new ways for libraries to reach library users through new communication channels, increased the technological competencies required for librarians and library staff, and introduced new ways to assist patrons, by adding both devices and software to the library's toolkit and also through teaching users how to utilize new technologies. However, library metrics have not necessarily kept up with the shift in how patrons use the library and library services. Showing the continued value in reference services and instruction makes it critical to document the types of questions being answered at all service points and defining what types of questions belong to each category. Technology has not replaced traditional library work, only augmented it through additional services and patron needs. Libraries need ways to account for the new ways librarians and library staff spend their time.

Technology instruction happens at several levels. The advent of makerspaces has created a new venue for instruction. The additional resources available to the public require library staff to develop expertise in the new technology they are providing. That may include tutorials and instruction on the operation of devices or peripherals, such as downloading plans and operating 3-D printers, or it may just involve demonstrations of what is now possible. Technology instruction can also occur in a formal teaching environment, in any type of library setting. Students in a school or academic library, community members in a public library, and employees in a corporate library may all turn to librarians for formal instruction on different types of technology, from basic computer skills to more detailed training on specific software, web design, or using their devices to access library material. The outcomes of this type of instruction, including the number of sessions offered and the numbers of attendees at each, are generally captured in statistics relating to programming rather than in conjunction with technology assistance and instruction offered at the reference desk, but they are still important measures to consider when looking at technology instruction in aggregate.

Technology instruction at services desks differs from more traditional reference in that it typically does not pertain to library content and resources. While questions regarding how to access and search the library catalog and databases, as well as guidance on how to conduct Internet searches, certainly have a technology aspect, they primarily refer to accessing content and require a degree of information literacy instruction, an area that has long been a part of reference desk activity and statistics. These questions can be viewed as subject reference, or another category as designated by the library, but fall into the purview of traditional reference work. Technology instruction, however, goes beyond locating information and applies more to using software and devices, either library owned or BYOD (bring your own device). But no matter how a library classifies questions, there should be a system in place to document the number and complexity of questions being asked.

Making Meaning from Statistics

The simplest method of keeping statistics is the hash mark method, which requires recording a hash mark each time a question is asked. This method is used so often because, while it is simple, it is also effective and easy to implement. It is easy to use paper and pencil to track transactions, but it also lacks some of the detail needed to show the value of library services or even to fully understand patron needs. To provide further information for those interpreting the statistics, it is possible to record hash marks for various types of reference activity separately. For instance, a library can track the number of subject reference questions, the number of database questions, the number of directional questions, the number of BYOD questions, the number of software questions, etc., in different columns or in different locations. In addition, individual hash marks can be made to represent questions of a certain difficulty or requiring a specific amount of time to answer, five minutes for example. If a librarian spent 30 minutes assisting a patron with setting up an account and downloading eBooks to a device, then that transaction could be represented by six hash marks in the statistics for that day. While that system may represent a more accurate view of the time and effort expended by those at the reference desk, it does not fully represent the complexity of the questions, or the type of knowledge required by those working at public service desks. In a hash mark system, even with modifications, there is no way to tell if those six hash marks represent six simple questions that require no specialized knowledge, or if they represent a single, complex transaction requiring in-depth knowledge and the ability to troubleshoot library systems and patron devices, or somewhere in between.

There are ways to address this lack of detail. Librarian have turned to technology to tackle this issue, using software designed specifically for the task, such as Springshare's LibAnalytics, or creating a homegrown solution using Google Forms, Google Sheets, Microsoft Excel, or employing other solutions. Once a more robust tracking system is in place it becomes easier to identify technology instruction questions and to assign a rating for difficulty or the amount of knowledge required to assist the library user, as well as record the amount of time, specifically or as a range, required to address the issue. Just as with subject-based reference questions where some questions are easily or quickly answered and in other cases the reference interview uncovers a thornier question, technology instruction at the reference desk varies quite a bit in time and knowledge required to address patron needs. Some questions may be familiar troubleshooting issues or frequently encountered tasks, such as downloading eBooks or formatting documents while others may involve unfamiliar software or devices and may take longer to unravel.

Tracking this type of data in statistics, particularly related to expanding services, can help justify the current staffing levels at public service desks based on the outcomes delivered to library users, but it may also highlight areas for staff development or even additional staffing needs to address these questions in addition to the other responsibilities of those staffing these desks, including content-based reference and formal instruction sessions and programming. Additionally, if the same types of questions are frequently identified in the analysis of the statistics, additional programming opportunities may also be identified.

Making a Plan

Once a system of collecting meaningful statistics has been implemented, it is possible to isolate and analyze the types of questions being asked. In addition to identifying trends in types and complexity of questions, it also provides the opportunity to look at how patrons are utilizing library services and determine if changes in staffing levels and expertise are needed. When considering the future of reference and technology instruction, there are many factors to keep in mind, including how to develop expertise, cross-train staff, draw the line when patrons' needs exceed staff knowledge or other resources, and keeping the library's mission in mind.

Develop Expertise

Keeping statistics on the types of questions received at service desks provides a wealth of information for planning. If the technology needs of the community align with current staff expertise and responsibilities, that's great. But if it doesn't, it might be time to take a closer look at staffing levels and develop expertise in new areas. This may require professional development for those in public service areas or may lead to the creation of a new position to address the technology training needs and also to keep an eye on emerging technologies and potential service expansions.

Developing expertise with technology is not that different from developing expertise in other library service areas. Just as it takes time to become conversant in all the reference sources, databases, and websites that can be used to assist members of the library's community, it also takes time to become familiar with the unique technology needs of the patrons. Some libraries may get a large number of questions related to downloading eBooks while other may get more questions about word processing, presentation, or even more specialized software. Some categories of technology instruction needs include

- eBooks—including accessing, checking out and downloading;
- devices—using tablets, phones, laptops, and desktops to access library resources;
- software—including training and questions on library provided software;
- specialized software and hardware—including accessing scanners, 3-D printers, or other technology provided by the library or in a makerspace;
- computer—including training on questions on basic computer and browser operation; and
- any other categories that are needed by library users.

Compare the categories with library staff expertise and identify any gaps in services provided. Fill any gaps in expertise through training or hiring. Depending on the distribution of reference questions to technology questions it may be possible to advocate for a new position or a redistribution of responsibilities in order to address the newly identified needs. No matter the solution to filling the gaps in technology expertise, the next step is to make sure that knowledge and expertise is shared across service points and shifts so the service level remains constant no matter what time or day of the week patrons are able to visit the library.

Cross-Training

Once expertise has been developed, it needs to be shared. Knowledge management and knowledge sharing is crucial to any organization, and libraries are no different. Knowledge sharing and cross-training can occur in many different forms, either face-to-face or electronically. Librarians and library staff like to share what they know, so face-to-face may be the most familiar option. Formal training or lunch and learn sessions can allow one-to-many knowledge sharing to take place if there is something many people need to learn. But due to public service desk staffing and other variables, that is not always a possibility. In the face-to-face format, information can also be shared during shift changes or in more serendipitous encounters.

However, due to the nature of library work, and the variety of questions that can be encountered, documenting instructions, tips, and tricks may be a more useful option. Using technology such as a shared document, Google Docs, a wiki, or other tools, a knowledge base can be created to help those staffing service areas troubleshoot issues or provide instruction on specific technology topics. Using the same categories that were identified when tracking technology instruction statistics, tip sheets and training materials for both library staff and library users can be accessed at the point of need. Rather than expecting everyone staffing a service desk to become experts with all the software and devices patrons might use, it is more effective to have a process for collecting information that can help those in service areas answer questions as they arise. Common problems, and hopefully solutions as well, can be outlined, and links to videos or other supporting documentation can be included as well. As technology and software continue to change, this documentation can be modified and updated to reflect the current technology as well as current user needs. Once the needs, and the ways in which the library can address those needs, have been identified, it also becomes easier to create training materials or instruction sessions that have a large audience, because the concepts have already been tested in the service environment.

Drawing the Line

While libraries are really great at finding ways to serve their communities, what they are not as great at is saying no. Technology is a term that encompasses many things. It can include things like providing computers in the library or offering basic computer classes. It can include assisting patrons with various computer tasks or pointing them to the right resources. But it can also include providing instruction or assistance on specialized hardware, software or patrons' own devices. There is a point when questions asked in the library are no longer library questions. There are boundaries that librarians don't cross when helping patrons with traditional reference questions, the most common of which is that library staff can't offer medical or legal advice. They can help you find the correct tax form or medical information, but they can't do your taxes or offer a diagnosis. Technology instruction should be addressed the same way, and the limits of library staff assistance should be clearly communicated to patrons. When a patron has a question that requires more expertise or one that crosses into the territory of the library staff doing instead of assisting (as in the case of patrons who want library staff to do their homework or design their website), then it is time to draw the line.

Keeping Your Mission in Mind

At the end of the day, technology assistance and instruction is a service that libraries offer to patrons, just like any other program or service. But rather than trying to make the library everything to everyone in the community, take a close look at the mission of the library and make sure any new offerings are tied to that goal. Use data gathered from transaction statistics to build a case for additional services, or to justify additional staff to take on these new challenges, but keep the needs of the community and the purpose of the library in mind.

Conclusion

Libraries have always adapted to the changing needs of their communities. Taking on the challenge of technology instruction providing another way for the library to provide importance services and to help patrons toward their hobby, career, and educational goals. Technology and technological literacy also relates very closely to information literacy and libraries' goals of providing access to information. Without the ability to use technology effectively, it becomes more difficult to access and use information. But it is possible for technology instruction to work alongside reference and instruction to address patron needs and continue to fulfill libraries' missions.

REFERENCES

Kenney, Brian. 2015. "Where Reference Fits in the Modern Library." *Publishers Weekly* 262 (37): 18. http://search.proquest.com/docview/1712837050?accountid=39642.

Saunders, Laura, Lillian Rozakus, and Eileen Abels. 2015. *Repositioning Reference: New Methods and New Services for a New Age*. Lanham, MD: Rowman & Littlefield.

Enhancing Pedagogy with Technology
Librarian-Guided Peer-to-Peer Instruction for Faculty

Emy Nelson Decker

College and university students are accustomed to using technology and have come to expect that their professors will use technology in the classroom as well. While many faculty members are comfortable trying new technology and incorporating its use in the classroom and in assignments, some prefer more support in regards to training prior to attempting to use technology in pedagogy. This essay describes the ways in which a unit within an academic library reimagined its faculty technology training workshops to help support faculty use of technology in the classroom. Instead of relying upon the traditional workshop model which featured unit members teaching faculty members how to use technology in training sessions, the workshops were redesigned and redeveloped to incorporate a faculty guest speaker to describe their own experience "from the trenches" in implementing technology in the classroom. The faculty speaker would also share the assignments he or she developed, any issues encountered in using the technology, and assist his or her peers in preparing to implement the technology in their courses. The addition of the peer-to-peer training component increased faculty confidence in teaching with technology and proved to be a successful new model that the unit continues to use for faculty technology workshops. In post workshop assessments, 100 percent of faculty respondents reported that they were more willing to try using new technology in the classroom after having heard successful accounts of it from their faculty colleagues. This essay will provide information about how to host workshops with faculty guest speakers serving as peer trainers and how to maximize workshop time to build faculty confidence in using technology. This program can be easily replicated and adapted to any library offering technology training workshops.

Overview

The Atlanta University Center, Robert W. Woodruff Library, Atlanta, Georgia, provides service to four historically black colleges and universities: Clark-Atlanta University, the Interdenominational Theological Center, Morehouse College, and Spelman College.

The E-Learning Technologies Unit is comprised of three paraprofessionals and the unit head librarian. The unit is tasked with designing, developing, and providing workshops for faculty that introduce them to emerging technologies as well as to new uses of existing technologies with the goal of enhancing the teaching and learning experience. A minimum of seven technology workshops are offered to Atlanta University Center faculty each semester and topics are determined by faculty request, current curricula or assignments, new learning technology trends, and hardware and software available to faculty in the library. The unit also provides workshops to students and library staff throughout the academic year. In addition, the unit is physically situated within the Technology Design Studio which is an innovative new space within the Woodruff Library that offers users an opportunity to work with cutting edge technologies including, but not limited to, digital drawing tablets, video capture robots, virtual telepresence machines, and touch screens. The Technology Design Studio also features Macintosh computers and software such as the Adobe Creative Suite, Final Cut Pro, etc., used for creative endeavors. The E-Learning Technologies Unit harnesses the Web 2.0 environment via social media to promote the unit's featured events, services, and initiatives. The unit itself maintains a blog that, in addition to communicating software tips and tricks, showcases the multimedia work created by the students who frequently use the Technology Design Studio in the library. Library users take advantage of the E-Learning Technologies Unit and the Technology Design Studio space in the library when seeking expertise in integrating technology and library resources into traditional, online, and hybrid courses.

Original Model for Faculty Workshops

When the E-Learning Technologies Unit was formed in 2012, the first semester's offerings of technology workshops were more theoretical than practical in nature. Prior to offering a workshop, all E-Learning Technologies Unit members would work together to compile the best and most up-to-date literature in the field about the learning technology at hand. From that, PowerPoint presentations about the technology topic of the workshop were developed for training purposes and related handouts were created for distribution during the workshop. Faculty members were then invited to come to the library for training on these various software programs and learning technologies. They sat at tables and listened to members of the E-Learning Technologies Unit describe or- in some cases-demonstrate how to use different types of learning technologies. The information being offered was helpful, but was offered in a manner that required faculty to later try the technology on their own instead of during the workshop.

A good example of this approach was the workshop we hosted that first semester called "Blogging for Faculty Who Don't Have Time to Blog." The workshop taught faculty how to use a classroom blog to save time and enhance the classroom experience. A blog can be a great way to organize courses and affiliated assignments and can also facilitate real-time, virtual communication, and serve as an effective learning portal. However, in presenting the workshop, the E-Learning Technologies Unit members logged into their own blog and offered faculty a tour of the "dashboard," various blog features, and provided information from recent scholarly literature about uses of blogs in the classroom and for out-of-the-classroom virtual communication. Receiving a tour of a blog can be helpful, but faculty likely needed more hands-on time with using a blog beyond the theoretical reasons why they should use one in order for them to feel inspired to try using one in their own classes. Nevertheless, faculty members were kind in their feedback of these early workshops, citing only a desire for more hands-on opportunities to gain a better understanding of the technologies being shown.

Characteristics of the original model for faculty technology workshops include

- theoretical;
- information based on current scholarship, not practice;
- faculty listening to information and watching demonstrations, no hands-on opportunities; and
- no success stories to draw upon of faculty colleagues who had tried using the technology.

Faculty Projects Born Out of Technology Workshops

Throughout the fall and spring semesters in 2013, faculty from each of the four campuses supported by the library, and in disciplines ranging from the humanities to STEM, launched classroom technology projects related to the topics of the E-Learning Technologies Unit's workshops. Some of the faculty who tried these projects had been attendees of the unit's technology workshops while others sought the unit's help independent of the workshops offered. Unit members worked with faculty to incorporate technology into the learning environment across this academic year.

Several faculty members tried flipping their classrooms. A "flipped classroom" is an instructional technique wherein instruction is given to the students outside of the classroom via multi-media and instructional videos and the related assignment takes place during class where students can work with their peers and the professor guides the active learning. So, in other words, instruction takes place "at home" and "homework" takes place in the classroom. Flipped classrooms are known by several different names, but this is the terminology commonly used at the Robert W. Woodruff Library. The first professor who tried flipping her class did so for an introductory level biology course. She selected a topic, created videos, asked E-Learning Technologies Units to assist her in reviewing and editing the videos, and then posted them to her Course Management Software so her students could login and review the videos at home prior to arriving in class to complete the related assignment. Working with this professor allowed us to learn critical skills in keeping videos short enough to hold the attention span of the student audience (Decker 2014). The following semester, we worked with a foreign language faculty member who recorded videos of herself speaking the language. Since mastering a foreign language requires hearing the language over and over, the videos she created aided her students in having a way to hear the language spoken. A third professor who had attended the unit's "Camtasia and Flipped Classroom" workshop the prior year flipped one class of his 19th century American history course. He used the library's recording studio which features Camtasia video capture software to record his videos and to add instructional graphics to his PowerPoint voice over presentation. The E-Learning Technologies Unit discovered the utility in having a faculty member flip one class out of a course with this experience.

Another faculty member approached the Unit Head for E-Learning Technologies seeking a creative and pedagogical method for incorporating social media into her classroom. She had been an attendee of the unit's "Social Media and Pedagogy" workshop. Across the two years, the activities developed for her included using a blog, using Pinterest, and using a virtual reality environment for her English courses.

Numerous faculty members had attended the unit's "Gaming and Gamification" workshop as it had been a popular trend in higher education. Several faculty developed online games, based on web apps, to serve as introductions and warm ups for exploring new topics within their courses. One professor taught mathematics and used games in the classroom to introduce advanced number theory and enhance the students' cognition of the lectures.

Librarian-Guided Peer-to-Peer Instruction

Fall semester 2014 brought with it an opportunity for the E-Learning Technologies Unit to revolutionize their technology workshops for faculty. While many faculty members had successfully incorporated technology into their teaching, very little of it except, perhaps, for the initial idea had been sparked by the workshops the unit was offering. In order to enhance the technology workshops, the unit decided to invite faculty members who had achieved success in using technology in the classroom to join the unit, in the form of peer trainers, in offering the workshop to their faculty colleagues. Keeping in mind the feedback from the workshops offered previously, the E-Learning Technologies Unit also decided to add more hands-on activities to the sessions as well.

Workshop topics conducive to having faculty serve as peer trainers include

- blogging for faculty who don't have time to blog;
- flipped classrooms;
- social media and pedagogy;
- best apps for the classroom;
- cloud applications;
- creating surveys / conducting assessments;
- presentation programs (Prezi, PowerPoint, etc.);
- gaming / gamification; and
- technology tools to enhance online courses.

Fall 2014 was the next time we offered the flipped classrooms workshop, and we invited the three faculty members we had worked with to flip their classroom to join us in presenting ideas and materials. Two of the three faculty members were able to attend during the scheduled time; the third sent us a five-minute video describing her experience that we would view during the workshop. This time, we arranged the library's workshop classroom chairs into a circle so that workshop attendees, E-Learning Technologies members, and our veteran faculty flippers-turned-trainers would all face each other. Members of the E-Learning Technologies Unit introduced the topic of flipped classrooms and presented an overview of the technology and resources the library offers faculty for flipping their classroom. During this discussion, unit members introduced Camtasia video capture software and announced technology desk drop-in hours for assistance in using the software or in previewing videos created by faculty for the purposes of out-of-classroom instruction. The workshop was informal in nature and faculty attendees were encouraged to ask questions and actively participate in the session. The faculty presenters who had experience in flipping their classroom shared what they had learned. One professor noted that the preparation work for flipping a class is the most time consuming part, but that once the videos were created and posted, she benefitted from having what seemed like more time with her students in the classroom as they worked on their biology lab. The professor who had flipped a history class recommended that faculty trying a flip for the first time adhere to flipping just one lecture or one topic, instead of attempting to flip an entire course for the very first time. He also shared with the workshop attendees that he found iMovie easier to use than Camtasia and recommended that faculty use whichever video recording software with which they are already familiar. A member of the E-Learning Technologies Unit recommended that faculty create several brief videos as opposed to one long video for out-of-classroom instruction. She learned that students respond better to brief video segments and can review them as they are standing in line at the bookstore, waiting for a bus, or in between preparing a meal at home. This information came from a conversation she had had with a student who was in the biology professor's course who shared how she used her time at home with the videos relating to her professor's flipped classroom.

The E-Learning Technologies Unit also hosted a workshop entitled "Social Media and Pedagogy" during fall semester 2014. The professor who had worked with the unit in developing various pedagogically sound projects on social media platforms agreed to partner with the unit and serve as a peer trainer for her colleagues looking to implement similar projects in their own courses. This workshop was set up similarly to the one on flipped classrooms wherein the unit emphasized a conversational-style, participatory workshop between the E-Learning Technologies Unit as workshop facilitators, the faculty member experienced in using social media successfully in her courses as a peer trainer, and the faculty workshop attendees looking for input in creating a similar project. During this workshop, the E-Learning Technologies Unit provided workshop attendees with some recommended social media platforms (blogs, Facebook, Pinterest, etc.) as well as some general projects that could be easily adapted to various subject matter and different disciplines. The professor who had used a blog, Pinterest boards, and a virtual reality environment encouraged workshop attendees to experiment with using various social media platforms. She told them that when she first set out to incorporate social media into the classroom, she had a personal Facebook account but never "friended" students and used it for personal communications only, never for classroom assignments. Moving to using social media in pedagogy was a new concept for her. She described in detail the blog project she assigned and touted its strength as a tool for an English course wherein students were evaluated on their writing. She did not have a very strong experience using Facebook as she felt that using this particular platform too closely merged personal life with coursework. She, however, offered a few tips for using Facebook if faculty wanted to try it for their own courses and recommended using Pinterest as it promotes visual literacy and visual thinking. The only drawback she noted, from an English course perspective was that Pinterest has character limits per "pinned" image. Therefore, she required a supplementary assignment of having students write a five-page paper to describe, in more detail, why they "pinned" what they did to their Pinterest boards. Social media can be a powerful learning resource because students are already using it in their social lives and bringing it into the classroom can further motivate student interactions (Morgan 2014).

During spring semester 2015, the E-Learning Technologies Unit offered a faculty workshop on Gaming and Gamification. Three faculty members from one of the library's member universities presented her work on gamification at a national conference. The unit invited the faculty member and two of her colleagues from the same campus, to serve as peer-trainers for this workshop. Faculty attendees of this workshop benefitted from hearing simple ways of implementing games into the classroom for the purposes of pedagogy. The faculty peer trainers encouraged faculty to try using simple games to get students engaged with the material and with each other. The professor of mathematics stressed the importance of mnemonics in mathematical formulas and shared that equations set to a beat or to a song has shown itself as having a significant impact on students remembering key formulas for exams in her experience.

Written assessments, collected after each E-Learning Technologies workshop from fall 2012 through fall 2015 indicated a positive change in faculty perception of the technology workshops. Faculty stated that they had benefitted significantly from the peer-to-peer training aspect of the workshops. One faculty member wrote, "Since other professors have had success in using this platform on our campus, I'm willing to give it a try, too." Another described the peer-to-peer training as being "a helpful and easy way to connect with colleagues and get some tried and true tips for using social media in class." As people begin to see results and share success stories, new methods and styles gain traction and come into more frequent use (Davis-Howard 2014). Since faculty members were hearing directly from their peers and receiving training from them, they reported experiencing a boost in confidence and an increased likelihood of trying a similar project in their own courses. In response to this feedback, the E-Learning Technologies unit kept this new workshop model that emphasizes peer-to-peer instruction for faculty.

Faculty Members as Peer Trainers Checklist

Remember the following when faculty members become peer trainers.

- Consider having faculty make a brief video (which will aid in scheduling concerns or if workshop will be held multiple times or across several semesters).
- Meet with faculty member beforehand to ensure that he or she will be offering information that will help other faculty members adapt the project for their own classrooms.
- Provide faculty peer trainer with guidelines as to what kind of project information should be communicated (e.g., what they did, how they did it, problems encountered, assessment).
- Remind faculty that they are training other faculty members, not teaching students.
- Thank the faculty peer trainer for participating and let them know that sharing their experience will help their faculty colleagues.

Implementing Librarian-Guided Peer-to-Peer Instruction on Technology

Peer-to-peer training is a useful method of instruction when it comes to teaching technology skills. While this essay focuses on a successful plan for an academic library, public libraries, other library types (e.g., public libraries, media centers in K–12 schools, and special libraries) may benefit from implementing a peer-to-peer training model for technology instruction as well. Technology continues to evolve and keeping abreast of new technologies as well as new methods of using current technologies is essential to the vitality of the library.

Steps for Setting Up a Peer-to-Peer Training Workshop on Technology

The following are useful steps in the process for creating a peer-to-peer training workshop on technology.

- Determine workshop technology topic.
- Identify individuals who have been successful in using technology.
- Request their collaboration in developing the workshop.
- Meet and design the workshop and determine learning outcomes.
- Develop workshop activities ("hands on," if possible).
- Assess workshop attendees' grasp of knowledge.
- Use feedback and assessment results to inform future workshop directions.

Conclusion

As described in this essay, peer-to-peer instruction can be an effective method of encouraging faculty to incorporate technology into their classrooms. Faculty who have had success in creating pedagogically sound technology projects have an opportunity to share their results with their colleagues who are, in turn, relying upon them to share hard-earned knowledge. The peer-to-peer training model was particularly rewarding for faculty workshop participants who benefitted from hearing about real-life examples of technology projects directly from their faculty peers. Receiving technology training from the unit and hearing practical experience from faculty colleagues bolstered the confidence of faculty who were willing to try undertaking a technology project for their classroom, but were perhaps unsure as to how to begin. This reimagining of faculty technology training workshops to better meet faculty needs and support them in their learning to use technology to enhance the classroom was a success and became the E-Learning Technologies Unit's preferred model for offering faculty technology workshops.

REFERENCES

Davis-Howard, Valerie. 2014. "Unleash Change Through a Peer-to-Peer Approach." *T + D* 68 (7): 76–77.
Decker, Emy N. 2014. "How to Flip and Land on Your Feet: Strategies for Empowering Faculty to Use Flipped Classrooms." *Making the Connection: Six Studies of Technology and Collaboration in Liberal Arts Institutions*, ed. Amanda Hagood, 9–18. Associated Colleges of the South.
Morgan, Hani. 2014. "Focus on Technology: Enhancing Instruction and Communication with Twitter." *Childhood Education* 90 (1): 75–76.

Information Literacy and Metaliteracy Are the Ties That Bind Librarians and Athletic Coaches

FORREST C. FOSTER, CARL LEAK *and*
TERRENCE JARROD MARTIN, SR.

It's no secret how (we) information specialists and librarians use information literacy skills on a daily basis. On any given day, one can find librarians designing a lesson plan for a semester course, helping a graduate student through the research process or even evaluating an employee for the ever so ambiguous work-plan review. At our library, C.G. O'Kelly, librarians are demonstrating how athletic coaches are encompassing information literacy skills to promote and market information literacy and library outreach efforts. What is information literacy? Information literacy is a set of abilities requiring individuals to recognize when information is needed and have the ability to locate, evaluate, and use effectively the needed information. However, did you know that for collegiate football coaches, exercising metaliteracy skills is no different? What is metaliteracy? Mackey and Jacobson describes metaliteracy as

> an overarching framework that informs other literacy type's e.g. visual, media, digital and others. Information literacy is the metaliteracy for a digital age because it provides the higher order thinking required to engage with multiple document types through various media formats in participatory environments. Metaliteracy provides an integrated and all-inclusive core for engaging with individuals and ideas in digital information environments [2011].

Many people are not cognizant of the research, assessment and schematics that are involved in creating a sound game plan for an opponent. Game planning, but more specifically the process of breaking down game film, can be meticulous and cerebral. What is the purpose of breaking down game footage of an opponent? The purpose is to seek out regular and irregular tendencies of your opponent, so that one can become familiar with what to expect from your opponent in contest. The art of game planning, which encompasses many of the old ACRL Information literacy strands and combined with some of the new ACRL frameworks ideologies, is analogous to the many of skills and competencies librarians exhibit. It is also the epitome of using metaliteracy literacy skills at its optimum.

Step 1: Authority Is Constructed and Contextual

Objectives:

- Recognize that authoritative content may be packaged formally or informally and may include sources of all media types (i.e., identifies the value and differences of potential resources in a variety of formats (e.g., multimedia, database, website, data set, audio/visual, book) [Association of College & Research Libraries 2000].

The defensive coordinator of a football team is the one who coordinates and strategizes a game plan to defend against the opposing team's offensive. The coordinator will need to know and comprehend the strategy and tactics of the opposing team's offense. He will need to know what type of plays they are creating and designing. He will need to know what formation or alignment these plays originate from. He will also need to know the best players and how often they are running or receiving the ball. In summary, the coordinator will need a complete analysis of the opponent's games to observe their strengths and weaknesses by analyzing the game footage and by other means if necessary.

The film or game footage of the opponent is the item that is usually the standard for extracting the information a coach needs. The film captures everything that takes places during a game. Another resource a coach will tend to use is other coaches! Many coaches rely on other coaches or "allies" from other teams to supply them will anecdotal information. "What do they do on 3rd down against your defense?" "Who was their favorite target to throw the ball to on 3rd down?" Some coaches, dishonorably, will even employ a spy. In 2007, the New England Patriots decided to incorporate a spy to scout their opponents by videotaping their opponents' signals. This however was deemed illegal and the Patriots were subjected to penalties. Many coaches will also use themselves as a source to gather information from prior and past experiences.

Step 2: Research as Inquiry

Objectives:

- Use various research methods, based on need, circumstance, and type of inquiry (i.e., *retrieves information online or in person using a variety of methods*).
- Deal with complex research by breaking complex questions into simple ones, limiting the scope of investigations (i.e., identifies appropriate investigative methods, laboratory experiment, simulation, fieldwork, selects efficient and effective approaches for accessing the information needed from information retrieval systems).
- Match information needs and search strategies to search tools [Association of College & Research Libraries 2000].

Once the desired information and its sources have been identified, the coaches will recognize the correct measures in obtaining this information. The method of obtaining film from the opponent has traditionally been to exchange game film with the opponent. Since the digital era arrived, the traditional method of exchanging VHS tapes via a courier mailing system has declined and now teams are sharing files more expeditiously via new digital applications. In today's era, the method by which most teams and coaches exchange game film is by a database called Hudl. Hudl acts as a database for coaches to view, record, borrow, lend, edit, search and store game footage of themselves and opponents. This exchange is every similar to the interlibrary loan process in which libraries borrow and lend resources to and from each other. These libraries usually are bound by a consortium. Much like using the league exchange pool in Hudl, it gives the teams the capability to share game footage with teams in the same league. When a request comes to exchange film, other teams will have immediate access to all of the film that has been implemented into the system.

Steps to add video to league pool:

- Click Exchanges at the top of the page, then select the League Pool tab.
- Click on the blue Add Your Video to the League Pool button.
- Select the playlist(s) you would like to add to the league pool. Click Next.
- Select the data and angles you would like to share with the league.
- Click Add Your Video to the League Pool. You now have access to the video that has been added to the pool.

Hudl is also very similar to a library academic database in that one can search for information within the database. This information can consist of video content or biographical content on an individual dependent upon the information inserted into the database.

- To find an athlete or a school, click the Search tab at the top of the page.
- On the Search page, you will see a search box at the top and criteria on the left which you can use to filter your results. The filtering criteria include:
    o Coach Rank
    o Graduation Year
    o Location
    o Position
    o Organization Level
- In the search box, you can find video by searching for an athlete or school name. The number in parentheses next to Teams and Athletes indicates the number of relevant hits.
    o You can also narrow your search by adding location (city/state) or high school to the athlete name in the search bar. Searching for "Seth NE" will return all athletes in Nebraska named Seth, rather than every athlete named Seth in our system [Hudl n.d.].

If a student was doing a research paper at this point, he would "hopefully" strategize search strategies to access the information they need from our wonderful academic databases. However, we're sure he would be on his way to type in his typical convoluted sentences in Google for a quick answer. Just like searching in the databases, there is no standard or correct method in seeking out the information you need from the game footage. Every coach has a different process in breaking down game footage to get what they need. The idea is to create a search process, format or a technique to extract the information you need.

Step 3: Searching Is Strategic

Objective:

- Use different searching language types (e.g., controlled vocabulary, keywords, natural language) [Association of College & Research Libraries 2000].

The Break Down of Game Film

When one is breaking down the game footage, he is not necessarily evaluating the footage initially. He is actually charting and tagging bits of information from the footage. Many coaches will create a customized chart sheet, personalized by the defensive coordinator. This chart sheet is designed to effectively and efficiently take notes of the game footage. From the notes, a coach will learn about the opposing team's strengths, weaknesses, run plays, pass plays, and trick plays. These notes are identified as major "bits" of information. Once the footage or film has been charted and tagged, the coach will input the desired or accessed information into a customized algorithm created by the defensive coach or a graduate assistant in a database comparable to Hudl. This algorithm is created to manipulate the accessed information into a more manageable comprehensive report. Again, the approach to access game footage does vary from coach to coach. In most instances, the data wanted is usually the same but the methods of obtaining it may vary. If one is using a database such as Hudl, the coach will denote which information he wants depending upon the information entered in as reiterated earlier. For example, if a coach was looking to see how many touchdowns were scored in a game, he would be able to find that by searching for that tagging or charting during the breaking down of the film session.

Hudl has the capability of offering custom-made or pre-designed reports. Hudl has several pre-designed interactive reports to help you quickly and easily generate powerful breakdowns without having to spend a lot of time creating a report. These reports can be created with just two clicks and generate in seconds. All of Hudl's reports are created in the video library, are available online, are printable, and can be shared to your entire team (Hudl n.d.).

Stats

This report will provide all of the basic stats for a football team. This report is based on information filled out in the participation columns (Passer, Receiver, Rusher, Tackler).

Stats will include the following:

- Passing Stats—Attempts, Completions, Completion Percentage, Yards Passing, Yards Per Attempt, Touchdowns scored, Fumbles, Interceptions, and Rating
- Rushing Stats—Attempts, Yards rushing, Average gain per rush, Touchdowns and Fumbles
- Receiving Stats—Receptions, Yards receiving, Average gain per reception, Touchdowns, Fumbles, Drops
- Defensive Stats—Tackles, Assists, Sacks, Tackles for Loss [Hudl, n.d.].

FORMATION REPORT

This report provides a comprehensive look at all the formations a particular offense has shown in the games being analyzed. The first page of the report provides an overall look at the top six offensive formations in the report. Each page after that is a detailed breakdown of every formation used. The report provides the following information on each formation:

- Run/Pass Breakdown
- Top Run and Pass Plays from the formation
- Hit Chart detailing the formation's running plays
- Pass Zone Chart detailing the formation's pass plays
- Breakdown of all MOTIONS used with the formation
- Breakdown of whether plays run from the formation were run into the Field or the Boundary [Hudl n.d.].

The objective in creating a custom report is to find tendencies not identified in pre-made reports. Custom reports should also be used when finding tendencies on breakdown data entered in custom columns.

CREATE CUSTOM REPORT

1. Check the box next to the playlist(s) you want to run a report on.
2. Click Report above the schedule entries and select Make a Custom Report at the bottom of the menu.
3. Choose up to eight columns to include in the report. The tendencies will generate from the data already entered in the selected columns.
4. Check Save this Report Template to save a template of your report. Find the template at the bottom of the Reports menu.
5. Click Create Report [Hudl n.d.].

Step 4: Research as Inquiry

Objectives:

- Synthesize ideas gathered from multiple sources *(i.e., summarizes the main ideas to be extracted from the information gathered and the information literate student synthesizes main ideas to construct new concepts, validates understanding and interpretation of the information through discourse with other individuals, subject-area experts, and/or practitioners)* [Association of College & Research Libraries 2000].

Let's see what the data says! Once the report has been amalgamated, the coaches will call a meeting to evaluate the report and the game footage simultaneously. Convening together allows all the coaches to assess and evaluate the data together to give a more comprehensive examination of the findings. Every coach has input and experience that is beneficial and vital. This new information will inform coaches of what the opponent's regular and irregular tendencies. Let's say through their findings, team x runs the ball 75 percent on 1st down when they are in Y formation. However, team x runs the ball 25 percent on 1st down when they are in X formation. Based on percentages, it's safe to say that when team x is in Y formation on 1st down, the coaches would need to prepare their defense for a run play against the opposing offense to defend the run, since 75 percent is a high percentage.

Metacognition plays a large role in information literacy and in sports. In library instruction preparation, it can influence your decision on how to present to a class, whether visually or kinetically. For the coaches, the data could show that team x runs the ball effectively to the left side of the offensive line, but for the defensive coordinator, the right side of his defensive line is the weak leak. So the defensive coordinator might have to counter attack that somehow by either changing his defense scheme or by calling different plays. The coordinator's ability to analyzing his defensive team's deficiencies is conducive for the team.

Another scenario is that initially you might have thought that team x was a pass heavy team, but the film illustrates or validates that they are a run heavy team. In information literacy, sometimes you have to synthesize main ideas to construct new ones, which is often prevalent in research and in the classroom. Sometimes the game plan changes depending on how the opponent reacts to the initial strategy, so change on the fly is inevitable at times. This could be similar to a library instruction class that loses Internet connection. What would be your back up plan? How will you counter this problem? Or what if the proxy server for one of your favorite databases you like to show is down? What do you do? How will you improvise? Or do you crack under pressure? Be prepared!

Step 5: Information Creation as a Process

Objectives:

- Recognize the implications of information formats that contain static or dynamic information (*i.e., applies new and prior information to the planning and creation of a particular product or performance*).
- Transfer knowledge of capabilities and constraints to new types of information products & develop, in their own creation processes, an understanding that their choices impact the purposes for which the information product will be used and the message it conveys (*i.e., communicates the message, product or performance effectively to others in a variety of ways*) [Association of College & Research Libraries 2000].

Once the data has been reviewed and evaluated, the formal summary of the research and analysis is referred to as the scouting report. The scouting report is a report of the opponent's strengths and weaknesses during certain parameters and instances on the field. It is also a strategy to attempt to defend and discontinue what the offense would like to do according to the game footage assessed. This also involves using information effectively by communicating the scouting report to the other coaches and players for practice. The scouting report entails the names of the opponents and heights, weights, and positions. It also includes the other team's favorite formations, plays and strategies. The scouting report will also usually have the opponent's weaknesses and flaws, sometimes called tendencies. The report is very detailed and immensely informative. Test your theories and adjustments to see what works. Practice could be a parallel for an experimental laboratory or it could a rough draft if one is writing a paper. Whether in meetings rooms or on practice and game fields, the use of signals cards, audibles, hand signals, headsets, and chalkboards are all mediums designed to help deliver the message to get to the end product and result. And finally, of course, the ultimate assessment in game planning is on the field. How well did the coordinator execute or amend the game plan during the contest by way of his defensive players based upon his research and analysis?

Step 6: Scholarship as Conversation

Objectives:

- Contribute to scholarly conversation at an appropriate level, such as local online community, guided discussion, undergraduate research journal, conference presentation/poster session [Association of College & Research Libraries 2000].

Many coaches and athletic personnel engage in scholarly communication in publication and in conversation. Many coaches attend annual workshops and conferences for their sports and engage in conversation about new techniques, strategies and schematics that were or were not successful for them. More specifically, this is a convenient time for them to be in a participatory environment to discuss and summarize changes in scholarly perspective over time on a particular topic such as a particular defensive scheme. Many coaches distinguish that they often enter into an ongoing scholarly conversation and not a finished conversation due to newfound knowledge or enhanced athletic performance that maybe has created a paradigm shift that changed their disposition on certain ways of thinking.

Information professionals and librarians have already initiated engaging initiatives in regards to librarianship and the inclusion of sports. Information literacy and fantasy football has become an intriguing trend over the past several years. Librarians have authored several books and articles about the lives of coaches and sports. So what's next? Who's going to be the brave envelope pusher? Librarians, ingenuity is the key, take chances by "assessing your library's strengths to determine whether you can offer any new services to your students and faculty" (Lacy 2011).

From a liaison standpoint, we would like to initiate outreach efforts with athletic coaches if possible. Why do we limit ourselves, in terms of outreach, to just strictly academic departments or technology-related sectors? Is it not possible for us to collaborate with the athletic departments, more specifically, athletic coaches in regards to information literacy? Why are we seen as two entirely different spectrums? Maybe we are!

Lastly, if you are passionate about marketing the library's resources and services, try making a connection with the athletic department. We all know most athletic departments have and hold a large voice on campus, especially if your school is considered a "football" institution. To create an ally with the athletic department by using information literacy could benefit your library in many ways. Side note—the daily housing of athletes for study hall does not count either!

References

Association of College & Research Libraries. 2000. www.ala.org/acrl. January 18. http://www.acrl.org/ala/mgrps/divs/acrl/standards/standards.pdf (accessed December 1, 2015).

Hudl. n.d. www.hudl.com. http://public.hudl.com/support/football/reports/using-football-reports/ (accessed 12 1, 2015).
_____. n.d. www.hudl.com. http://public.hudl.com/support/recruit/search-and-filter-in-recruit/ (accessed December 1, 2015).
Lacy, M. 2011. "The Virtues of a Committed Dilettante: Embracing Nonexpert Expertise." *College & Research Libraries News* 72, no. 11: 646.
Mackey, T.P., and T. E. Jacobson. 2011. "Reframing Information Literacy as a Metaliteracy." *College & Research Libraries* 72, no. 1: 62.

Tech Training and Library Advocacy
Linking the Academic Library with the School Library and Turning Pre-Service Teachers into Lifelong Library Users

HEATHER BEIRNE *and* CINDY JUDD

The relationship between K–12 teachers and their school librarians is essential to student success. As times change, school librarians are rapidly becoming the technology leaders of their institutions, building and managing Makerspaces, providing information literacy and digital literacy instruction, and training busy teachers on the latest educational technologies. However, many teachers, even recent graduates, are unaware of the changing role of the school librarian and how the school librarian's information literacy (IL) and technology expertise may support them and their students. This is an important issue as the acquisition of so-called 21st century skills become increasingly emphasized in K–12, and as our world grows increasingly complex (Latham 2013). These skills are at the core of current educational initiatives like the Partnership for 21st Century Skills and the Common Core State Standards, as well as the American Association of School Librarians (AASL)-authored 2007 initiative *Standards for the 21st-Century Learner*, among others.

Unfortunately, as a recent study indicates, more emphasis is being placed on teacher-librarian collaboration in the Library and Information Science literature and in LIS education than in the education literature and in education classes, despite the fact that an interest in 21st century skills is evident in the literature and content of both disciplines (Latham 2013, 2). The same study reveals that teachers working in the field often view school libraries not as resource hubs or technology centers, but as "extra space where student detentions or faculty meetings could be held," and that collaboration between teachers and school librarians is either "nonexistent or difficult to achieve" (Latham 2013, 10). Latham concludes that "incorporating instruction in teacher-librarian collaboration into education and LIS curricula, and, in particular, developing cross-disciplinary courses that model and facilitate such collaboration for pre-service teachers and school librarians are important steps in overcoming these challenges and achieving these goals" (Latham 2013, 15).

While not generally part of the curriculum construction process for pre-service teachers, education librarians can do their part to make teacher candidates aware of the possibilities of 21st-century skills-focused teacher-librarian collaboration. Initiating a "librarian as educational technology leader" model within a university's education program can set a precedent for the way teacher candidates view their school librarians in future jobs, leading to future collaboration, library use, and library advocacy, which can only benefit their students. Hunt (2013, 14) suggests that "by initiating library-classroom collaboration early in a teacher's development it is possible that student teachers will embrace the school librarian as an instructional partner throughout their career."

This essay will cover the ways in which two Eastern Kentucky University (EKU) Education Librarians have worked with pre-service teachers in ways that model the ideal collaborative relationship between K–12 teachers and school librarians. Throughout the essay, the authors will discuss the use of various technology tools and techniques in library instruction to help model innovative teaching strategies and cultivate teachers who are lifelong library users and advocates, and who will take full professional advantage of their school librarian's skills and support.

Background and Context

Eastern Kentucky University (EKU) is a mid-sized, regional, comprehensive, public university located in Richmond, Kentucky. EKU offers a variety of undergraduate and graduate degrees taught at the main campus, several regional campuses and centers, as well as online.

The Learning Resources Center (LRC) is EKU's education library (curriculum materials center), located on the third floor of EKU's main library. Two full-time education librarians work in the LRC, which houses both youth and professional materials for pre-service teachers, including K–12-appropriate books and manipulatives, teaching materials, puppets, games, puzzles, models, kits, textbooks, and many other items that circulate to students, faculty, and staff. The LRC also facilitates access to EKU Libraries' online education databases via online research guides, tutorials, and library instruction, typically performed in a one-shot session. The two education librarians provide information literacy instruction for education students at all levels, including pre-service teachers, on topics such as using the databases to find articles, evaluating information, and selecting appropriate and relevant K–12 books and materials, both online and physical, for classroom use.

Planting the Seed for Library Advocacy and Collaboration: Technology-Based Approaches to Library Instruction

For pre-service teachers being taught IL skills by education librarians, the mindful and intentional connection of IL skills to their future professional lives in the K–12 classroom may be enhanced by the deliberate use and modeling of relevant educational technology tools for learning, collaborating, and teaching to ground IL and digital literacy concepts. Immersing teacher candidates in a technology-rich classroom experience results in more engaging IL instruction and models the use of educational technology, spotlighting the librarian as a technology leader and digital literacy expert to whom they can go for technology training, both now and in the future. Instruction sessions themselves can be thought of as functioning as pre-service professional development, setting a precedent for the technology-based and instructional professional development that the students may receive from their future school librarians as teachers.

Google Drive

For pre-service and in-service teachers, Google Drive holds many pedagogical as well as organizational and collaborative possibilities. Essentially a free productivity suite which is similar to Microsoft Office, Drive is hosted in the cloud by Google, allowing for real-time collaboration by two or more users. (Free apps are, of course, always preferable in K–12 education since teachers are not always guaranteed a steady technology budget.) Drive allows a document's owner to control viewing, editing, and commenting rights for all collaborators, as well as to view the revision history, making it ideal for classroom active learning and group activities.

Google Drive apps can be incorporated separately or together to enhance in-class instruction and facilitate active learning. According to Beirne, Cole, and Richardson, Google Drive helps instructors "promote digital literacy while providing a highly collaborative learning environment. These apps help facilitate brainstorming activities and group work, allow for quick and easy feedback, and aid in planning and assessment" and "can be used to engage and teach our students by immersing them into a learning process which allows everyone to explore, create, and share information" (Beirne, Cole, and Richardson 2015, 3). Teachers can easily use Drive to create, share, access on any computer, and collaborate on documents without having to pass around multiple versions using e-mail.

Teachers can use Drive to push multiple links or share prompts with students without printing paper handouts or worksheets, and guide students through online or face-to-face class activities. When projected onto a screen or SmartBoard, teachers and students can discuss answers that appear in a document as they are added in real time, giving students the benefit of having their work shown on the board for their classmates to read, "creating an 'authentic audience' for their work and motivating them to contribute meaningfully" (Beirne, Cole, and Richardson 2015, 5). Responses to Google Forms are automatically saved as spreadsheets in Google Sheets, making assessment and the collection and sharing of class data very simple.

Modeling pedagogical use of Google Drive establishes the librarian as a technological and instructional leader. In one activity for a children's literature course, the education librarian was tasked with teaching the database NoveList Plus, a nearly comprehensive source of information about books that includes book reviews from the major review sources, information about age appropriateness, readalikes for particular titles, and more. Rather than lecturing on the ins and outs of the database, the librarian flipped the classroom by sharing a pre-made NoveList Plus video tutorial for the students to view before class. She then utilized the limited class time to teach the more critical skill of evaluating picture books for classroom use using the book reviews contained in NoveList Plus. In groups, students then used a shared Doc or Form to consider specific, real-life classroom scenarios in which they would need to identify, select and evaluate children's literature connected to various science, social studies, and math content. Together, the student teachers recorded their responses to questions on a Doc, which are projected up onto the screen in real time and visible to their classmates for discussion. This models not only Drive and its role in the classroom, but the concept of the flipped classroom, an instructional strategy which involves pushing course materials, such as readings, videos, or websites to students before class so that class time can be dedicated to activities that promote higher learning (EDUCAUSE, 2012; Davies, Douglas, and Ball 2013, 565).

Students are then taught how to use Google Sheets to keep track of various pieces of information (title, author, major themes, reviews, etc.) for a class picture book assignment in which they review and evaluate 30 picture books that they have read. In this way, they become familiar with it as a spreadsheet tool for organizing information they need to do their job. In sharing it with classmates and their instructor, they learn the important capability of collaboration with other teachers. EKU education librarians have also used Google Forms as a mechanism for administering pre- and post-tests for one-shot instruction sessions, modeling its assessment capabilities for pre-service teachers. Again, having this information presented by the librarian technology expert also lays the foundation for pre-service teachers to consider librarians as go-to colleagues for introduction to and help with technology.

Padlet

Another online tool that can be used to promote interactive learning is Padlet. A Padlet is an online "wall" on which users can post ideas, solicit feedback, gather input from participants, share videos or images, and add links to many different file types. The walls, which are like an infinite canvas, can be customized and shared with others via e-mail and various social media sites as well as by embedding into a blog or website. Users can password-protect a Padlet and moderate a post before it appears on the wall. Padlet can be a wonderful tool to use during a class in which students are brainstorming or creating a concept map. Students post content to the wall in real-time, making it convenient to work on during class or even at a time that is convenient to users. Content can also be added outside of class as part of a homework assignment and be viewed later by the instructor to assess participation and/or attention to details as required by the teacher.

Padlet has been a wonderful tool to introduce education students to as it fosters interactive learning with a flexible format that invites all different types of content to be shared by students. For one instruction session at EKU Libraries, the librarian asked students to break down a research topic into keywords and develop a search statement. The students were offered a laptop provided by the librarian or could use a personal electronic device. The librarian shared the Padlet web address with students and asked them to post their responses which were projected on the screen for the entire class to view. Padlet provided the perfect opportunity for the librarian to act more as a facilitator by letting the students present their ideas and solicit feedback.

Padlet allows for real time sharing of ideas, which makes for an interesting experience as students see each other working through an assignment. They realize that others may be making the same mistakes that they are, that their thought processes are similar or that others went in a direction they had not thought of, which could challenge them to think differently about their work. When pre-service teachers use Padlet, they can learn the benefits of having their own students collaborate and be led by their own ideas; the teacher then serves as a facilitator rather than the sage-on-the-stage who directs the learning. The ability to share Padlets provides numerous advantages: teachers can use information from a Padlet to build on a previous activity, students can reflect on progress made throughout the year, parents can see what their children are working on at school, and teachers can assess where their students are in order to help determine future assignments, just to name a few.

Socrative

Socrative is an online student response system that allows an educator to collect feedback and assess learning using any Internet-connected device. It is an excellent tool to increase student engagement and to help teachers quickly and efficiently receive information on students' progress. Teachers can use Socrative to measure acquisition of information throughout the entire instructional unit as well as assess learning at the beginning or end of a unit or presentation. Socrative is a quizzing system that allows for real-time feedback and collection of data that can be shared live, in class, or later in a report. Participants log into Socrative using their designated room number/code and begin answering questions almost immediately.

Socrative offers teachers a variety of quiz options to best meet their educational needs. Quizzes can contain multiple-choice, true/false, or short answer questions. Teachers can require students to enter their names to tie responses to a specific student or they can choose to anonymize answers. Quizzes can be student-paced or instructor-paced allowing for flexibility of delivery. At Eastern Kentucky University librarians have used Socrative with several different education courses. LRC librarians have opened instruction sessions with Socrative to gauge background research experience, knowledge of a specific topic, familiarity with research tools, and to solicit questions for the librarian to answer regarding the research process. The ability to save the responses and filter them into a report is especially helpful because it gives feedback for improving future instructional content. It is also information that can be shared with the course instructor regarding students' prior research experience and as a demonstration of what was learned in the library session. Socrative offers an Exit Ticket as a formative assessment that gives students a set of three questions to help the teacher collect feedback from the students about what they learned, how well they learned the material covered, and a custom question for the teacher to define related to their instruction. EKU librarians have used the Exit Ticket function at the end of a class as well as through a course management system so students can complete the questions within a set time frame after a class session has ended.

Socrative is a way to have students productively use mobile devices in a classroom setting. Its features allow instructors to incorporate metacognitive strategies to help students consider their own learning as well as demonstrate their progress through each new unit.

Social Media

Social media tools are used by people of all ages for creative and personal expression along with building connections with a local and global community. In an educational setting, "social network sites such as Facebook may serve as invaluable tools for teacher educators to encourage collaborative approaches to building knowledge" (Schieble 2010, 108). Unfortunately, most K-12 schools have blocked popular social media outlets, including Facebook, Instagram, and Twitter, over concerns about privacy and appropriate use of these tools in an educational setting. Such concerns regarding student safety are not invalid, but preventing students and teachers from having access to tools that they get excited about and use regularly "communicates the idea that how students use literacy as a social practice outside of school has no place *in school*" (Schieble 2010, 211). More and more faculty in higher education, however, are incorporating social media tools in their courses, including posting to blogs, viewing YouTube videos, and posting comments on Twitter, because they offer a more collaborative learning experience. Faculty in teacher preparation programs recognize that modeling use of social media in an educational setting can equip future teachers be advocates and creative users of tools that have great instructive potential.

In EKU's Learning Resources Center, librarians have adopted this same modeling philosophy in their approach to incorporating flipped classroom strategies as well as active learning strategies through the use of social media. For example, when introducing students to the spaces, services, and resources available in the LRC, librarians assign students to locate specific materials and to record their findings through photos on Twitter. The librarian encourages students to use a common, pre-determined set of hashtags that can be viewed by the libraries' Twitter followers as well as through a search of common library hashtags in those same social media outlets. Users who follow the LRC's Twitter account as well as those who search for EKU-related hashtags on Twitter can discover information about the educational materials and resources available in the LRC.

In EKU's graduate programs, faculty have used blogs, discussion boards, and Google Drive as a means of fostering community and shared learning experiences within their classes. Other social networks, such as Twitter, have given students an opportunity to not only connect outside of the classroom but also as a way to see the professional value of social media. For example, one professor has used Twitter as a tool to share important articles, highlight trends, and introduce students to education leaders and organizations. One EKU education librarian has participated in those online Twitter discussions by offering encouraging comments as well as sharing resources connected to the course readings, class discussions, and students' research interests. This gave the librarian the opportunity to model this sort of interaction between a librarian and the course instructor.

Interacting with students within a social media context and/or providing learning opportunities for education students allows the librarian to demonstrate his or her technology expertise as a model for a future relationship between the classroom teacher and school librarian. Providing the opportunity to use tools that students get excited about using outside of school can increase intrinsic motivation as well as a willingness to participate in classroom activities that may not have existed prior to using social media. Using interactive and collaborative tools such as social networks in an educational setting helps students think about their own learning while they learn in front of, with, and from their peers (Anderson and Justice 2015).

Digital Storytelling

Creating a digital story is a common assignment for students in education programs, mirroring its practice in the K–12 environment. In both contexts, digital storytelling allows students to demonstrate a blend of 21st century and traditional skills such as information literacy (research, digital citizenship and ethical use of information), technology skills, creativity, organizational skills, collaboration, writing and speaking skills, and more. Heo defines digital storytelling as "a branch of storytelling that uses digital media resources to tell a story" that may be "expressed through art, oral history, creative writing, speaking, photographs, music, news clippings, digital video, the Web, graphic design, sound engineering, or animation, and thus involves multiple modalities" (Heo 2011, 64). Heo goes on to explain that "this technique fosters higher order cognition and helps students with various learning styles by utilizing multimedia technology" (Heo 2011, 64). The assignment helps teacher candidates learn to make instructional videos, and to teach K-12 students to use the same tools to make videos on virtually any topic. Possibilities for K-12 classroom assignments include student-made tutorials, book trailers, multimedia poems, and much more.

EKU education librarians' strategic instructional support of the digital storytelling projects assigned by several EKU education courses has been an opportunity to showcase both the tech-leader and professional development capacities of school librarians. For example, the librarian flipped the classroom and encouraged students to teach themselves how to use Windows Live Movie Maker or iMovie via a series of videos viewed before class. During class time, the librarian taught about "big picture" concepts such as the importance of attribution of multimedia used, and to introduce the ideas of copyright, finding copyright-friendly media and digital citizenship (defined by Moreillon as "necessary and safe online behaviors" within the elements of digital "access, commerce, communication, literacy, etiquette, law, rights and responsibilities, health and wellness, and security") (Moreillon 2013, 26). The act of shifting responsibility for learning the tools onto the teacher candidates helps build pre-service teachers' confidence in their ability to "teach themselves" a tech tool, an important skill in and of itself and one they will use again and again in the classroom. Willis states that "training programs that improve technology self-efficacy of teacher candidates will better prepare candidates to overcome technology challenges with greater levels of confidence" (Willis 2015, 1).

The act of modeling digital storytelling instruction for education students coupled with the intentional close collaboration of the librarian acting in the role of an instructional coach also helps them to think not only about the implementation of the technology, but the way in which the technology might enhance their pedagogy. Heo asserts that technology integration in the classroom is effective when it helps to construct an authentic and meaningful learning experience for students and is not just incorporated for its own sake, a difficult concept for pre-service teachers and young educators to grasp (Heo 2011, 65). It is also important for students to overcome internal barriers such as fear of and resistance to learning new technology (Heo 2011, 62). The act of learning about digital storytelling tools and their applications in the classroom both boosts self-efficacy in teacher candidates and helps them think pedagogically, all while involving their librarians.

Conclusion

In conclusion, education librarians in EKU Libraries' Learning Resources Center believe strongly in teaching education students the information literacy skills they will need to be successful teachers. The librarians are intentional in demonstrating effective pedagogical use of educational technology in a way that cultivates a strong, collegial relationship between teachers and school librarians for years to come. This relationship benefits teachers and librarians, but first and foremost, generations of K–12 students.

REFERENCES

American Association of School Librarians. 2007. "Standards for the 21st-Century Learner." http://www.ala.org/aasl/sites/ala.org.aasl/files/content/guidelinesandstandards/learningstandards/AASL_LearningStandards.pdf.

Anderson, Janice L., and Julie E. Justice. 2015. "Disruptive Design in Pre-Service Teacher Education: Uptake, Participation, and Resistance." *Teaching Education* 26 (4): 400–421.

Beirne, Heather, Ashley Cole, and Sarah Richardson. 2015. "App It Up: Using Google Apps in Library Instruction." In *The Complete Guide to Using Google in Libraries: Instruction, Administration, and Staff Productivity (Volume 1)*, ed. Carol Smallwood, 3–12. Lanham, MD: Rowman & Littlefield.

Davies, Randall S., Douglas L. Dean, and Nick Ball. 2013. "Flipping the Classroom and Instructional Technology Integration in a College-Level Information Systems Spreadsheet Course." *Educational Technology Research and Development* 61 (4): 563–580.

EDUCAUSE. 2012. "7 Things You Should Know About Flipped Classrooms." *EDUCAUSE Creative Commons*, February. https://net.educause.edu/ir/library/pdf/ELI7081.pdf.

Fourie, Ina, and Anika Meyer. 2015. "What to Make of Makerspaces: Tools and DIY Only or Is There an Interconnected Information Resources Space?" *Library Hi Tech* 33 (4): 519–525.

Heo, Misook. 2011. "Improving Technology Competency and Disposition of Beginning Pre-Service Teachers with Digital Storytelling." *Journal of Educational Multimedia and Hypermedia* 20 (1): 61–81.

Hunt, Rebecca. 2013. "The Insider: School Librarians as Part of a Blended Professional Learning Community for Student Teacher Development in Technology Integration." *School Libraries Worldwide* 19 (1): 13–27.

Latham, Don, Melissa Gross, and Shelbie Witte. 2013. "Preparing Teachers and Librarians to Collaborate to Teach 21st Century Skills: Views of LIS and Education Faculty." *School Library Research* 16: 1–23.

Moreillon, Judi. 2013. "Leadership: Teaching Digital Citizenship." *School Library Monthly* 30 (1): 27.

National Governors Association Center for Best Practices, Council of Chief State School Officers. 2010. "Common Core State Standards." http://www.corestandards.org/.

Partnership for 21st Century Learning. "Overview: Framework for 21st Century Learning." *Framework for 21st Century Learning*. Accessed November 18, 2015. http://www.p21.org/about-us/p21-framework.

Schieble, Melissa. 2010. "The Not So Digital Divide: Bringing Pre-Service English Teachers' Media Literacies into Practice." *Journal of Media Literacy Education* 2 (2): 102–112.

Willis, Jana. 2015. "Examining Technology and Teaching Efficacy of Preservice Teacher Candidates: A Deliberate Course Design Model." *Current Issues in Education* 18 (3): 1–17.

About the Contributors

Rachel Warriner **Bartron** is the director of the Louis Maslow STEM (Science, Technology, Engineering, and Math) School at Wyoming Seminary College Preparatory School in Kingston, Pennsylvania, and has been since its inception in 2012.

Heather **Beirne** is an education librarian at Eastern Kentucky University Libraries. Her research interests include information literacy, web 2.0, digital literacy, digital citizenship, and digital storytelling.

Melissa **Bernasek** is the director of information services at Gail Borden Public Library in Elgin, Illinois. On a daily basis, she oversees operations of in-house services for adults while leading a team of 19 people to provide customer-focused, responsive services.

Aaron J. **Blodgett** is assistant professor of mathematics at the University of Findlay in Ohio. His research interests include algebraic number theory, covering sets, and cohomology.

Laura **Bohuski** is the special formats cataloger and an assistant professor at Western Kentucky University where she catalogs materials that are not monographic in nature. Her research interests include innovation in technology, cataloging, and Japanese history.

Dongmei **Cao** is a tenured science librarian at the College of Charleston Libraries and has been a reference librarian since 2001. She has been an active member of Chinese American Librarians Association (CALA) since 2001.

Ashley J. **Cole** is a reference and instruction librarian at Eastern Kentucky University specializing in student engagement and the first-year experience. She has conducted workshops at the Kentucky Library Association and Pedagogicon, among others.

Julia J. **Dahm** is the technology services librarian of the Health Sciences Library System at the University of Pittsburgh. She is the instructor of several software classes, liaison to 3-D printing services, and manager of the Technology Help Desk.

Jennifer L. **Dean** is the library director and an assistant professor at Siena Heights University in Adrian, Michigan. Her research interests include organizational theory, communication, and leadership.

Emy Nelson **Decker** is the unit head for e-learning technologies at the Atlanta University Center, Robert W. Woodruff Library. Her interests are centered on emerging technologies as well as new uses of existing technologies within the modern academic library setting.

Jezmynne **Dene** is the director of the Portneuf District Library in Chubbuck, Idaho. She enjoys enabling her staff to succeed and moving her library into the future while staying relevant and important to her library's community.

Monica M. **Dombrowski** is the technology education manager at Gail Borden Public Library in Elgin, Illinois. In her role she creates, plans, and oversees all public technology classes and trains staff on new systems and software.

About the Contributors

Samantha **Duckworth**, is the science and technology librarian at Portland Public Library, in Portland, Maine. Her background in technology instruction has shown that access, freedom, and privacy are traditional values of librarianship that are paramount to the digital arena.

Danielle M. **Duvall** has been with the King County Library System in Washington state since 2004 and serves as the public service specialist for mobile services. She has created, developed, and taught computer and job searching skills programs for refugee centers, homeless shelters, and safe houses.

Christine **Elliott** is research and instruction librarian at the College of Charleston Libraries. Her research interests include instructional technology, library outreach and marketing, first-year student education and experience, information literacy for diverse and under-served populations, disability services, and women's and gender studies.

Michelle **Emanuel** is the head of cataloging and metadata services and the subject selector for media and modern languages in the University of Mississippi Libraries. She has published in *Collection Management*, *Cataloging and Classification Quarterly*, and the *Journal of Electronic Resource Management*, among others.

Francisco J. **Fajardo** is the clinical engagement librarian for the Herbert Wertheim College of Medicine at Florida International University. He has published in the areas of access services and outreach/collaboration between academic medical libraries and partner hospital libraries.

Jennifer Bunton **Forgit** has worked in public and academic libraries for 15 years as a page, interlibrary loan assistant, museum cataloger, reference librarian, serials cataloger, and teen services librarian. She is the teen services manager at Cary Memorial Library in Lexington, Massachusetts.

Forrest C. **Foster** is the head of information commons/access services at C.G. O'Kelly Library at Winston-Salem State University. He is heavily involved in teaching information and digital literacy to the university community.

Deloris J. **Foxworth** is a lecturer in information communication technology in the School of Library and Information Science at the University of Kentucky. She also serves as advisor of the Information Communication Technology (ICT) Student Association.

Lisa **Fraser**, services implementation coordinator for the King County Library System in Washington state, has taught at the Information School of the University of Washington. She has co-edited a number of titles on librarianship.

Sara **Frey** is an instructional media specialist/librarian and technology integration coach at Plymouth Whitemarsh High School, in Plymouth Meeting, Pennsylvania. In 2015 she received the Pennsylvania Library Association High Best Practices Award for high school librarians.

Nicole **Helregel** is a reference and web services specialist at the University of Illinois at Urbana-Champaign. Her memberships include the American Library Association, Association of College and Research Libraries, Illinois Library Association, and Health Science Librarians of Illinois.

Kathryn M. **Houk** is the health and life sciences librarian at San Diego State University. She has several years of experience teaching information literacy, research technique and theory, and various new technologies to faculty and students in the life sciences and health fields.

Amy **James** is an emerging technologies librarian at Spring Arbor University, in Spring Arbor, Michigan. She is also a member of the American Library Association, Library Instruction Round Table, Mi-ALA, and the Association of Christian Librarians.

Heidi R. **Johnson** is the social sciences librarian at University of Nevada, Las Vegas, where she is the liaison to the anthropology, political science, and sociology departments. Her memberships include the American Library Association and Association of College & Research Libraries.

Joshua K. **Johnson** is a branch librarian and systems librarian for the Davis County Library in Farmington, Utah. His memberships include the American Library Association and Utah Library Association.

About the Contributors

Cindy **Judd** is an associate university librarian for Eastern Kentucky University Libraries. She serves as the team leader for the Learning Resources Center, overseeing the area of the library that provides a variety of services and diverse collections for the College of Education.

Hazel **Koziol** is a library technical assistant at Portland Public Library, in Portland, Maine. As a member of the library's Science & Technology team, she maintains that libraries are powerful centers for encouraging and enabling digital citizenship.

Kate **Lambaria** is the fine arts librarian at the University of Nevada, Las Vegas, where she is the liaison to the departments of art, dance, film, and theatre, and the schools of architecture and music.

Carl **Leak** is the associate director and health sciences librarian at C.G. O'Kelly Library at Winston-Salem State University. His research interests are health sciences librarianship, health disparities, library leadership, assessing value in libraries, library instruction, and genealogy.

Courtney L. **Lewis** is the director of library services and innovative research at St. Catherine's School in Richmond, Virginia. She has authored articles appearing in *Knowledge Quest* and *Young Adult Library Services*.

Shana **Lopez** is the technology education associate at Gail Borden Public Library in Elgin, Illinois. Her specialties include research, designing class material, and one-on-one technology training.

Cara **Marco** is the assistant library director at Sullivan University in Louisville, Kentucky. She is a member of the American Library Association, the Library Leadership & Management Association, and the Kentucky Library Association.

Brad **Marcum** is the distance and online education program officer at Eastern Kentucky University Libraries. He recently conducted workshops at the Kentucky Library Association annual conference and Pedagogicon.

Terrence Jarrod **Martin**, Sr., is the OK Scholars coordinator at C.G. O'Kelly Library in Winston-Salem, North Carolina. He provides faculty members relevant information about combining effective teaching strategies, library resources and services to accomplish the goal of producing information literate graduates.

Elizabeth Tarski **McArthur** is the access services librarian at the Blumberg Memorial Library at Texas Lutheran University. She is a member of the American Library Association, the Texas Library Association, and the Association of College and Research Libraries.

Elizabeth **Nelson** is the cataloging and collection development librarian at McHenry County College in Crystal Lake, Illinois. Prior to this she spent seven years as a special librarian working on knowledge management and knowledge sharing projects and also worked as a reference and instruction librarian.

Jordan M. **Nielsen** is the business data librarian at San Diego State University. He studies how technology is changing librarianship, including examining what technology skills are required of modern research librarians, how technology can be used to provide library support to distance education students, and how to motivate online learners with digital credentials.

Jorge E. **Perez** is the digital learning and information technology librarian for the Herbert Wertheim College of Medicine at Florida International University. He is a contributor to an upcoming Library Information Technology Association (LITA) Guide on Digital Visualization, LITA blog contributor, and greatly interested with topics within technology and mental health.

Christa E. **Poparad** is the head of research and instruction services at the College of Charleston. Her research interests include scaffolding information literacy instruction throughout the curriculum, providing research and computing services to diverse user communities, and practical assessment of library resources and services.

About the Contributors

Lura **Sanborn** is the research and instruction librarian at St. Paul's School in Concord, New Hampshire. She is an 11-year reviewer for *Library Journal* and in 2015 was named the ALA's "Reference Reviewer of the Year."

Carol **Smallwood** has edited and coedited a number of books on library and librarianship topics. Her library experience includes school, public, academic and special as well as administration and library systems consultant.

Mark A. **Stoffan** is the head of digital, access and technology services at Hunter Library, Western Carolina University. His expertise includes digital curation and preservation, information technology, and services to distance education students.

Amanda **Toth** is a public services librarian at Lane Public Library in Fairfield, Ohio, where she is also the resident eBook guru, training both staff and patrons in new technology and downloadable tech offered by the library.

Index

academic libraries 65, 74, 82, 101, 104, 139, 148–150, 185, 190, 195, 205
active learning 6, 12, 13, 15–18, 99, 192, 207, 208, 210
Adventures in Access! (game) 74, 75, 79, 81
advertising 46, 51, 125, 127, 128, 129, 141, 154, 155, 157, 179
Amazon 49, 50, 52, 122
American Association of School Librarians (AASL) 22, 205
American Library Association (ALA) 16, 46, 163
Android (operating system) 48–50, 52, 53, 118, 120
Association of College and Research Libraries (ACRL) Framework for Information Literacy for Higher Education 8, 13, 82, 86, 87, 146, 197
Association of College and Research Libraries (ACRL) Information Literacy Competency Standard for Higher Education 15, 88, 87, 88
apps 6, 8, 9, 23, 50, 52, 53, 86, 97, 98, 101, 102, 118, 119–121, 123, 193, 207
Atlantic University Center, Atlanta, Georgia 190, 191
audiobooks 48, 49, 50, 118

Baby Boomers 51, 52
badges (digital) 80, 139–145
behaviorism (learning theory) 12, 75
Blackboard 6, 8, 147, 150
blogs 13, 14, 15, 17, 31, 71, 111, 118, 191, 193, 194, 208, 210
Boolean 17, 18, 148, 172
Boopsie 118, 119
budget 10, 11, 28, 41, 42, 53, 57, 62, 111, 181, 207

Camtasia 10, 147–149, 192–194
California 181
Canvas 6
C.G. O'Kelly Library (Winston-Salem State University, Winston-Salem, NC) 197
chat 8, 53, 76, 111, 149
chemistry 21, 149, 150
Chromebook 23, 156
circulation 32, 67, 68, 72, 101, 121, 149, 150, 165
citations 15, 22–24, 25, 32, 84–86, 149

CMS (Content Management System) 6, 92, 111, 112, 116
coaching 45, 59, 96–102
code 78, 79, 104, 107, 136, 152–158, 209
Coggle 16
collaboration 20, 25, 28, 30, 32, 78, 86, 87, 107, 112, 113, 115, 136, 139, 144, 164, 165, 179, 196, 205–208, 211
college 20, 21, 28, 41, 56, 61, 68, 83, 85, 89, 90, 95, 105, 139, 146, 152, 153, 155, 157, 171, 190
College of Charleston Libraries 89–95
ColonelSmart (program at Eastern Kentucky University (EKU) Libraries) 82–88
constructivism 12, 13, 75
copyright 15, 16, 22, 25, 86, 87, 107, 178, 211
Creative Commons 15, 177–179

databases 9, 10, 16, 18, 22, 25, 35, 37, 38, 57, 74, 76, 82, 92, 93, 104, 106–109, 118, 123, 144, 147, 148, 150, 162–164, 170–172, 177, 185–186, 198–200, 202, 206, 207
Desire 2 Learn 6
device club 118–124
digital divide 48, 56, 58, 59, 62, 63
digital literacy 27–33, 56, 58, 60–63, 71, 119, 160, 175, 205–207

Eastern Kentucky University (EKU) Libraries (Richmond, Kentucky) 82, 83, 84, 85, 87, 206–212
eBooks 22, 35, 38, 48, 50, 118, 121, 122, 162, 163, 185–187
Edge Impact Survey 43
email 50, 60, 149, 160, 163, 165, 207, 208
evaluation 15, 22, 33, 125, 129–131, 143
Excel (Microsoft software) 35, 36, 40, 41, 45, 63, 132, 134, 144, 186

Facebook 14, 15, 37, 51, 53, 68, 118, 152, 179, 194, 210
faculty 6, 10, 11, 27, 29–31, 33, 65, 69, 77, 79–82, 84–88, 93, 101, 104–109, 132, 140–144, 146, 149, 175–177, 179, 181, 190–196, 203, 205, 206, 210
fair use 15, 16
fantasy football 203

Feedback 8–10, 42, 45, 53, 68, 69, 79, 80, 100, 123, 128, 129, 131, 166, 192, 193, 195, 196, 207–209
Final Cut Pro 10, 191
flipped classroom 9, 13–15, 98, 147, 192–194, 207, 208, 210, 211

Gail Borden Public Library (Elgin, Illinois) 40, 41
gamification 74, 75, 140, 193, 195
Girls Who Code (GWC) 152–158
Gizmo Garage program (Idaho) 48–53
Google 16–18, 22, 23, 25, 49, 50, 52, 69, 77, 82, 84, 85, 100, 104, 106–109, 112, 119, 123, 134, 186, 187, 199, 207, 208, 210
Google Drive 84, 207
Google Scholar 17, 18, 69, 84, 85, 106
graduate students 28, 74, 76, 77, 79, 80, 81, 83, 84, 105, 149, 197, 200, 206, 210

handouts 35–38, 42, 45, 125, 127, 128, 130, 131, 138, 172, 173, 191, 207
high school(s) 20, 25, 152, 157, 162, 199
homeless 58, 159, 160, 163–166; *see also* tent cities
homework 9, 17, 52, 72, 162, 188, 192, 208
Horizon Report 27, 69
Hudl 199, 200
Hunter Library (Western Carolina University) 27–32

iBook 21–25
Idaho Commission for Libraries 48, 53
Illustrator (Adobe software) 34, 35
immigrant(s) 41, 56, 61
information literacy 8, 12, 13, 15, 16, 18, 20–22, 25, 28, 32, 42, 82, 83, 85–88, 144, 146, 175, 183–185, 188, 197, 202, 203, 205, 206, 211, 212
Instagram 179, 210
Institute of Museum and Library Services 28, 119
Internet 28, 35, 40, 45, 48, 50–52, 58, 63, 65, 74, 78, 79, 82, 106, 107, 109–112, 144, 154, 160, 163, 165, 185, 202, 209
Intranet 24, 66, 90, 110–116, 164
iTunes 49, 50, 52

Jing 10, 144, 148

Kindle 49, 52
King County Library System (KCLS) (Washington State) 159–166

Lane Public Library (Fairfield, Ohio) 34, 35
laptops 34, 37, 38, 52, 59, 68, 155, 156, 160, 164, 187, 208
learning management system (use for LMS) 6, 8, 9, 22, 100, 101, 141
LibGuides 6, 7, 9, 66, 69, 71, 89–95, 150, 180
librarians 6–10, 15, 20–25, 27–29, 31, 32, 34, 39–46, 57, 58, 61–70, 74, 76, 82–88, 89–95, 98–102, 104–109, 113, 139, 144, 146–151, 152, 157, 158, 164, 168–174, 178, 180, 183–188, 190, 191, 193, 203–212
library advocacy 205, 206; *see also* advertising; outreach

library cards 162, 166
library catalog (use for OPAC) 65, 69, 72, 76, 91, 93, 100, 111, 118, 149, 185
library director 49, 51–53, 154–156
Library of Congress classification system 69, 72, 149, 150
Library Services and Technology Act 27, 48
library website 66, 69, 76, 122, 179
LMS *see* learning management system

Mac (use for Macintosh, use for MacBooks) 21, 23, 31, 191
MacArthur Foundation 139
MacBooks *see* Mac
Macintosh *see* Mac
makerspaces 28, 29, 31–33, 82, 99, 176, 178, 184, 187, 205
Microsoft Word 42, 127, 132, 148
middle school 20, 152
Millennials 8, 168
Moodle 6
music 11, 68, 121, 161, 172, 211

Noodletools 22, 24, 25
North Carolina 28, 29

Oakland University Libraries 7
One-shot (library instruction) 7, 11, 83, 85–87, 146–148, 206
online classes 8–11,
OPAC *see* library catalog
Open Access 177–179
outreach 52–54, 105, 146, 162, 163, 166, 168, 179, 197, 203

Padlet 208, 209
patron(s) 28, 29, 34–46, 49, 57–63, 65–71, 74, 76, 77, 80, 82–86, 90, 102, 118–124, 138, 140, 141, 144, 145, 152, 157–166, 168–174, 183–188
PDFs 15, 29, 127, 132, 134, 137, 149, 150, 154
Pew Research Center 118
phone (any) 9, 48–50, 52, 53, 72
Photoshop (Adobe software) 35, 129, 144
physics 20–25
Piaget 12
Pinterest 15, 41, 193, 194
policy 59, 68, 69, 110, 113, 155, 156, 162, 163
Poll Everywhere (software) 9, 15
polls 6, 9, 15, 93, 114, 115, 121
Portland Public Library (PPL) (Portland, Maine) 56 63
Portneuf Library (Chubbuck, Idaho) 48, 53
PowerPoint 10, 35, 42, 45, 91, 127, 129, 132–138, 172, 177, 191–193
Prezi 84, 95, 125, 127, 129, 131, 193
printers 31, 62, 65–67, 71, 72, 137, 178, 184, 187
professional development 56, 57, 83, 96, 97, 99, 100, 141–144, 186, 207, 211
promotion 49, 114, 115, 121–123, 143, 163, 179, 180
proxy server 76, 77, 149, 202
public libraries 34, 35, 40, 41, 44, 56, 58, 62, 101,

102, 119, 120, 139, 141, 152, 155, 156, 161–163, 165, 185, 196
publishing 15, 22, 176–179

quizzes 8, 9, 10, 69, 147, 150, 209

reference 32, 48, 52, 65, 69–72, 74, 76, 80, 113, 144, 147, 150, 168, 173, 183–188
robot 150, 191
rubrics 7, 22, 24
San Diego State University (SDSU) Library 175, 176, 180, 181
Saujani, Reshma 152
scaffolding (educational technique) 6–11
scanners 31, 67, 72, 187
school libraries 99, 143, 144, 152, 155, 156, 205
school librarians 22, 96, 101, 205–207, 210–212

Seattle Public Library 162, 165
Skokie Public Library (Skokie, Illinois) 44
Skype 41
social media 9, 14, 31, 38, 60, 62, 63, 82, 84, 118, 122, 143, 144, 155, 177–180, 191, 193–195, 208–210
Socrative 209
sports 20–25, 202, 203
staff 27–35, 36–39, 40–46, 48–53, 56–63, 65–71, 74, 76, 76–82, 84, 89–95, 98, 100–115, 118, 119, 121, 123, 132, 140–144, 150, 152, 154, 157, 159–166, 178, 179, 183, 184, 186–188, 191, 206
statistics 9, 35, 60, 120, 121, 123, 165, 166, 184–188
STEM (Science, Technology, Engineering and Math) 20–25, 27, 152, 157, 192
students 6–11, 12–18, 20–26, 27–39, 56, 61, 65–71, 82–88, 90, 99–101, 104–109, 118, 125, 127–131, 132–138, 139–144, 146–150, 152–158, 163, 168–174, 175–181, 185, 190–195, 197, 199, 201, 203, 205–212
subject specialists 49, 52, 54, 180
surveys 6, 7, 9, 12, 21, 27, 28, 31–33, 42–45, 47, 60, 70–72, 92, 93, 95, 100, 119–121, 129, 147, 166, 193

tablets 9, 36, 38, 40, 48–50, 52, 53, 68, 99, 102, 118, 136, 156, 163, 164, 187, 191
teachers 8, 9, 21–25, 40, 41, 58–60, 71, 82, 96–101, 139, 163, 169, 170, 205–212
TechSmith 10, 147, 148
tent cities 159–166

3-D printing 29–32, 82, 181
train the trainer 36, 61, 86, 114
training 27, 35–46, 48, 49, 51–53, 56–58, 60–65, 67–72, 74, 77, 80–84, 87, 89–95, 110, 112, 114, 118–121, 123, 141–145, 152, 154, 160, 161, 163, 172, 178, 185–188, 190, 191, 195, 196, 205, 206, 211
Tumblr 41
tutor 34, 35, 37–39, 58–62, 118, 163
Twine (software) 74, 77–81
Twitter 14, 15, 118, 179, 210
Typeform 69–72

undergraduate (students) 28, 82–84, 90, 104–106, 108, 149, 176, 203, 206
University of Illinois at Urbana-Champaign 74, 75, 76, 79, 83, 85
University of Pittsburgh, Health Science Library System 125–131
University of Mississippi Libraries (UML) 147
usability 69, 113, 115

video tutorials 6–10, 13–15, 98, 119, 125, 146–150, 173, 178, 187, 192–195, 207, 208, 211
virtual reality 193, 194
virtual reference 74, 76
volunteers 61, 62, 84, 121, 122, 140, 152, 154–157, 159, 160
VPN (Virtual Private Network) 76, 77
Vygotsky, Lev 6

Web 2.0 13, 14, 83, 110, 191
Western Carolina University 27, 30
Wi-Fi 49–52, 121
widgets 6, 23, 91, 93
Windows (operating system) 10, 50, 118, 211
Wordpress 32, 66, 112, 116
workshops 29, 31–33, 57, 58, 82–90, 95, 97, 119–121, 125, 126, 129, 139, 140, 143, 175–181, 190–196, 203
Wyoming Seminary 20, 21

XMind 75, 78

YouTube 9, 14, 15, 68, 118, 127, 147, 148, 210

Zotero 31, 32, 84–86